3

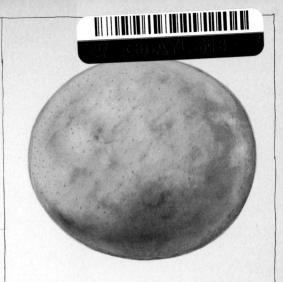

iral forms in Nature the shells of the sea
e among the most beautiful.

TORTOISE a fresh water TURTLE
sea and on land for about 200 million years.

FLUORITE crystalizes in a form
milar to gold and diamonds.

SILK WORM COCOON (life size)
beautiful filament of great value to man
nce first used in China in 2600 B.C.

Wing of the ARCTIC TERN, bird of
gest annual flight 22,000 miles.

Tree SEEDS: Acorn of Live Oak;
one of Largest Tree-Sequoia Gigantia.

5

7

6

BEAUTY FOR THE SIGHTED
AND THE BLIND

OBJECTS OF WONDER AND BEAUTY

This painting suggests a few of the unlimited number of objects that are
beautiful to see and also to touch. About half of them are man made, described
in pages that follow; most of the others are in the Collection now being
formed, of "Objects of Beauty and Wonder from the Great Storehouse of
Nature." All have been enjoyed by sighted and blind persons together.

BEAUTY
FOR THE SIGHTED
AND THE BLIND

BY

ALLEN H. EATON

Author of Immigrant Gifts to American Life,
Handicrafts of the Southern Highlands, Handicrafts of New England,
Beauty Behind Barbed Wire

FOREWORD BY

Helen Keller

ILLUSTRATED

ST MARTIN'S PRESS · NEW YORK

701
E

I Dedicate This Book

TO THE VOLUNTEER WORKERS FOR THE BLIND EVERYWHERE

Without them few programs for the blind could be sustained. Their help and encouragement can not be measured, but it shines through the lives of countless persons without sight; and, through their service, their friendship and their love for those who can not see, they are helping those who can to understand the most important truth there is to know about blindness, which is, that blind persons are just like other folks except they do not see with their eyes.

A heart in love with beauty never grows old.

ANCIENT TURKISH PROVERB

Art is the one form of human energy in the whole world which really works for union and destroys the barriers between man and man. It is the real cement of human life; the everlasting refreshment and renewal.

JOHN GALSWORTHY

Art when really understood is the province of every human being. It is simply a question of doing things, anything well. It is not an outside extra thing . . . He does not have to be a painter or a sculptor to be an artist. He can work in any medium. He simply has to find the gain in the work itself, not outside it.

ROBERT HENRI

To me the greatest thing is to live beauty in our daily life and to crowd every moment of our life with things of beauty . . . As long as beauty abides only with a few articles created by a few geniuses the kingdom of beauty is nowhere near realization.

YANAGI

The things which men have made . . . are inevitably the best witness. They cannot lie, and what they say is of supreme importance. For they speak of men's soul and they show who are his gods.

ERIC GILL

So act as to bring out the best in others and thereby bring out the best in ourselves.

FELIX ADLER

Strong bonds with life is the finest feature of our art.

D. KABOLENSKY

God grant me the courage to change the things I can change, the serenity to accept those I can not change; and the wisdom to know the difference.

ST. FRANCIS OF ASSISI

It ain't what we don't know that hurts us; it's what we know that ain't true.

JOSH BILLINGS

The significance of man is not what he attains but rather what he longs to attain.

KAHLIL GIBRAN

If I only had one wish, I wouldn't waste it on wishing I could see. I'd wish instead that everybody could understand one another and how a person feels like inside. Bob, 12 years old, blind from birth.

AS QUOTED BY DR. HOWARD RUSK IN NEW YORK TIMES

CONTENTS

ILLUSTRATIONS

FOREWORD

IT GIVES me great pleasure to write a foreword to Allen Eaton's "Beauty for the Sighted and the Blind." The collection, which the book describes, of objects to charm and instruct the blind and their seeing friends is one of the most constructive and far reaching developments in the relations of people in the dark and those with sight. The bringing together of such a collection for the blind by a person of fine sensibilities is a gift of a rare and precious kind. It seems strange to sense-arrogant persons that the blind man should talk about enjoying beauty of which he can have no visual perception. But those with eyes in their minds will realize that some elements essential to beauty are order, proportion and form, and that the intelligent blind man has access to these elements. Touch is the feeler with which through darkness he obtains many aesthetic pleasures. The dainty motion of a bird in his hand, the leaves of the willow, the wind blowing against his face messages of heat and cold, the streets and roads he treads and the combinations of ideas to which those impressions give rise, make up his conception of beauty, which is as real to him as if his eyes responded to the light. His world may not have color, but if his brains are alert, it breathes and pulsates with meaning.

His interest is also excited by the flow of straight and curved lines in all surfaces he can touch. The manifestations of their variety, eloquence and sweep are infinite and amazing. In this respect he is at home with the sculptor, the observant surgeon and the skilled mechanic. So it is evident that lack of sight need not shut him out of God's world of beauty.

The artistic blind man (or woman) is doubly thrilled when through his hand he meets the imagination of another bodied forth in a graceful statue, an exquisite vase, an ancient implement endowed with poetic symbolism. The process by which he has attained this ability is the same as training a child's sight to an appreciation of art. Truly his friends who are both normal and sensitive can share the aliveness of his world and intensify his joy by furnishing details that will carry his interest beyond his touch.

The motive of Mr. Eaton's book is to encourage "more and happy communication between the sighted and the blind." He affords an impressive, concrete realization of life that will enrich the blind and discard the remoteness which used to be their lot. In his exhibits and the information they spread among the public Mr. Eaton will build up delightful subjects of common interest between the blind and their seeing fellows. From my own experience I warmly support his assertion that the appreciation of beauty is as vital to the blind as to those who see, and that every person without sight, but with the insight, "has within his reach, has for the claiming, a kingdom of beauty that is inexhaustible in any lifetime."

HELEN KELLER

Arcan Ridge
Westport, Connecticut

PREFACE

ON A winter night long ago in Boston, a little girl, just begin-
ing to sense the wonder of life's adventures, was taken to
see Helen Keller and her teacher, Anne Sullivan Macy. As they
showed the audience how a deaf, blind woman could "talk" without the power of speech, and understand without sight or hearing, the most vivid impression of that night was one of vitality in
the face of inexpressible handicaps, and the joy in what life can
bring in spite of them.

The girl could not know then that she would some day be a
fellow alumna of Helen Keller's college—Radcliffe—and that the
next time they would meet face to face would be after the girl
had become Director of the Federal Government's program for
the rehabilitation of the disabled, and on that occasion, in Louisville, Kentucky, she would be participating in a ceremony honor-
ing that same Helen Keller at a gathering of devoted rehabilitation
workers to give to Helen Keller the highest honor they could
bestow—the President's Award of the National Rehabilitation
Association. From Boston, Massachusetts, to Louisville, Kentucky,
is a long bridge in time and space, but it had been used by both
of us in a sustained effort to give millions over the world the
opportunity to achieve what Helen Keller has achieved—maximum
fulfillment in life.

To meet again between the covers of Allen Eaton's book is not,
therefore, to meet as strangers, but as devoted missionaries in the
cause to which he has devoted his life—the intrinsic importance
of beauty in all of life's aspects, and the moral obligation to go
out of our way to insure for those denied its appreciation, in usual
or conventional ways, an opportunity to compensate for this and
thus remain wholly a part of the total community life.

The program for the rehabilitation of the disabled of our country—and indeed of the world—has as its obligation the restoring

of every physically or mentally disabled human being to the highest point of well-being possible for that individual—physically, intellectually, vocationally, socially, and spiritually. The official United States Government program of vocational rehabilitation is one of the major parts of the Department of Health, Education, and Welfare and is committed totally to making the ideal of the dignity of the individual, no matter how seriously disabled, paramount in the regard of his government for him.

In carrying out its mission, the Office of Vocational Rehabilitation does many things. It provides the structure for the Federal-State program of service for disabled people so that they can achieve productive employment, which tens of thousands do every year. It conducts extensive professional training programs to continue the flow of trained dedicated workers to help accomplish this mission. It assists communities to build and equip rehabilitation facilities, large and small, where the service given takes on the aura of miracle-working in the modern age.

Perhaps most important of all it encourages research through grants and fellowships to find new knowledge with which to combat disability and compensate for it, and new ways to help people understand each other—the sighted and the blind; the hearing to probe the lonely fortress of the deaf; all of us to feel the kinship of the human family. In this subtle field of increasing awareness of each other, in making the spiritual contact that is the spark of understanding, is there a better seed to sow and cultivate than beauty and the feel of beautiful things enjoyed together?

On the February afternoon three years ago when I first met Allen Eaton, I caught the vision of the possibilities of this project —Beauty for the Sighted and the Blind. As he unfolded his dream that the sighted and the blind together could share the common experience of appreciating beautiful things, by the sense of touch, I began to see an almost limitless significance in his idea. We tend to place so little emphasis and importance on the role of beauty in life. Do we neglect it—or take it for granted? Agencies organized to give service to people have usually neglected the therapeutic role of aesthetics—as important to the whole man we strive for as competency in anything. As Allen Eaton unfolded his dream, showed his objects of beauty and took me in imagination through the museums of our country with our blind friends, I began to see something even more rewarding for programs of rehabilitation—a unique and untried vehicle to increased understanding.

So it was that Allen Eaton was awarded a Research Fellowship by the Office of Vocational Rehabilitation to complete his book, perfect the collection of objects of beauty, and at the same time advise and work with the Office of Vocational Rehabilitation to begin the projects outlined here.

It was a happy moment to be present as a partner as we opened a new door to our many blind friends. With them many of their sighted companions will have a new sense of enjoyment of objects they have seen up to now only with their eyes. If the museums of our country, and indeed of the world, find ways to broaden enjoyment of their treasures through this book we will have another example of making art—and service to the disabled —a universal language.

It is not my place to make acknowledgments, but I cannot resist a few: To Helen Keller—a lifelong beacon—because she inspired this humble contribution to the fulfillment of her dreams; to the Russell Sage Foundation for encouragement in the pioneer days of the experience; to the American Foundation for the Blind for making possible the building up of the collection and cooperating throughout this enterprise; to the friends and colleagues at the Kansas Rehabilitation Center for the Blind, representative of the whole public program, for their encouragement, help and interpretation. We are grateful to all who helped but to these especially, as we go about making real for more of our people here and over the world the motto of the Department of Health, Education, and Welfare—Spes Anchora Vitae—Hope, the Anchor of Life.

MARY E. SWITZER
Director, Office of Vocational Rehabilitation,
U. S. Department of Health, Education and Welfare

INTRODUCTION

*There is no wealth but life. Life, including all its powers
of love, of joy, and of admiration. That country is rich-
est which nourishes the greatest number of noble and
happy human beings.*—JOHN RUSKIN

THIS is a book of experiences with beauty. It is about the
aesthetic responses of both seeing and blind persons to
the wonder and beauty of the world about them, a response which
enriches each one who has it without taking anything away from
another. "The perception of beauty," says Dr. Berthold Lowenfeld, Director of the California School for the Blind, "is one of
the most useful of man's experiences." And when this useful experience is shared with another, it can be one of life's most
treasured communications.

If all the blind persons of the earth could find a single voice to
express their greatest wish, it would surely be that everyone
could understand the most important thing to know about blindness, that while it is one of the most severe of human handicaps
it is in no sense an impairment of the mental and spiritual resources of the individual.

As the brilliant blind scholar and pioneer psychologist, Pierre
Villey, said in his great work, *The World of the Blind,* "Before
anything else it is necessary to establish the fundamental truth
that blindness does not affect the individuality, but leaves it intact.
Its sources remain healthy; no mental faculty of the blind is
affected in any way, and all of them, under favorable circumstances, are susceptible of blooming out to the highest degree of
development to which a normal being can aspire."

If a second wish could be granted to those without sight, it
would be that society do whatever it can to open and keep open
for them all the avenues of perception and of learning. For the

greatest need of those who cannot see is, and always will be, communication on all levels of human interest with those who can see, and the emphasis here is on *all* the levels.

This book aspires to encourage communication between the sighted and the blind on one of the highest levels of human interest, the appreciation and enjoyment of beauty. Its purpose is to help bring to blind people everywhere a larger measure of beauty than they have ever known, by opening many doors and windows heretofore closed to them. The medium for opening the first door of this experience is a "Collection of Objects of Beauty for the Sighted and the Blind," objects which are beautiful to behold through the sense of sight and also beautiful to behold through the sense of touch.

These objects and some of the experiences had with them will be described in the text and illustrations, but it should be noted here that this kind of communication through selected objects, is not a one-sided experience; its values are not for the blind alone but quite as much for those who see. It brings to the seeing not only a better understanding of the great power of touch in the lives of the blind, but a clearer idea of how their own aesthetic lives can be enriched by cultivating this sense. This reciprocal experience of learning from the blind has, for many sighted persons, proved one of the finest of their lives.

Perhaps not more than one in a thousand of those of us who see has ever had the opportunity to associate with blind persons, yet to do so is a great need for each and often a privilege of rare quality. It is hoped that the time will come when, in the education of sighted children, they shall have a chance to know and to have for a time, as companion, schoolmate or friend, some blind child or adult. Not only will the gain be to the blind child, but to the seeing one as well; for he will come to understand, as he cannot so well in any other way, the position of at least one blind child in school and in society; and he will also come to prize more highly the perceptive senses with which he himself by nature is usually endowed, and thus be stimulated to strengthen and refine them. Perhaps the greatest gain to him will be that he will learn how very alike sighted and blind people are and, instead of having the timidity which many people, undoubtedly a great majority, feel throughout their lives toward those who cannot see, he will be drawn closer to them and through understanding come to feel at home with them, realizing a truth not well enough known, that his blind friend has something, often very much, to share of his own individuality. He will realize, too, the part which blindness may have played in the development of that individuality.

The idea around which this book is written, that is the mutual enjoyment of beauty by the sighted and the blind, and the communication between them which such an experience evokes, had its beginnings several years ago when I was a member of the Staff of the Russell Sage Foundation and our family lived not far from an institution for the blind in the Bronx borough of New York City.

One evening just before Christmas, on dropping into our neighborhood store, my attention was arrested by the sight of several blind persons, perhaps half a dozen, enjoying the holiday display of merchandise as they took into their hands or ran their fingers over the various objects, especially those in the toy department. I remember well their delight in a furnished doll house, their pleasure in some of the dolls and other toys, and the enthusiasm of one over a pair of child's ice skates.

Apparently they were shopping for their children or small friends, but they were also taking advantage of the invitation of our storekeeper to have a "look" at everything. One or two were very serious as they took their time to explore new articles with deliberation. Others were talking and laughing and informing one another of what they were seeing, and saying how pleased so-and-so would be with this or that; and sometimes one would pass an object to another to examine and enjoy. Never before had I realized how much blind persons could see and enjoy through their sense of touch.

I watched them as long as I felt I should, wandering around among the merchandise as though examining it, but really seeing nothing but them and the things they were looking at. All that evening and for several days and evenings afterwards, I thought of the good time those blind folks were having because of the understanding generosity of our modest storekeeper; and later I learned that every year this was one of his ways of extending the Christmas spirit. How I wished that other storekeepers everywhere would do likewise, but the improbability of it, the impossibility of it, especially in the larger and more efficient stores, depressed me.

Finally, the thought came. Since we cannot expect many merchants to invite the blind to their stores to enjoy the sights so freely open to the rest of us, isn't there some way that we sighted people can make available to those who cannot see, objects of interest and beauty and meaning, which they may experience and enjoy through their sense of touch?

The practicability of this thought was no doubt subconsciously influenced by experiences I had had as National Field Secretary of the American Federation of Arts before I joined the Staff of the Russell Sage Foundation; I had organized and directed a number of handicraft exhibitions, some local, others national in scope, but all containing some objects which, on reflection, I thought would appeal to blind persons, as they had to thousands who could see. Thus my thoughts began to run in the direction of "small exhibits," a name first used to describe the exhibitions.

Later, the better term "collection" was substituted. The word "exhibits" had proved less effective because it carried with it the thought that these objects might be brought together and sent from place to place, as is done with other shows to be viewed by sighted persons only, but, as will be seen, there are such differences in the techniques of showing the articles to sighted and to blind persons that the term "collection," which is more elastic and general, seemed preferable and it will be more frequently used here, although either term is representative of the idea.

The idea took the form of bringing together objects suitable for the blind, as we have been doing for the sighted, with such modifications as common sense, experience, and circumstances should dictate.

Perhaps I should explain at this point that I had never had the privilege of knowing blind persons as individuals; and therefore to learn of their ability to get very definite notions about objects by handling them and to derive pleasure from them through the sense of touch, as I was convinced on that winter evening that they had. This ability was a great revelation to me. If many blind people could do this, then there was surely something solid to build on. We who had sight must take the initiative.

Never having had the pleasure of sharing a beautiful object

with any blind person, I did not feel too competent to proceed, yet the urge was strong to try.

Perhaps someone had already done what I had in mind—that often happens, and so I consulted the Library of the American Foundation for the Blind to find that there was no such experience on record. Then, what I had thought of as a privilege was turning in my mind toward a responsibility, and I resolved to begin work on the idea as soon as possible. It would have to be, to begin with, on evenings and free days; and, fortunately for me, one of my daughters, Betty, was interested and would help; so we were soon thinking and working together. This was in the winter of 1931.

Although a search in the literature of the blind reveals no earlier attempt to use objects of beauty as a medium of communication between them and the sighted, it seemed a natural step and a timely one in the evolution of the efforts that society has made, and is making, to bring into the lives of the blind, the rights and privileges and opportunities enjoyed by the vast majority of mankind which possesses the priceless gift of sight. Because it is a new step in this evolution, of opportunities for the blind, it seems fitting that brief references be made here to the progress of work which has led toward it; and into the scheme of which it seems to fit so well.

One of the superb achievements in human culture of the last two centuries is what society has done to help the blind in their adjustment to the social, cultural and economic life of our time. More has been accomplished in these two hundred years than in all the previous ages of man's existence.

For the pioneer beginnings in this great social advance, the world will always owe its greatest debt to France, first to that live-minded philosopher and scholarly encyclopedist Denis Diderot, who, in his now immortal "Letter on the Blind for the Use of Those Who See," published in 1749, revealed to the public for the first time, the personalities and the extraordinary accomplishments of several blind persons. He expressed the belief that there were many other not yet identified blind persons who were capable of intellectual and moral development.

Then about a third of a century later emerged Valentin Hauy who, touched by the helplessness and misery of the blind and

fired by Diderot's revealing "Letter," declared that the rank and
file of them could and should be taught, and in 1784 opened in
Paris, the first school in the world to prove it, the National Institute for the Young Blind.

Then, forty-five years later, came Louis Braille, in 1829, with
one of the most unique inventions in the history of the human
race, an embossed alphabet and numerals of magic points or dots
which many of the blind could learn to write with a simple tool,
and which could then be read with the tips of the fingers, opening gates to knowledge, and providing a key to written communication for every blind person who could use the alphabet.

Other countries, including our own, have since made splendid
contributions to the education and welfare of the blind, but to
France and her great genius must go the credit for the pioneer
work. Soon after Louis Braille's great invention in 1829, but not
influenced by it, the first schools for the blind were established
in our country.

The New England Asylum for the Blind, now the Perkins Institution and Massachusetts School for the Blind, opened in
Boston in 1832, in the same year the New York Institute for the
Education of the Blind was opened in New York City; and in
1833 the Pennsylvania Institution for the Instruction of the Blind
was opened in Philadelphia. These are the pioneer schools for
the blind in the United States.

The French Academy of Moral and Political Science, about
eighty years later, in presenting Pierre Villey its award for his pioneer work "The World of the Blind" cited that book as saying, that
contrary to the opinion widely spread, "the blind man's intellect,
intelligence and personality is equal to that of the man who has
his sight." The purpose of this present book, "Beauty for the
Sighted and the Blind," is to give further support to the French
Academy's declaration. And it will add a new chapter to prove
that the enjoyment of beauty through senses of perception other
than sight can be as genuine, as sensitive, as deep as human beings
can experience.

Thinking of Louis Braille to whom the blind probably acknowledge their greatest debt, I am reminded of an interesting event
in the use of his alphabet:

Columbia University was celebrating the 200th Anniversary of its life and work. A group of blind scholars had assembled to make their plea for the "right of the blind to knowledge", and their papers were read from the braille manuscript with an exactitude and at a speed differing not at all from the scores of papers presented in other seminars by speakers who had the full use of sight.

It was a long time before Braille's system of writing was finally adopted in America. The dots were too foreign in appearance to the sighted teachers of the blind, who clung to the idea that the Roman letters of the alphabet, so familiar to them, were the only ones which would convey meaning to others. But after experiments and experiences over many years it was at last realized that raised dots were the medium for the finger tips as Roman letters, so agreeable to the eye, never could be; and these tiny keys to knowledge were finally accepted never to be abandoned.

One of the main purposes of this book is to encourage blind persons to explore objects—especially through the sense of touch—the oldest method of perception to the blind, and for ages the only one. But it is, as practiced here, also a new and most discriminating way of communication, for, while it opens many doors to knowledge, it seeks especially to open those to the enjoyment of beauty, thus bringing to all, the aesthetic experience so prized in the highest, indeed in all human cultures.

We have just spoken of experiencing beauty through feeling the objects, through the sense of touch, but that is not quite accurate; the statement is not quite enough. There should be added that ever present indispensable aid, the sense of hearing, through which sighted and blind persons communicate most fully and frequently. The verbal interpretation of the objects by the sighted person is of greatest importance, in this exercise of communication. If, however, hearing is absent, as in the case of the deaf-blind person, this fact will not deprive him of the experience of beauty, for the sighted person will provide himself with another means of communication than his voice; he will, in such a case, have to employ writing in braille, a manual alphabet or a mechanical aid such as the Tellatouch typing machine.

The most important thing that can be said about experiencing beauty is that it is a personal, a subjective experience; it cannot be experienced by proxy. The importance of this fact is stressed here because there should be no intention by the sighted, at any time, to impose their choices or preferences upon the blind persons who participate in the experience. The fact is, however, that generally the objects which appeal to the sighted as beautiful, appeal likewise to the blind, especially if the objects are well presented and well interpreted. And whenever a sighted and a blind person, or any two persons, discover beauty in the same object a new bond is thereby created, congenial for the moment or the hour, and to be recalled time and again with pleasure.

That the blind are as much in need of the influence and the experience of beauty as are the sighted, no thoughtful person will question. But, that beauty in many of its forms is beyond the immediate reach of the blind is obvious, because so large a percentage of the objects in both nature and in the arts are perceivable only through the sense of sight, and many of them hard to get at in any other way. However, it is not what we do not know that we cherish; it is what we do know and love, and the objects of charm and fascination and beauty in the world of nature and in the kingdom of the arts, the things which are waiting for our eager minds to see through touch, are inexhaustible in the longest lifetime. One who cannot see a ray of light or hear the faintest sound has said, "I want to live forever; there is so much that is beautiful to see."

The fact that so much wonder and beauty is easily perceivable through sight has by no means resulted in all persons who have it, appreciating and enjoying the magic world which surrounds them. But to those who do, no one will question the gain. And one of the trends which our western civilization is now encouraging, and which is growing, fostered by our increasing knowledge of, and contact with the cultures of the Orient, is the conviction that we must give beauty a larger and more conscious place in our own thinking and living, and thus help extend its blessing, as far as we are able, to humanity everywhere.

The principal obstacles which have seemed to be in the way of bringing beauty in larger measure into the lives of the blind, summed up, are: First, a general indifference to aesthetic values on the part of a large number of the seeing public; second, the very common belief that beauty is reserved only for those who have the sense of sight; third, that it is not practical or that it is a nonessential in general vocational training, especially of the blind; and fourth, is the failure to realize that the experience of beauty is indispensable to balanced living and to normal growth. To each and all of these obstacles there is a practical, constructive, and inspiring answer in the experience and the testimony of the blind themselves; some of this testimony will be found in the pages which follow.

There are two common misconceptions concerning blindness, which should be corrected early in order to make it easier for the reader to understand the message which this book seeks to convey. First is the often expressed opinion that blind persons possess a sixth sense; that when sight is lost another useful and protective sense takes its place. There is now universal agreement among scientists, and among most of those who work or live with the blind, that blind persons are usually equipped with the same set of senses as those of us who are reading this printed page; that is, with hearing, feeling, smelling and tasting; lacking only the sense of sight, but possessing no additional sense of perception.

The nearest substitute, or sixth sense which a blind person can have is the one which he alone can develop by training, by cultivating his remaining senses to perceive more keenly, more fully, for him. And this he often does to what is an amazing extent, or so it seems, to us who see. But any sighted person could, if he desired to—and if he had the will—bring these same four senses with which he is usually equipped, up to the same degree of acuteness.

A second misconception is that there is such a thing as an "art for the blind." Much has been written and much more spoken on this subject. The fallacy is dissolved when it is realized that the blind people of the world are as varied as the sighted, and in the same ways.

Music, the art in which blind persons have become so appreciative and proficient, is an art for all. It will encourage us to remember that when the prophetic Valentin Huay established his first school for the blind, he was thinking of music's therapeutic value, its benefit as an outlet, frankly saying that we could not expect the blind to become fine musicians. Now millions of people are charmed by the music of the blind composers and performers.

Literature, now available to and practiced by the blind as was never dreamed of a century ago, is for all.

Even the arts of form with which we are most concerned here, and which we commonly designate as the visual arts, sometimes as the plastic arts or the spatial arts, are for all; and ways are being found, and more will yet be found, to bring these arts and other forms of beauty to the blind, and the blind to them.

And as the sense of touch comes to be better understood by the creators of forms and textures, more fine forms will be created; and they will be for the enjoyment of all who cultivate the great sense of touch. One of our first steps toward strengthening and refining this superb sense of touch is to make accessible the things which are now available.

The things which men make with their hands have a deep abiding value. First, they are letters and words and phrases in a great universal alphabet which all can understand. Then, too, they speak the truth for all to experience, and often, when beautiful, to be moved by them. Eric Gill has expressed it so well: "The things which men have made are inevitably the best witness. They cannot lie, and what they say is of supreme importance." The experiences recorded in the following pages are mainly reactions to things which men have made with their hands.

The opening chapter of this book deals with the "Sense of Beauty for All: Age Long—World Wide." A chapter on "Touch as a Way to Knowledge and a Way to Beauty" is an obvious inclusion, leading toward the heart of the work, which describes "The Collection of Objects of Beauty for the Sighted and the Blind," the origin of the idea, the uses made of the collection, and some details of the experiences of the blind with these objects, which were selected largely for their tactile qualities.

But, preceding the central chapter is one on "Some Abilities and Achievements of Blind Persons," with short life and work sketches of several persons, not generally known to the public, who are making their living and spending their lives much as the rest of us do—only they work and live without sight. A reason for including this Chapter at this point in the book is that extraordinary achievements of blind persons in many walks of life are overwhelming evidence of their normality, hence their capacity to enjoy beauty. But there is an even more basic fact to which this work would attest, namely that blind persons are just like other persons—except they do not see with their eyes. Or, to quote the words of a blind man, Robert Barnett, Director of the American Foundation for the Blind, talking to some of us who see: "Gentlemen, I beg you to remember that the eye is not all of a man."

A special chapter on "Beauty for Those Who Neither See Nor Hear: the Deaf-Blind," is included because they are the blind of whom we know the least, yet their need for beauty and their capacity to feel its inspiration have been proved, even though some of their perceptions are beyond our understanding.

There is a chapter on "Writing and Thinking Toward Beauty for the Blind," in which some of the literature on beauty for the blind, and their ability (or lack of ability) to enjoy it is quoted and discussed.

Other chapters deal with suggestions of how museums, libraries, rehabilitation centers and schools may serve the blind more adequately, by adding to their books, objects which, through the sense of touch plus verbal or written interpretation, will convey knowledge, beauty and charm to blind individuals, and which will often act also as stimuli to communication between sighted and blind persons. No American museum has yet developed a sustained program of service for the blind, although there are signs that this may be on the way. To encourage this, a chapter on "Museums and Their Possible Service to the Blind" is included.

Whatever museums, schools, rehabilitation centers and other institutions may do to bring knowledge and beauty to the blind, perhaps the greatest single need is for those sighted individuals closely and continuously associated with them, to realize how much of their own environment and aesthetic experiences can be shared with blind persons; and how they can encourage blind persons to develop special interests and hobbies, especially collections, for their contributions to personal, social and aesthetic growth; therefore a chapter is included on "Individuals Sighted and Blind, Sharing Objects of Beauty Together."

And toward the end of the book is a special chapter which explains itself, on "A Collection of Objects of Wonder and Beauty from the Great Storehouse of Nature." This chapter contains some suggestions on a collection now in the making, and a few of the objects are illustrated in the end papers of this book, and in the frontispiece.

Alexander Bain of the University of Aberdeen, writing a hundred years ago in his pioneer work, "The Senses and the Intellect," said, "The human hand is invested with the character of a special organ of touch. . . . Through this matchless instrument we can tell substances by touch, and decide upon qualities of texture and merits of workmanship." And, in concluding his monumental observations on the senses, he wrote: "There is nothing essential to the highest intellectual processes of science and thought which may not be attained in the absence of sight."

It is a logical step in the reasoning, though it has been a long and slow one, from the conclusions of the pioneer Scotch psychologist Bain, to the conclusion recorded within the pages of this book, that is, that the experiences of beauty, in its tangible forms, is well within the circle of these "highest of thought processes" and that, contrary to the opinions held by many laymen and by some workers for the blind, the truth is that beauty is a heritage in which both the blind and the seeing may share; the blind not in all the experiences which are available to those with sight, but in very many of them, in enough, and many times more than enough, to last the longest life time.

BEAUTY FOR THE SIGHTED
AND THE BLIND

CHAPTER 1

BEAUTY: THE AESTHETIC EXPERIENCE—
AGE LONG; WORLD WIDE

*The Evolution of the New Era rests on the corner-
stone of knowledge and beauty.*—NICHOLAS ROERICH

TO ONE who loves beauty—and who does not, in some measure?—the word needs no definition, for one has only to
perceive some fine thought, hear some favorite sound or combination of sounds, touch some lovely surface, or behold some thing
which is beautiful to him, to feel its pervasiveness. William Ralph
Inge, the "gloomy Dean" of England, expressed one of its attributes when he said, "Nobody is bored when he is trying to
make something that is beautiful or to discover something that
is true." And thousands of miles across the sea, Granny Jude, an
old weaver of coverlets in the mountains of North Carolina, confirmed the Dean's opinion when, warping up her loom for a new
pattern which a neighbor from over the ridge had brought her,
said: "I'm a-rarin' to draw it in to see how the spots come out.
Shucks, ain't it grand the things they is to do and to find out
about?"

Because beauty is a gift for every human being, the poets, the
philosophers, and the music makers have spoken and sung its
praises throughout the ages. Plato said, "Beauty is the splendor of
truth," and Keats was enraptured by this definition. Beauty is "a
happiness," as Dimnet puts it so simply, "of which we never feel
doubtful. Its effect is always to raise us up, without any sensation of effort, to our highest level." One does not have to be a
poet, a philosopher, or an artist to know what beauty is and to
welcome it. We need only to be our true selves; to be sincere.

Beauty manifests itself both to those who create it and to those who contemplate it; hence its enjoyment is a gift to every human heart.

Long ago an ancient writer summed up the finest aspiration of the human race as the quest for "the good, the true, and the beautiful." That summary has never changed. Centuries, yes ages, preceding this utterance, long before written communication was invented and human history first recorded, we know from artifacts which archeologists have uncovered, and which they and the anthropologists have interpreted for us, that the urge to create beauty was one of the early conscious efforts of man.

The arts of man did not wait for wealth and leisure for development, as some would have us think; they were born of necessity, always of the people and, then as now, advanced through intelligence, skill, and taste to meet the needs of their time. When they came to flower in profusion in the Far East, the Near East, and in Egypt, they had not suddenly sprung into existence but were the result of long evolution in which the sense of beauty has always been a part of man's development of conscience.

Today one of the needs for all of us is to be sufficiently aware of the power of beauty to look for it day by day, for the enrichment it can be to our own lives and the lives of others, and especially as a means of communication, with our neighbors at home and our far neighbors throughout the world. This book is particularly concerned with beauty for those who perceive it in different ways, through different senses yet without difference in the quality of the feeling evoked, so that shared beauty becomes communication of a high order.

Beauty is first of all a personal, subjective experience; therefore in some form or forms it is probably an experience of every human being. But there are those who are not conscious enough of it to count it as important for themselves, or for their fellows; to them it may seem a matter of comparative indifference. Others give it a high rank in their catalogue of choicest things; and some give it the highest place in their experiences. The aesthetic experience can be felt far beyond our ability to describe it; as Santayana, its best exponent among modern philosophers, says: "To feel beauty is a better thing than to understand how we come to feel it." The aim of this book is to help give the aesthetic experience a high place in the esteem of our people, by extending the circle of its boundaries a little further than is usual and concentrating on its role in the world of the blind. First, to show that the need for beauty is as great for the blind as for those who see; second, to bring out clearly how the aesthetic experience can be brought within their reach; and third, to suggest the mutual gain to both the sighted and the blind in sharing this enjoyment together.

The principal inequality with which this mutual experience with beauty begins is that the stimulus to it is not equally within the reach of each; though sometimes it is. But usually, the initiative must be taken by those who have the convenient sense of sight, by bringing together attractive and stimulating objects where they may be mutually enjoyed. But once this opportunity is provided, the aesthetic experience is as possible for a blind as for a sighted person, because the experiencing of beauty is a response, not to the special sense which perceives it, but to the whole intellectual and emotional being; it is a response of the full personality.

Responsiveness is a main concern of this book, which undertakes to prove that any one of the senses of perception: sight, hearing, touch, smell, or taste, through its recognition of a beautiful stimulus, is sufficient to set the whole intellectual and emotional life into vibration and thus bring about the aesthetic experience. But it is the sense of touch, mainly, through which this experience for the blind is evoked, and the stimulus an object selected for its aesthetic appeal.

The most important thing to know about beauty for the blind, as for those who see, is that it is a personal and subjective experience; it can not be conferred upon one individual by another by wishing or by insisting.

There has never been, in the experiences related here, any attempt by one person to impose upon another a preference or a choice. The most that has been done by way of communication concerning an object has been to name and describe it, to give its historical and social bearings, its attributes, and sometimes to mention qualities and associations which appealed to the one who assembled it or the one showing it. But in presenting any part of the collection for observation it is always explained that "there is nothing here which anyone thinks you ought to like, or that you are expected to like."

One of the most embarrassing situations in which anyone can find himself is to be expected to like a thing of which he has no knowledge, for which he has either no feeling or possibly even a distaste. Enjoyment of the arts is often spoiled by those who insist that we like what they like. An aesthetic experience of beauty in nature or the arts cannot be other than an individual reaction to a stimulus. When any two of us react happily to the same stimulus, it is an event of importance, but it is nothing to be insisted upon. Sincere enthusiasm for a thing of beauty should not, however, be suppressed, for often it leads others into pleasurable moments and toward permanent and satisfying preferences of their own. We may wish that others could feel as we do in the contemplation of something that is beautiful to us; but the only wish that can not fail is that someone shall find, somewhere, an object which will evoke in him a response of the same high quality as the object of our choice evokes in us. It is freedom to choose which has given beauty its transcendency through the ages, often lifting us above futile controversies about the arts. In this spirit, sighted and blind have together profoundly enjoyed this collection of beautiful objects which are described in later chapters.

Someone may ask why the term "beauty" was chosen to designate this collection instead of "art" or "the arts." The answer is that beauty is a better understood term, is less controversial, and has a definitely pleasure-giving connotation. However, each object in the collection is an object of art in the broad sense of that term and in the opinion of him who selected it. Therefore it will be possible and pleasant often to use the terms beauty and the arts interchangeably.

The word "art" means so many different things to different people that some explanation of what it means to him who assembled this collection may be appropriate. We are here concerned mainly with the visual arts which man, for his convenience, separated a short time ago into the fine arts and the minor or "useful" arts and has ever since been further subdividing. These divisions are sometimes a convenience in conversation and also in critical writing, but they are not of much help in the effort to understand the place of beauty in all the arts or in their relation to each other. The forty-some articles included in this collection can all be classified as handicrafts, but they are objects of art as the assembler understands the term; for art is just the excellent way of making something or doing something that needs to be done—and each object selected comes clearly within that category. But the more the arts are divided and subdivided the more confusing they become to the layman, and we welcome Emerson's voice as he says, "Beauty must come back to the useful arts and the distinction between the fine and useful arts be forgotten."

No one has ever spoken more clearly or given us a better definition of the arts, especially the visual arts with which we are mainly concerned here, than the eminent American painter and great teacher, Robert Henri, who said:

"Art when really understood is the province of every human being. It is simply a question of doing things, anything well. It is not an outside extra thing. . . . He does not have to be a painter or a sculptor to be an artist. He can work in any medium. He simply has to find the gain in the work itself, and not outside it."

Accepting this definition we shall be at home with the arts and with beauty, and our concern will be with their inspiration in the lives of all.

The project under consideration here we call, "The Collection of Objects of Beauty for the Sighted and the Blind." The collection includes about forty beautiful and significant objects chosen from a very broad field of handicrafts in the hope that there would be some things of unusual interest for each person who beheld them, and possibly several favorite objects for all. Each object was chosen for its appeal to both sight and touch. It goes without saying that each object had beauty of its own for the one who assembled them.

Although the sense of sight and the sense of touch, plus that of hearing, will be the principal perceivers of beauty recorded here, it is important to remember that the total response to the stimulus in any case is not what the perceiving sense registers but what the brain or the mind makes of this perception. Thomas Cutsforth, psychologist and author, who incidentally is blind, states this fact clearly in the chapter, "The Aesthetic Life of the Blind," in his book, *The Blind in School and in Society.* He writes: "Aesthetic growth does not take place so much through the senses as it does through the entire intellectual development. Aesthetic appreciation is always related to the wealth of effective relationships it organizes about the stimulus pattern."

One of the strong reasons for recognizing the urge to beauty as an instrument of high social value, is its universality. We of the Western world are likely to attribute the need and practice of the aesthetic experience to a few special individuals and institutions in the upper brackets of culture: artists, a few teachers, scholars, philosophers, and art museums. We too often overlook the fact that our natures are such that no one can live a full life without a deep consciousness of beauty, and that many people in every corner of our country and the world walk with beauty and are symbols of its ancient and present-day urgency, although this may be known only to their families, their neighbors or nearest friends, and sometimes only to themselves.

Dr. Alexis Carrel, a great scientist, a native of France but a citizen of the United States by choice, in his book, *Man the Unknown*, writes eloquently and convincingly of the universality of this persistent human quest:

"Esthetic sense," he says, "exists in the most primitive human beings as in the most civilized. It even survives the disappearance of intelligence . . . The creation of forms, or of a series of sounds, capable of awakening an esthetic emotion, is an elementary need of our nature . . ." and he adds: "Esthetic activity manifests itself in both the creation and the contemplation of beauty. . . . Beauty is an inexhaustible source of happiness to those who discover its abode."

If Dr. Carrel is right, and no well-informed person will doubt the truth of what he says, how can we escape the obligation of seeing that everyone has an opportunity to cultivate this sense and to experience it from day to day throughout life? It is one of the "inalienable rights," and a blessing which can be had in abundance without taking anything of worth away from other people. Even more, beauty enriches all who see it enjoyed or who learn of its enjoyment by others.

What then are beauty's principal manifestations? Where is it to be found? It appears for us in two great kingdoms, both of which are ours for the caring, the kingdom of nature and the kingdom of the arts: the world as man finds it, and the things that he shapes from it.

Nature comes first, with its magnitude, its wonder, its beauty. Every civilization has registered its reaction to the beauty of nature but none, in modern times, with more sensitiveness than the people of Japan where "children are taught from infancy to use their imagination, especially in the perception of hidden beauty. The poorest, unable to buy any work of human art, becomes independent of such extraneous aids by learning to recognize in the most commonplace of objects—a water-worn stone, a shadow on a wall, a fallen leaf—a beauty transcending the works of man."

Then come the arts of man, the things in which he reflects best his own image, his imagination. It is only a small segment of the things he makes with which our theme has to do, but how important they are, how significant, especially those artifacts which reflect his sense of use and beauty, beginning with the simplest tools man shaped to extend, strengthen, and make more perfect the work of his hands. One of these tools we have in our collection, dates back, we guess, ten thousands years; others are in use today, when the number of products from his tools and machines on this continent alone, bewilders a modern world. Of these artifacts, many, very many, are beautiful, and from this great store we select a few for our contemplation and appreciation, for aesthetic activity manifests itself in the contemplation as well as in the creation of the beautiful.

There were several reasons for choosing, for this first collection, articles from the great storehouse of the arts, rather than a similar number of objects from nature's unlimited world. First, the things which have been shaped by the hands for the use and enjoyment of man are the things with which the blind are, as a rule, most familiar. And a good place to start any experiment or experience is with the familiar, with people where they are.

A second reason is that there are so many available artifacts which in size, form, texture, and other qualities, meet the requirements of such a collection. Many of these are also comparatively inexpensive.

A third reason is that the things which man has made often inspire others to make things like them, or suggested by them. Moreover, as will be noted in detail in a later chapter, a separate and special collection of objects in natural forms for the sighted and the blind is now in process; this will open many new doors and windows for blind persons on the wonders, beauties, and miracles of nature.

Sometime there will be collections of objects where the works of nature and the arts will be shown together. This is a new field for aesthetic appreciation and one of promise. One notable instance of this principle, carried out for those who see, is the superb collection of "Objects of Nature and of Art" in relationship to each other, originated and worked out by Mrs. Fiske Warren of Boston. This beautiful and unique collection was shown first in the Fogg Museum at Harvard and later at the Boston Museum of Fine Arts; then in other cities throughout the country. The basis for the nature forms was Mrs. Warren's fascinating collection of shells, and examples of sculpture and architecture using shell forms as motifs were shown in excellent photographs. This exhibition was designed to be looked at; but a similar collection utilizing some models which could, like the shells, be handled, would be practical for the enjoyment of both sighted and blind persons.

To a blind person every object in a collection such as those described here, comes out of space, and by itself, with no relationship to anything else in its environment or surroundings unless someone indicates it through verbal description. This means that undivided attention can be given to the object itself, and that the beholder, examining it carefully, can usually sense everything that a sighted person can, except low-relief decoration and color. To this, someone will say, "But color is everything, it is to me the chief element in any article." That may well be, but if it is the only element you enjoy, then your seeing is not complete, for there is the whole form, the flow of line, the texture which can never be fully sensed except through touch, sometimes the smell, and the temperature, as the cold of crystal, the warmth of amber, elements which can never be seen and some of which are properties of every material and artifact. Even the form and texture which the eyes see clearly in a Chinese porcelain vase can not be fully experienced until you can take it into your hands and feel it through your palms, fingers, and finger tips. This you will do and more, if you are blind, but will often neglect if you can see, because it seems unnecessary to you for your comprehension. Color, in any object, means much; but it is far from being all.

It will simplify our thinking if we omit here any discussion of the several degrees of blindness that are legally recognized, and think for the moment of the term "blind" as referring to those who do not see at all. Of those who are entirely without sight, some, congenitally blind, have been so since birth; others, who have once had vision, remember some visual images; but even this difference, which is sometimes very great, need not concern us at this point. We are for the moment thinking of all who can not see and who get their knowledge and impressions of objects, such as those in this collection, mainly through the sense of touch, plus what they hear or read about them.

One can not generalize too much, but there are instances in which the qualities that a blind person can perceive in an object make it more prized to him than to one who can see. There is the possibility too, that because of his deep interest in, and perhaps affection for, only a few things, those for which he does care will mean more. Of several persons who own or have access to pieces of the beautiful Royal Copenhagen porcelain, it is a blind friend who seems to enjoy them most.

It is never possible to know whether an object would have meant more to a blind person, if he could have seen as well as felt it; but that is not relatively important. What we need to know and do know, is that some objects evoke in blind persons aesthetic responses that mean a great deal to them, and that therefore many more opportunities should be placed within their reach, or better, shared with them, for it is increasingly clear that the mutual enjoyment of objects of beauty by sighted and blind persons can bring satisfactions comparable to the best experiences between two persons with sight. This is a fact of basic importance, for it means that a sighted person may bring to his blind friend, companion, or associate a continuing flow of beautiful objects.

The sharing of objects of beauty by two or more persons is a mutual privilege. There is a deep and long established urge on the part of human beings to share with others the things which move them most. This urge must have been the greatest single contributor to the invention of speech and other forms of communication. Cicero said of it: "Though a man should climb up into heaven and behold universal nature and the beauty of the stars, yet if he had none to whom he could relate it, that would be to him but a tedious spectacle."

When one sees the eagerness with which many blind persons welcome the chance to know things of beauty and take them to their hearts, one wonders why this privilege of tactual perception has not been more thoughtfully and systematically extended to them through the schools, the art museums, and the libraries. Also, and this is what we wish to encourage above all else, between persons and persons.

Some of the explanations for these delays are given here briefly, because they still exist and are likely to continue for a long time. One is, and it is basic, that a very large part of the seeing world has not felt the importance of a knowledge and practice of the arts in their broad sense, either in their own lives or in the lives of their children. There is evidence now that attitudes are changing, but many adults can remember, a generation ago, the resistance that was put up to any inclusion of the arts in the local school curriculum on the grounds that they were not practical for life; and how troubled parents and neighbors often were when any of the children showed a dangerous leaning toward the arts as a vocation. It has been largely the great wave of adult education or, as John Cotton Dana preferred to call it, "informal education," in our country which has helped bring parents to a wiser and better point of view on this subject, as they thought back over their school days and realized some of the things they missed which could have contributed to their taste and culture.

We now have what was never dreamed of at the beginning of this century, unlimited numbers of people playing in the arts: "Sunday painters," craftsmen, and tinkers in attics and basements, and others working at many things wherever they can find room, and some places where they can't, all helping toward the realization that there is something of the artist in most of us and to let it come through occasionally isn't too dangerous. All this activity is related to, and preparation for, the aesthetic experiences of everyday life, in which many can have a part either in the practice of some art or skill or, what is sometimes more important, in the contemplation and enjoyment of the beautiful around us.

Coming closer to the special question of why the arts, in their broad meaning, have not been given a larger place in the education and the lives of the blind, the first reason is obviously that suggested above, that their importance in life has lagged in the general development of our education.

But there have been some special and definite obstacles, three in particular, that are more directly connected with work for the blind. The first of these is the almost universal belief that the aesthetic experience is one reserved only for those who see with their eyes. This is natural enough, for most of the aesthetic experiences we have with objects or scenes, come to us through our sight; and we can not imagine ourselves able to enjoy them if we can not look at them with our eyes. We are usually quite unaware of the fact that if a blind person can get his hands on some object of his liking he not only can get a good understanding of it, but may, through tactile exploration, get a good or a fine feeling for it. This is possible for the reason, as already stated, that it is not the sense of perception, in this case the hand, which sees it, but the brain or mind to which it has been brought. And we can say with assurance that many objects can be sensed or felt and understood as well through touch as through sight, and some better.

A second reason is that in the training of the blind for vocations, where they can hope to earn a part or all of their living, any attention to beauty is not considered practical. It is commonly felt that there is so much to be learned in preparation for any trade or profession that time can not be spared for anything which can not actually be used—and of course beauty, it is usually thought, can not be used. But we are beginning to see that anything which contributes to the peace, stability of mind, and good spirits of the individual can be used, because it does contribute to his equipment for daily tasks and living. Moreover, if one is conscious of beauty, and the sense of order upon which it is based, he will probably find practical uses for it in whatever he is doing.

More than one observing employer has testified that in the mechanical trades the one who has a sense of the beautiful about his work, and carries it on with an aesthetic feeling, has a real advantage over the one who lacks it. The wise teacher and employer therefore encourages the development of the intellect and the taste of his blind employees, knowing that here are two spheres of the mind open to unlimited growth.

A third and ever present obstacle in the way of the development of the aesthetic sense among the blind is the limitations which those who can see, place upon them and their potentialities. It is well to remember that it was only a hundred and seventy years ago that, stirred by the now famous letter of M. Diderot known as "The Letter on the Blind for the Use of Those Who See," Valentin Hauy established in Paris the first school in the world for the blind. With great foresight he encouraged music, especially instrumental music, for his pupils, saying at the time that, although of course the blind would never become accomplished musicians, the outlet, the exercise, was unquestionably good for them. The achievements of blind persons in the field of music, so very far beyond Hauy's expectations, are now known to millions of people throughout the world. No informed person would now think of placing limitations on the development of a musician because of his blindness.

It is a reasonable hope that we are entering a period of development in our culture in which the interpretation of the arts and the advocacy of beauty as essential elements in all our lives, will have a much wider acceptance. Let us not underestimate the part which blind persons can take, and some are taking, to help usher in the new day. That we shall before too long have blind persons who can qualify as guides and docents in our museums and schools as interpreters of the wonders and beauties of nature and the arts of man, is an intelligent hope. Their paths to these positions of leadership and happiness will be partly cleared by the kind of communication on the aesthetic level which this book is encouraging between sighted and blind persons.

But besides these activities in the field of the professions, it is hoped that people in all walks of life will share their aesthetic treasures and experiences with each other. And that they will encourage the love and practice of beauty in the lives of all who feel it, and in the way that is best for them, whether through the sense of sight, or the sense of touch, or through any or all of the other senses of perception.

The cultivation of the aesthetic life by the sighted and the blind together will bring to both the realization of the best that has

been said about beauty, the immortal words of the English poet
John Keats:

> "A thing of beauty is a joy forever
> Its loveliness increases, it will never
> Pass into nothingness."

CHAPTER 2

THE SENSE OF TOUCH: A WAY TO
KNOWLEDGE—A WAY TO BEAUTY

*My hand is to me what your Hearing and Sight are to
you. In large measure we travel the same road, read the
same books, speak the same language, yet our experiences are different.*—HELEN KELLER

WITHOUT attempting to delve into the voluminous literature on the human hand and the sense of touch, which to
most blind persons is the chief sense of perception, the effort here
will be to note a few important facts concerning this indispensable
aid in the life, the progress, and the welfare of all mankind both
in acquiring knowledge and in the enjoyment of beauty; and to
understand something of the indispensability of touch to both
sighted and blind.

Too much credit cannot be given this superb sense of perception with which most of us are endowed, but it is well always to
realize also its relationship to the other senses, particularly the
sense of hearing, in the lives of most of the blind.

Touch is usually considered in connection with the hands and
perhaps more especially the finger tips, for it is the latter with
which first contacts are usually made, and through them that the
blind now have access to the world's written knowledge through
the almost universally used alphabet, Braille. It is also through
the finger tips that much of the exploring of objects is done. And
it is through the hand, its palm, fingers, and finger tips, that
exploration into the realm of the beautiful is made possible,
although the lips and the tongue, the feet and other parts of
the body are all employed in the sense of touch, and may also
play their part in aesthetic experience. In fact, our whole bodies

16

contribute through touch to our aesthetic feelings. Mark Shoe-smith, the teacher and sculptor who, although blind himself, yet taught many young people how to get pleasure through the practice and appreciation of sculpture, said in substance: "Sitting in a comfortable chair is an aesthetic experience which I very much appreciate and enjoy." But with the blind the touch of the hand is usually the beginning of knowledge.

It is well known that the hand, with its opposing fingers and thumb, is one of the most distinctive features differentiating the human from other animals. Man's high proportion of achievements, especially in the shaping of things, can be traced to this remarkably controlled articulation of thumb and fingers. It was through the liberation of his hands when man first stood erect, that he took his first definite steps toward civilization. And it has been largely through the perfecting of the functions of this great tool, or instrument, that cultures have been built, layer upon layer, and in variety beyond the power of any early imagination to foretell.

Professor Robert McDougal, in his book, *The Significance of the Human Hand in the Evolution of the Mind*, writes: "Since every intellectual advance is conditioned on the possibility of realizing in concrete form those more elementary conceptions from which it proceeds, it is perhaps not too much to say that the hand, through which alone this embodiment of thought and purpose is mediated, is of all bodily members the most human and the most noble; and that in its features and its adaptabilities is symbolized all that man has achieved in his long upward march from the primitive ooze."

The same idea is conveyed by Victor Perard, in the Foreword to his book, *Hands and Their Construction*, when he writes: "The sense of sight, smell and hearing are, in general, much keener in animals than in men. Man, however, excels in the sense of touch. Since it is through this sense that the recognition and appreciation of smoothness, roughness, size, texture, temperature, dimensional values, are transmitted to the brain, man's superiority in this sense has been an important factor in his mental development."

Since the hand has been so important in man's intellectual development and in his claims to superiority over other animals, it seems reasonable to believe that it can function freely and almost to the fullest satisfaction of some without the support of that other vital sense, sight. The confidence which some blind persons attach to this organ of perception is well exemplified by the blind-born Indian youth who, when told that an operation could be performed which could give him sight, said that he was not interested. And when the doctor attempted to describe the vast new world that would be his, he remained indifferent, and said that he would much rather be given a longer arm and a larger hand.

In such matters, no one can speak for a blind person except the blind person himself, and no one should generalize about a subject so vital. It is true beyond a doubt that many persons have found adequate compensation for the loss of sight in the knowledge, pleasure, and inspiration they have been able to get through touch and the power to manipulate and shape things with their hands.

If a large part of mankind had from the beginning been without sight it is obvious that civilization would not have developed in the manner we know it. It is, of course, futile to speculate on what it might have been or would be even now in such a contingency. But without speculation one can assuredly state that within our present civilization the blind, largely through their extraordinary use and development of the power of touch, have improved immeasurably their opportunity to understand the world about them, and to contribute their full share to shaping the culture we all enjoy. Possibly in proportion to their numbers, and in view of the opportunities available to them, the blind have done more than their share.

Although some may believe that the world of the blind is blurred and dim at best, it is well to recall the assuring words of Pierre Villey, himself blind, who wrote: "In a man's mind there are few notions that a blind man cannot acquire, because there are very few which come to us uniquely by means of the eyes." And he continued, "The mind of the blind man, which we are apt to think of as sober, is penetrated through and through by the light from outside . . . It [the mind] has the sense of hearing and that of touch, the former for spoken thought, the latter for written thought, both of them precious for making exterior objects known." And then this splendid spokesman for the blind says, for himself, what is undoubtedly the sentiment of many, perhaps of most, blind scholars and philosophers: "Through these two windows opening wide on the world, multitudes of ideas enter. What does it matter if the blind is down at the third window. Daylight has penetrated sufficiently within for everything to be in complete activity there."

It is somewhat ironical that, touch being the blind person's sight, it is not the *inability to learn* or to experience which stands in the way of his progress, but the lack of opportunities to use fully this very sense which he has. The sense of touch is the next best, and often the best, avenue of human perception. Elsewhere in this book reference will be made to the superior qualities of touch as a medium of perception, whether for the sighted or the blind; but here we may note briefly the process of letting the light of knowledge into the mind of a blind person through the window of touch.

The process by which one perceives objects through touch can be quite well understood if one will observe his blind friend explore an object, especially if it is one entirely new to him. Through feeling, tapping, pressing, and otherwise carefully examining with the fingers and tracing with the finger tips, the mind gains through touch a notion of the form, the structure, the material, and other elements of the object: a set of impressions of relatively great importance, and usually to be definitely remembered.

The recognition of objects, unless very familiar ones, does not take place instantly. It often requires many times of touching, and if the object is unfamiliar or unknown, the process of analysis is sometimes very long. If the examination fails to identify, or is too long drawn out, it may be necessary to have interpretation of the object before it can be well understood; this may be given through the verbal explanation of a sighted person or through written communication.

It should be remembered, too, that the perceiving hand will often recognize an object not so much by thoroughly feeling its structure and forms, as by recognizing its location or position and by its relation to other objects. This could be illustrated in many ways, as for instance that a blind man when dining with a friend should come in touch with the back of the dining-room chair. This contact would enable him to know where to sit, and the edge of the table would open the picture to much else he would need to know. A sighted person may get a still better idea of touch exploration if he watches his blind hostess set the table; the edge or rim of the table is her guide, and she places each dish and piece of silver exactly where it should be that it may be readily found by a blind guest, and in the conventional position for a sighted one.

The quest for knowledge through touch (and this chapter is especially for the layman who may not have had an opportunity to observe a blind person closely) may be divided or thought of both in terms of manual exploration of the physical world as illustrated above, and as acquiring knowledge by touch through the reading of Braille, now the standard form of written communication, which substitutes dots for the letters of the alphabet with some supplementary symbols or signs.

Although the number of talking books is increasing rapidly, and other mechanical methods for hearing are being devised, and although the great majority get their knowledge through sound, yet blind persons are dependent upon touch as a way to most of the recorded writing of the present and past, and of course are dependent on it for any correspondence or written messages which they may send or receive.

Hence whatever of man's experience and knowledge is acquired by the blind through reading, must be by the sense of touch. The writing now available to the blind covers thousands of books and other publications, and much more is constantly being brailled by volunteer workers the country over. Summing up, then, the blind discover and explore the physical world through touch; and touch is their way of interpreting all that has been set down in Braille for them. Therefore touch is, for the blind, the surest and best way to knowledge, and for the deaf-blind it is the only way.

Since a joy ranking high in the life of the individual is the quest for knowledge for its own sake, a sharp line between this quest for knowledge and the quest for beauty can not in reality be drawn. There is nothing which gives man greater distinction than his insatiable search for knowledge and his right of access to it must never be denied because he may through no fault of his own lack one of the chief means of inquiry, eyesight. Whatever way may be devised for conveying knowledge to the blind in the future must, as at present, be through the sense of hearing or the sense of touch. The sense of touch is the only one which he can employ at will and by himself, independent of another. Even with the talking machines, be they records on tape or disk, in order to hear them he must adjust them through his sense of touch.

Finally, the sense of touch should be thought of as having at least two functions: one for discovering or identifying, the other for appreciating or enjoying. As a blind friend put it, "A keen touch, a utilitarian touch is not the same as an appreciative touch. The consciousness of tactile beauty is a flower which will have an unusually rich soil in which to grow once the seed has been planted in a blind person's mind. The latent capacity is there." But whether we are thinking of the utilitarian touch or the appreciative touch, there is one fact we must always keep in mind, that with touch as with sight there are many grades of perception. I have in mind one person especially who, on a walk or observing a special spot or object, will see many details which I can not see at all until she points them out and I focus my eyes on them. Sometimes, in order to get them, I have to use a magnifying glass. Such a person we say is myopic, or nearsighted. I believe there may be just as much difference in the gradations of touch as of sight. I have observed many gradations; some persons will through touch perceive objects so small that others can not perceive them at all. Therefore we whose sense of touch is quite crude should be careful not to place any limits on the tactual perception of any blind person.

In discussing touch we will sometimes use the words "beauty" and the arts interchangeably; so we may well recall a sentence from the report of the "Harvard Committee on General Education in a Free Society": "Precisely because they wear the warmth and color of the senses, the arts are probably the strongest and deepest of all educative forces."

If we are conscious of touch as a way to knowledge we are, perhaps without knowing it, on our way to beauty; for while all knowledge is not beautiful, much that is pervading, uplifting, and enduring is; and without knowledge, however gained, our powers of aesthetic experience would be very limited. It is from knowledge that we make our choices, among them our choices of lovely thoughts and things.

Our question here is, can we in the absence of sight, assisted by verbal or written interpretation, and relying mainly on the sense of touch, find our way to a world of beauty satisfying to the mind, or intellect, and to the spirit, often filling our cup of happiness and delight?

The testimony is overwhelming that we can. The testimony of persons who have never seen a ray of light, and of those who have lived part of their lives in light and part in darkness, and of some who can neither see nor hear, all convinces us that the fullest lives have been lived by persons who lacked not sight alone, but also other senses of perception. With this knowledge one is almost constrained to believe that as long as one of the senses of perception remains intact and active as a line of communication to the brain, the personality lives and functions.

We are not here considering the doubly handicapped, those who can neither see nor hear; they are reserved for the chapter on beauty for the deaf-blind. The problem here is very much simpler, where we are considering only those who, although they can hear, have lost or have never had their sight. And we return to the basic point, the sense of touch as a way to beauty.

Every sighted person, if he thinks at all, will recall some instances in which he has gained a good idea of an object through touching it; perhaps a better idea than he could gain in any other way, and many sighted persons will testify to the same thing. It is then but a short step from these experiences of seeing persons to that of the blind person who, not seeing at all, must rely mainly on the sense of touch to get a general notion of the nature of the object and to gain from it any pleasure or enjoyment.

The three main qualities which a sighted person seeks in an object and which are at the root of his aesthetic experience, namely, material, function, and form, are perceivable and knowable through touch; therefore they are often as comprehensible to the blind as to those who see. Let us try to consider these basic elements or attributes of beauty both through the eyes of the sighted and through the perceiving hands of the blind.

It is difficult to get at the root of the aesthetic experience through words alone, although good writing helps and thoughts beautifully expressed are fine contributors. But it is doubtful if seeing a material, or hearing of it, or reading about it will exceed in satisfaction the experience of recognizing and classifying it in our minds by touch. From infancy to maturity we will wish to get our hands on a material for which we have any feeling. If we cannot touch it we are apt, at a very early age, to cry for it, and at any age to be disappointed if we are thwarted in our desire to get it into our hands. Why? Because with most of us, feeling it is our best way to know it, and in the absence of sight, it is almost the only way.

The reason for our desire, and often our insistence, that we identify ourselves with the material in an object, is because it is an essential contributor to our knowledge and understanding of it. It is a part of the experience through which we convince ourselves as to the fitness, the appropriateness, of the object for its avowed purpose.

Santayana says of the importance of materials in the sensuous experience, "However subordinate the beauty may be which a garment, a building or a poem derives from its sensuous material, yet the presence of this sensuous material is indispensable. Form cannot be the form of nothing. If, then, finding or creating beauty, we ignore the materials of things, and attend only to their form, we miss an ever present opportunity to heighten our effects. For whatever delight the form may bring, the material might have given delight already, and so much would have been gained toward the value of the total result."

And he continues; "There is no effect of form which an effect of material could not enhance, and this effect of material underlying that of form, raises the latter to a higher power and gives the beauty of the subject a certain poignancy, thoroughness and infinity which it otherwise would have lacked. The Parthenon, not in marble, the King's crown not of gold, and the stars not of fire, would be feeble and prosaic things. The greater hold which material beauty has upon the senses stimulates us here, where the form is also sublime, and lifts and intensifies our emotions. We need this stimulus if our perceptions are to reach the highest point of strength and acuteness. Nothing can be ravishing that is not beautiful pervasively."

The observation of the aesthetic value of materials points to a fact of great importance in a democratic society, namely, that these types of enjoyment are within the reach of all or almost all.

They do not require a special training or wide travel or priority advantages to be enjoyed, because they are within the common knowledge or at least within reach of most persons; and as we shall see when reporting the experiences with blind persons, the mere mention of the material, the fact that this object is crystal, amber, jade, or coral, that it is made of clay or ebony or amethyst, excites the desire to feel it and explore its qualities more fully than the eye would ordinarily do. Because one who sees can often get a partial effect of the material at a glance, his eyes, always roving, will travel elsewhere; but when the blind person senses this same material through touch he will often make much more of it. He will get its hardness, its temperature, and other qualities, enjoyable at the moment, and pleasant to look forward to again and again. And if it be a material which is new to him, it adds an item of importance and sometimes of delight to his collection of pleasant feelings and remembered things, and he is sure that touching it is the best way to experience it.

Everyone who sees or feels a man-made object will wish to know very early what its purpose is. When he knows this he begins to form his considered judgments as to how well it fulfills its function. The more he knows about the use of an object the better able he is to appreciate the qualities it has, and as he compares one object with another, he becomes sensitive about the one which responds best to his needs and his thoughts. All this is an aesthetic exercise; it may be in connection with a single sheet of paper on which he has printed or written some thought by hand; or in connection with a piece of leather of morocco or calf to be used in binding his completed book: or in the selection of a fine tool with which he is to shape a piece of wood or carve an inscription on stone. It might be a special chair on which he prefers to sit, a "settin' chair" from the Southern Highlands which fits him, and his mental concept better than anything else he knows. Every person who is at all sensitive will have his feelings about the function or purpose of the object, and a blind person who is to determine that point for himself will often give function a major consideration in the object he makes for himself or for someone else; or the object which comes his way to use and to enjoy.

There is that third aesthetic consideration about which a blind person will have as deep a conviction as any sighted person could have: the form which the final product takes. To many designers, sculptors, painters, authors, architects, and laymen, form is the great end; and in many cases it says the most that can be said of an object. There can be no color, no decoration or ornament which exceeds the importance of the form; it is of all qualities the most definite and lasting; it stands out in every light for what it is, no accident but the carefully thought-out end which the object must say or be.

Forms of reasonable dimension which can be felt without changing the position of the body or which can be held in one or both hands comfortably, even down to miniature forms in which the elements or the directions can be sensed, are often as perceivable to one who can not see as to one who can; and therefore can be as well judged for their appropriateness. I am certain that these three basic elements of an object are thoroughly comprehensible and enjoyable to the blind, through the sense of touch mainly, but supplemented by whatever other qualities and associations thought will bring to the object. Therefore the blind person can have a good and satisfying hold on beauty.

These three elements, that is material, function and form which we have found essential to the comprehension and the enjoyment of objects of beauty, are elements which are clearly perceivable to blind persons, mainly through the sense of touch. But there are sometimes other elements in the experience of beauty which are perceivable to touch; order, proportion, motion, temperature, rhythm, flow of line, and especially textures.

Whatever name we may give it, "tactile beauty" or something else, we must admit that it can be an aesthetic experience of a high order, comparable to that enjoyed by a sighted person who attains it through another avenue of perception.

The number of objects he can enjoy will surely increase with each generation, for of the making of things by hand there must be no end, and no one doubts the continuance and increase of beautiful things made partly or entirely by machinery. So there will be no end to their enjoyment by the blind, if those who see them with their eyes will help place them within the reach of those who must know them best through their hands. The number of beautiful things which sighted and blind can enjoy together are far beyond the limitations of figures to suggest. The way to beauty is on the highway of knowledge and of thinking, of which there is no foreseeable limit as human communication is increased, improved, and enriched.

The aesthetic response is a subjective one to which the whole gamut of personal impressions and experiences make their special contribution. It is a response for which all of our life has been preparing. It is for us to attain not only for present enjoyment, but to cherish for its recalling power. We leave beauty as we leave a friend, anxious and ready to return.

It was for all, that John Galsworthy left this message, "In these unsuperstitious days, no other ideal seems worthy of us, or indeed possible to us, save beauty—or call it, if you will, the dignity of human life . . . the teaching of what beauty is, to all . . . so that we wish and work and dream that not only ourselves, but everybody may be healthy and happy, and above all the fostering of the habit of doing things and making things well, for the joy of the work and the pleasure of achievement."

CHAPTER 3

SOME ABILITIES AND ACHIEVEMENTS
OF BLIND PERSONS

There is no man living who can not do
more than he thinks he can.—HENRY FORD

ALTHOUGH the main theme of this book is the sharing of beauty between sighted and blind persons, there lies behind it an even broader purpose: to help reveal how much alike in interests, tastes, aspirations, abilities, and accomplishments are those of us who see the world about us mainly through our eyes, and those who see it through other senses of perception.

The more alike we come to know sighted and blind persons to be in many and diverse ways, the easier it is for us to understand how they can be alike in particular ways; and how, for instance, the blind can derive pleasure from many of the same things which bring pleasure to seeing persons. If it can be shown that blind men and women do well the same things which seeing men and women do to make a living or to realize dreams, the way will be partly cleared for the belief that beauty is something which both need equally and which they can experience together.

As countless persons without sight throughout the ages have said, with imploring earnestness, "We who are blind are just like you, except that we do not see with our eyes." And anyone who knows a blind person well, knows that this is true.

But the vast majority of us have never had the opportunity to know blind persons well, and because they are so few in comparison with the whole population, and because until very recently the age-old beliefs persisted that there was something about blindness which cut the individual off from the sources of perception and learning essential to a normal, useful, and full life,

27

I bring in at this point some evidence that blind persons are just like other people except for the lack of sight.

It was not until after the date of our Declaration of Independence that any provision was made, anywhere in the world, for schools or other facilities for learning which would help the blind become useful and productive members of society with the hope of sharing the privileges and responsibilities of other citizens.

The first school ever established for the blind was in Paris, France, in 1784. It is therefore considerably less than two centuries ago, to quote a great French scholar, Pierre Villey (himself blind), "since the sun rose for the first time, on the little world of the blind." Valentin Hauy, founder of the school, declared that the rank and file of those who could not see with their eyes were nevertheless capable of receiving the moral and intellectual culture which, as Villey said, "has not only brought into their darkness light for their souls and fortified so many hearts and minds, which until then were barren; it also brought in a laborious hive of workers who endeavor to ensure for its members hitherto outcasts of society, more and more every day, so that, with more complete development of their faculties, they may know the dignity and the joy of useful activity.

"Until then the blind had led isolated lives. The conquest of each one of them had been lost for his brother in misfortune. By inviting them all to enjoy the benefits of Instruction, Valentin Hauy created a bond between them. Common interests now unite them. . . . What one discovers for the improvement of his own fortune or welfare is conveyed to them all."

What has been accomplished for and by the blind in less than one hundred and seventy-five years since Hauy founded "L'Institution Nationale des Jeunes Aveugles" (The Institution for Young Blind People), surpasses the imagination of any one person. Hauy's path was far from smooth in combating the prejudice in his native France and other countries, but he somehow kept his school going, and before he died he had established another school at St. Petersburg (now Leningrad) in 1807. Other countries followed his lead—England at Liverpool in 1791; Scotland at Edinburgh in 1793; Austria at Vienna in 1804; Germany at Steglitz in 1806; Switzerland at Zurich in 1809; Denmark at Copenhagen in 1811;

Ireland at Dublin in 1815; Spain at Barcelona in 1820. These were of course only the first schools for the blind in these countries.

Forty-eight and forty-nine years after Valentin Hauy established that first school in France, America came into the picture with three schools: in 1832, the New England Asylum for the Blind, now known as Perkins School for the Blind; in the same year the New York Institution for the Blind, now known as the New York Institute for the Education of the Blind in New York City; and in 1833, the Pennsylvania Institution for the Instruction of the Blind in Philadelphia, now the Overbrook School for the Blind. Since these three pioneer schools for America were established, the United States and Canada have written some of the great chapters in the world's work for the blind.

Society, and the blind especially, owe a great debt to those blind persons of many countries who have clearly demonstrated their ability to think through problems and perform tasks commonly supposed to be beyond the powers of those without sight. "What man has done, man may do" has been demonstrated over and over again by thousands of blind persons, and probably never so often as in our time and in our own country. There are also the pioneers who go ahead of what has yet been done; as Helen Keller says, "While they were saying among themselves, 'It can't be done,' it was done."

In searching for material to support the thesis that the blind are just like other people except that they do not see with their eyes, I expected to find a book somewhere, in addition to occasional magazine and newspaper articles, on the achievements of blind persons from which I could draw examples to illustrate how very alike are the blind and those who see. The quest led me back to the first book ever written on that subject in America or, as far as I know, in any country, a quaint but enlightening small volume, *Beauties and Achievements of the Blind,* the manuscript of which was finished just over one hundred years ago. It was printed twelve years later, in 1869. And the reason prompting the two young authors, both of them blind, to write their book was to help clear the way for the development of persons trained and qualified to work, but who, because of the prevailing ignorance about blindness, were denied the opportunity to make a living. The authors believed or at least hoped that if the world could know what blind persons had already accomplished it would open the doors of opportunity for those qualified to make a living but who were at the time neither socially nor economically acceptable.

Beauties and Achievements of the Blind was respectfully inscribed, "To the American Public Whose Philanthropic Heart Ever Moves at Humanity's Call." The authors, William Artman and L. V. Hall, were two young graduates of the then twenty-four-year-old New York Institution for the Blind (now New York Institute for the Education of the Blind, New York City). In their short and modest Introduction they wrote, "Upon the history of our lives we shall say but little" but "for the satisfaction of the curious, we were born in Western New York within the vicinity of 24 years ago, that Artman lost his sight at the age of 18; that Hall's privation was congenital; that we were both educated at the New York Institution for the Blind, and have for the last four or five years been endeavoring to force a subsistence from nature and society, in various and of course *honorable* occupations."

"Reason as well as experience proclaims to us," says the Preface, "that until the efforts of the blind are weighed in the balance of merit, it is impossible for us to succeed in any undertaking. Sympathy like the atmosphere, surrounds us on every side, but like this, it is too light to sustain life." To meet this situation and problem, the authors "have deemed it expedient to give the facts we wish to illustrate in connection with the lives of some of the most distinguished blind persons."

The characters were "chosen from almost every age, century, occupation, and class of society and we have imported from Europe for this purpose, numerous valuable works written by the blind, never before possessed by the American public."

If such a book were written today, it would differ greatly from this volume of a century ago. There would be now a much longer list of the things which blind persons do to make a living, because there are now so many more opportunities which factory and mass production has developed for labor, especially in the United States; and because our blind citizens have worked themselves up and into many trades, skills, and professions. And there are now so many kinds of work which blind persons can do, of which our authors of the 1850's could not have dreamed, fine dreamers as they were.

In addition to the great changes in work have been equally great changes in recreation and sports, in which the activities and achievements of the blind in our country have far exceeded those of any other land. These indoor and outdoor sports include fishing, rowing, horseback riding, bowling, wrestling, ice and roller skating, skiing, golf, track athletics, dancing, walking, mountain climbing, and others.

Nation-wide statistics on the work activities of the blind are hard to come by, but various informants give the impression that there is hardly a trade or profession in which some blind persons are not engaged. The men and women employed in industry, in the trades, and in office work are so many that it is not possible even to begin a list of them here. There are possibly several hundred teachers in public and private schools and colleges of the country; there are many musicians of all kinds, both teachers and performers; the National Federation of the Blind has compiled a list of more than a hundred practicing lawyers, and there is an estimate of about fifty practicing doctors.

Probably the largest number of blind leaders in any of the professions is in the general field of social welfare; especially in those divisions of the work dealing directly with the blind. Many of the leaders and others who work for and with the blind are well known to the public, and to mention any of them here would mean leaving out many who merit inclusion. Therefore, that perhaps most notable group of blind servants of society is omitted here; but we will choose a few examples from other "workers at large" to illustrate the wide participation of the blind in many walks of life. Of those included, eight are from the United States and one from France. These may be considered symbols of the blind in the work of the world.

From a long list of distinguished, though not widely known blind persons, I have selected, as a very inadequate cross-section: a house builder from New Jersey, a farmer from New York State, a minister from Kansas, an electronics engineer from New York City, a teacher from Illinois, a Friend of Indians from Arizona, a lawyer from Rhode Island, a gardener from Pennsylvania, and a doctor from France.

THE HOUSE BUILT IN THE DARK
BY FRANCIS BURDETT

"A person never knows all he is talented to do until he tries," explained Francis Burdett when someone asked how he, sixty-five years of age and totally blind, ever managed to build his two-and-a-half-story, seven-room Dutch-Colonial house, without any help except from the mason who made the concrete foundation and the brick chimney.

Several blind persons in the United States are credited with building their own houses, quite a number have built barns and constructed shelters for animals and poultry, but since only one blind house builder could be included in this chapter, I have selected Francis Burdett.

I went all through and around his house after he had finished and was living in it. Although I did not see the house when it was going up, I knew several who did, and the details of his work and the stages of progress are admirably recorded. Not only did he build it entirely by himself, except the foundation and the chimney, but he and his wife dreamed it; he designed every detail of it, including the mason work, installed the plumbing, amazed the neighbors by sawing and hammering on nights so dark you could not see your hand before you, causing many a listener to hold his breath; he framed the roof and moved all over it, twenty-five and thirty feet above the ground, with no more concern than if he were on the first floor.

The roof was the only place where the closest inspection could find evidence that the builder of this house could not see. Two short stretches of the asbestos shingles with which he had covered it came out finally a little different color from the others. This had happened on an icy winter day—or night—when he was working on the roof in a sleet storm, his fingers so numb from cold that he failed to distinguish the right side of the shingles from the wrong side, as he had in all other cases by a slight difference in the sanded texture of their sides.

Francis Burdett was not a carpenter during the fifty-odd years in which he had his sight. He was a skillful and successful jeweler and watchmaker, a fine craftsman in gold and silver, with an established business in Providence, Rhode Island, when one day a truck ran into him, causing injuries which brought about blindness, and changed much of the course of his life. While learning to be a blind man he taught himself how to use carpenters' tools and did cabinetwork, made children's furniture and novelties, which he sometimes sold, and with his wife's earnings as a trained nurse, they together made the income for the family.

From the beginning of Mr. Burdett's handicap, they began to dream of a house of their own, and their thoughts turned toward the Colonial Dutch type, similar to one they had once had in Rhode Island. However, this type of house seemed at first quite beyond them in several ways, the financing being one. But whatever their house might be, it was agreed that Mr. Burdett, who had become quite skillful with carpenters' tools, should build it. And so first he built a two-room bungalow on the outskirts of Wayne, New Jersey, which served as temporary quarters until the new house was finished.

The new house (illustrated here) when finished—and it took Mr. Burdett two and a half years' steady work without vacations —was two and a half stories, or three, if the attic counts for one, of Dutch-Colonial type with living room, dining room, and kitchen downstairs, four bedrooms, three closets, a hallway and bathroom upstairs, a basement, and enclosed back porch. The house completed was 26 feet wide at the front, 30 feet deep, and 29 feet high.

The dream began long before the two-room bungalow was built, but it was in this very small house of two rooms, the building of which had been an encouragement toward the great house, that everything was thought out by the architect and builder, while his wife was away much of the time, nursing in private houses or hospitals, earning much of the meager family income. And thinking it out required something more than is usual in the planning of a new home. Instead of spending days, yes weeks, as a sighted person would, deciding on plans and specifications, making numerous visits to an architect's office, finally selecting just the type of house desired, the materials to be used, and the hundreds of details that go into the building, and then making blueprints without which the contracting builder could do nothing; instead of this, the blind builder had to bend his mind from the first stake to be driven for the foundation to the completely finished house, with every detail included, and he had to do all this without a single outside suggestion, and store away in the pigeonholes of his mind the complete plans and specifications as he thought them out. And he must hold them in his head until he could pull them out again, one by one, as needed, and put into final form, not on blueprint paper but in bodied form, the details and unity of the house itself.

This he did with the help of a piece of cardboard which he shaped with his hands and made his mind follow; not through the eye, which usually follows patterns, but through feel in his sensitive finger tips. The first part of this process was to determine the scale which his simple model would take; he set it at one inch to the foot. The first shape he cut out was the elevation of the front of the house in the form of a silhouette. That is, the cardboard was exactly the shape he intended the front of the house to be—only it was one-twelfth the size. Into the cardboard, which was very heavy, he placed a tack at each bend and angle, and working from such guides he constructed the house timber by timber until it was completed. Not able to see a level, he made all angles in his house correct with the use of his steel square. When a variation from a right angle was required, as in the pitch of the roof, he figured out how it should feel, made a templet of cardboard or of wood and followed that in his construction. Of course for lengths he used a special yardstick and his steel square.

It is not possible here to follow all the details of the building through, but it will help if one understands that the carpenter ordered his lumber in the rough, as any contractor would, and shaped it into the forms needed with his saws, planes, and other woodworking tools—no power tools or machines on the job. Most of the doors, the door casings, and the window frames were finished at the mill, but such work as the stairs between floors and into the basement Mr. Burdett shaped up and built himself.

Almost all the lumber, the joists, beams and rafters and other timbers for the framework he handled alone; and with heavy timbers and large window frames used a block and tackle. I believe it was seventy-six floor beams of 2 x 10 timber that he sawed, fitted, and fastened in place. The construction of the roof frame in this house was far from simple for any builder, but with patience, skill, and the lifting help of his block and tackle, he accomplished it—the last part of the framework to be done. Emphasis is on the "last part" here, because the blind builder working alone could not proceed as a group of sighted workers could do—erecting the whole frame of the house, including gables, first. Our blind builder first laid the rough floor of the building so that he could have a solid place to stand and work on. Then he built the frame of the first story complete; then laid the second floor, built the frame of the second story, and laid the floor of the attic; and from this floor and scaffolding, which he erected himself on the outside of the building, he was able to construct the roof.

The imagination will help picture the thinking and the action of our blind house builder, if we visualize him day after day and night after night in the bungalow, holding in his hand the cardboard model, or silhouette, of the front end of the house, 26 inches wide, in the center about 29 inches high to the top of the ridgepole; and the length and directions of the framing timbers indicated by the outside lines of the pasteboard model. From this he would see in his mind's eye the entire structure, first from the front, then straight back to the end of the house. Each timber that went into the structure he would have to memorize and know where to find. In the same way he would memorize all the materials to be used—nails, screws, etc. And of course he always knew where his tools were, and he had facilities for sharpening his chisels, filing his saws, etc. He built a tool shed immediately back of the house, where he kept both tools and some materials, and where, when storms came, he could rest and eat his lunch. He built himself three ladders of different lengths, six wooden bucks, a workbench, and many contrivances to save his time and make for accuracy, one being a simple wooden form, which he used hundreds of times to give him the exact distance between studs, rafters, and other free timbers, since he could not see to measure them with his rule.

To the question often asked of the builder—how he ever did it, he would reply, "To succeed at anything, be it a large, intricate undertaking, or of less significance, a person must have first a reason, second a purpose, third an interest in the objective, and fourth, a determinate will to do it. In my case, the first three points I mentioned were very clear to me; and, I believe, my own self-will to do something worth while, and my condition, forced me to do it. I am totally blind, and sixty-five years old; for years my wife found it necessary to work at her profession as a nurse to support us both. This necessitated her constant absence from home. Neither of us had any real comforts. I learned to cook my own food, bake bread, and do about everything needed to be done around the house. But circumstances made it necessary for Mrs. Burdett to pack her grip, rush off to some hospital or private home, and leave me stranded in the dark alone. Often I wouldn't hear her voice for a whole month." Then they decided on a plan to work together, and this called for a house they had long dreamed of—the house which their neighbors named the "Miracle House."

"I have been asked many times how I can plod away here on this building early and late, wet and dry, hot and cold, making slow progress, and still remain cheerful. I always felt that cheerfulness is an asset to success, and is needed to reach a goal, whether a man can see or not, and it is an encouraging sound that is heard by himself in humming a tune as he works. A person never knows all he is talented to do until he tries.

"Many people have told me that the building is a credit to the community. Of course I cannot see it, but I have a fair conception of its appearance. I have felt every inch of it with my hands and kept the finished house in my mind as I worked. My hope is that it will help others . . . to reach some worthy goal."

THE BLIND FARMER OF THE CATSKILLS: JOSEPH MCDONAGH

Joseph McDonagh, the blind farmer of the Catskills, was born on a farm in County Roscommon in the middle of Ireland in 1889. "When a lad of sixteen, I came to America to make my own way in a wonderful new land. I came into the new country alone, and purposely, to 'find myself,' and to prove to myself that I could survive by my own hands. . . . Work was found for me on the docks of New York City. Here I was for near ten years when, in 1916, a serious work accident blinded me.

"It was seven years later in 1923 that friends took me to the Catskills, and we found a small shanty in the foothills, where they left me, and where I made myself at home for over fifteen years.

I was often cold, and more than often hungry. One time there was so little food that we, my dog and I, shared a dog biscuit between us. Just dog biscuit and coffee. It was soon after this that Bozo, my favorite dog, and I came together. I have had several dogs, good and faithful, before and since; but Bozo was 'The Dog'." Pausing for words to express his feelings, he said simply, "No dog could do more for a man than Bozo did for me."

Mr. McDonagh explained how a friend in New Jersey told him about this dog when it was less than a year old; because no one seemed to be able to do anything with him it had been decided to destroy him. But this friend, believing him a very intelligent puppy, and remembering Joe's way with animals, asked Joe if he would like to take him on and train him. So Bozo joined his master in rural New York just in time to help him in his early experiments and experiences as a blind farmer.

Incidentally, Bozo was a mongrel, but very intelligent and loyal; his likeness appears on another page in the photograph of the farmer at the barn door with a favorite calf. Joe and Bozo lived and worked together for over fourteen years. When Bozo died, the farmer had a village stonecutter make a modest granite monument to mark his grave in the yard, a few paces from Joe's bedroom. Into the granite the stonemason carved this inscription:

In Memory of
My Faithful Dog
Bozo
Joe McDonagh
1947

Although Joe's early years were spent on a farm in Ireland, and though often while in New York he longed to get back to the soil, it was not so easy for a man who could not see and who had no capital for employing help. Moreover, his ambition was not to have someone work for him but to do things with his own hands and to have the closest association with farm animals, for he understood them and knew that they would understand and co-operate with him. The question was how to begin.

"Finally I bought ten hens, and in time, from this start, we, Bozo and I, were able to increase our flock to a hundred layers.

For feed we secured our grain in a town four miles away in hundred-pound lots, the miller dividing it up into bags of fifty pounds each, which I carried on foot—one bag today, the balance the next, Bozo showing me the way over the rough terrain and the road. At this time we cut up from twenty-five to thirty cords of wood each year, and piled it for winter fuel to burn in our shack, and some to sell for income. I carried our eggs to market in pails and baskets, Bozo leading the way. Every Sunday he would take me along three miles of mountain roads to Mass, leaving me at the church door; he waited for me outside and then took me home.

"One day a good neighbor gave me a Jersey calf to raise. Then a summer resident boarded a three-quarter Jersey cow with me, and that was the start of my dairy herd. Cows of other breeds have been in the herd from time to time, but Jerseys have predominated, and they are my favorite strain; they respond to my personal care. My Jerseys eat less, are gentle, and there is a ready market for the quality of milk. Each has its individual personality and character, its own beauty and form of refinement. I enjoy their company, often talking to them. Keeping a cow in the barn a few days trains her to my ways and wishes. She is turned out to pasture, and returns with the herd. Ten of the cows carry bells, but not Shamrock or Killarney! The pasture fence has but one strand of wire. And not a cow has left me in seven years."

And the calves are still closer to him, for he, and no one else, touches them from the time they come into the world until he weans them. "I let them nurse all they want from the cow for four days," he explained, "then I take over with two quarts of milk of an even temperature and warm pails. And I have never lost a calf." He not only talks to his cows and calves, but sometimes sings to them, and when a famous Irish folk singer and accordionist visited Mr. McDonagh, he was invited to come to the barn and play for the animals, which he did with fine feeling while Joe did the milking.

The Green County Farm Bureau reports that "his cows are healthy, well cared for, and produce well above the average. They know him well, and he knows them. The stable, the milk house, and the utensils are clean and tidy. He keeps from ten to fourteen head of milking cattle, breeds artificially, feeds scientifically, attends dairy Grange meetings faithfully, and by his neighbors is judged an all-around good dairy farmer." Since this account was written, he has also stepped up the quality of his herd, has received special awards of merit from the Department of Agriculture, and is in the forefront of progress in dairy farming in the Catskill area.

"My calves do not realize it, but my cows know I am blind as well as I do, but they never take unfair advantage of their knowledge." He has fond names for them all, usually Irish in character, from a song or a poem, and they come to his call. There is Wild Irish Rose, Killarney, Irish Eyes, Buttercup, Palmela (born on Palm Sunday), Kathleen, Erin Go-Bragh (Ireland forever), Shamrock, and others. The relations between them would probably have been the same had Joe been a sighted farmer, for he says, "I love all animals. A blind person can make friends with animals easier than sighted people, strange as it may seem. I feed the birds in winter when their pen is empty—they fly about me and chirp as though to say, 'Feed me!' The only time I left my animals was in 1941. The cows and Bozo and Happy [his son] were left with Miss Watson. 'Kitty Bang,' our cat, and her kittens were at my former home half a mile away, with plenty of food. But Kitty Bang brought her kittens, one by one, to be with her dogs and cows. And there I found them all together when I returned."

When Joe McDonagh was asked if he was ever lonely, he replied, "Me lonely? I should say not! I have friends in my neighbors, and my visitors have been as many as 3500 a year." And he continued, "Blindness is not bad. You have to take your afflictions, if there is anything wrong with you,—never mind what it is. Have faith in God, confidence in yourself. No self-pity, and the world will smile with you."

JOHN URICH, THE BLIND BOY WHO WANTED TO BE A MINISTER

John Urich was born in Kansas City, Kansas, the only sightless child of a family of six. His parents were poor, his father a laborer in a packing plant, but they all pulled together, and when John was nine he knew what he wanted to do, and why. He told their family pastor that he wanted to be a minister, so that he could help other people, as the pastor was always doing. But as he grew older he heard much arguing about it, and when he had finished high school and it came time to go to college he was about convinced that the people were right, that a minister ought to be a man who could see. But if he could not be a minister he would try to find other ways to help people and he was encouraged by the promise that if he earned his university degree he might become a worker in the social welfare field.

He earned the degree in the University of Kansas School of Social Sciences, and while in college he married a blind student who shared his ambition. After graduation they settled in Kansas City, their savings nearly exhausted, awaiting the job he had been promised. John Urich filled out all the papers, and then waited for a long time for the expected call, finally to be told that he lacked the qualifications. The reason for the turn-down was not specified but it was final and both John and Carole knew that the disqualification was blindness.

He then decided to try his luck in another city, one where he knew jobs were plentiful, for we were in a war. This was in 1942, and with all his savings, a total of forty-five dollars, his belongings in a small suitcase, his seeing-eye dog Bonnie as his companion, he took the cheapest transportation route, a bus, to Washington, D.C. Here he knew there was work for everyone, and, thrilled by the prospect of joining in the war effort and hopeful of having his wife Carole join him soon, he and Bonnie set out on their hunt for employment.

It was hot summer, the pavement blistered Bonnie's feet as they walked from one building to another filling out papers, answering questions, and wondering why—and yet knowing why—there was such waiting and hesitancy about giving a strong, capable, and willing young man in his prime, work that he was so anxious and able to do. All he could do was to leave the address and telephone number of the inexpensive hotel where he was staying, in case anything should develop.

This tragic story of looking for work in the capital city and much more is well told, and in detail, by A. E. Hotchner in the *Saturday Evening Post*, where Urich says, "There were any number of clerical jobs I could have performed, but no one wanted to take a chance on a blind man." But one morning as, tired and discouraged, he was waiting for a heavy rain to stop so he might start another day's search, the phone rang and he was offered a job of transcribing letters. "What will you do if you make a mistake?" he was asked. "I won't make any," he said quietly, and set about to type his first letter, and when finished he called the supervisor to inspect it. "It's fine," she said, "but it's in red." The typewriter, as nobody had told him, had a black and red ribbon.

John Urich held this job for four years, and he and his wife were happy in living and working with people who treated them as equals. The young man's longing for the ministry was as strong as ever, but the minister of the church with which they were affiliated in Washington told him, "Whatever work you do will be Christian work. I am afraid you will have to be contented with that."

But later, when John got a job as counselor to blind soldiers in the Lutheran Church, the Presbyterian minister was so sympathetic with his longing to get into the ministry that he got in touch with an old friend, Professor Paul Scherer of the Lutheran Seminary, and soon John was invited to appear before the United Lutheran Synod of New York and New England, which governs the Lutheran Church of that area. He passed the oral examinations and asked for a chance to prove himself worthy of his ambition, pleading, "I want to be a minister because that's the best way there is to help people."

A majority of the synod voted to send him to the seminary; but Dr. Frederick R. Knubel, president of the synod, said, "I think it only fair to tell you . . . that knowing your limitations, I shall never in good conscience be able to give you a church. But if you wish to go to the Seminary, knowing this, I shall not stand in your way."

John and Carole Urich moved to Philadelphia in 1947 where he entered the Lutheran Theological Seminary in September. Here they lived frugally, and to help out she took in ironing. Then occasionally they earned a few dollars by entertaining at socials, Mrs. Urich at the piano accompanying John's fine baritone voice, their repertoire often including songs of their own composition.

At the end of the three-year course John Urich graduated second in his class. The Lutheran custom is for a pastor to go to a church

which needs a minister and preach a trial sermon; after this the
church, if it wants him, extends him an invitation to return. But it
was a long time before the blind minister received an invitation
to preach. Finally a young pastor, a classmate of John's at the
Seminary, was leaving his church in Brooklyn and asked John if
he would be interested. Urich asked Director Knubel if he might
try a few sermons on the Brooklyn congregation and the latter,
rather reluctantly, agreed. John preached three sermons and on
the fourth Sunday the church took a vote; it was twenty-nine
against to twenty-three for. But the young minister was not discouraged, he was elated. "It means," he said, "that twenty-three
of those parishioners wanted me as pastor. That's a good sign."

However, he did not get a church, nor was he often asked to
preach a supply sermon. One day he asked his friend Dr. Allen
if he thought there was any possibility of his entering the Presbyterian ministry. The Presbytery invited him to appear before them,
and agreed to accept his Lutheran study as requisite for their acceptance. "They seemed eager to have me," the young minister
said, "and there seemed to be no prejudice against my blindness.
I would be recommended to churches on an equal footing with
other seminary graduates. While I deeply regretted having to
switch churches . . . I decided I would rather be a Presbyterian
minister than a Lutheran layman."

The young minister began studying Presbyterian doctrine which
he concluded was not as different from Lutheran as some of his
professors at the Seminary had seemed to think. About this time
he received a telephone message from Doctor Knubel, telling him
there was a Lutheran church in New York City, the Grace and
St. Paul's Church on West Seventy-first Street, needing a new
pastor, and asking him if he would care to talk with them. He
met with the church council and they had a long discussion about
how he could manage to visit their widely scattered members.
After he had explained his ability to get around, and that visiting
members would not be a great difficulty, the council still seemed
skeptical. Finally Urich said, "Give me a trial. Take me on for
six months; if by then I don't measure up to what you want in a
preacher, you have simply to tell me and I will go. Is that fair?"

On March twelfth, the day before he was scheduled to appear
before the Presbytery, the full council of Grace and St. Paul's met

for final consideration. One of the elders, in a long written statement, set forth reasons why a blind minister wouldn't do; he pointed out that the applicant had been rejected by Brooklyn, and he felt a blind pastor would give his church a "crippled" appearance.

"Maybe what you say will come to pass," the chairman of the Pulpit Committee replied, "but that would be closing our minds. I do not think turning our backs on this man because he is blind is a Christian thing to do. I, for one, am in favor of giving Mr. Urich a chance."

The vote went fourteen to three in favor of the chance. The elder who lost said he would read his statement again to the whole congregation when they convened at the end of six months for the final decision.

The Urichs were joyful, but there were misgivings in the congregation. One member said, when he heard a blind pastor was coming; "I could not possibly get the right values out of a service, if I were worrying all the time that the pastor might fall backwards or knock down the candles. I want a pastor I can look up to, not one I pity."

But the first Sunday the members of the congregation were amazed at the sureness of the minister in conducting the service, moving about without groping from the altar to the chancel rail, up the steps to the pulpit, and down the center aisle to the door, where he spoke personally to many and bade them good morning. But it had taken the new minister long hours of practice to accomplish this.

He delivered a most effective sermon. He had a fine, deep, rich voice, a relaxed manner; he was, in appearance, a very normal person. In a few weeks his congregation were so absorbed in his sermons they seemed to have forgotten his blindness. The minister had a subway guide made up in Braille and was soon making home calls; Mrs. Urich organized a choir, played the organ, assisted in the Sunday school, helped form a young people's group, played the piano on social occasions.

Everything worked out well and the day before the trial period ended, the elder who had opposed him came to see the pastor. "I do not know how your congregation will vote tomorrow," he said, "but I want you to know that I think you are eminently qualified to be a pastor. I have been wrong in my judgment. You have proved that your lack of sight is in no way an impairment of your ability as a minister of God. I promise you that if this congregation won't have you, I shall do everything in my power to find you another."

Almost the entire congregation turned out for the special meeting. The minister knew he had made many friends, yet he was not sure that a clear majority of the congregation would want a blind man as a permanent minister. And to add to the uncertainty it had been decided to vote not by a showing of hands but by a secret ballot, so that no one would be pressed to vote against his convictions.

Mr. and Mrs. Urich waited in their apartment that Sunday morning, beside the telephone, while the voting was going on. At last the phone rang; the vote had been concluded; would they please come to the church right away?

"I somehow managed to get Bonnie's harness on," Mr. Urich explained afterwards, "and we entered the meeting room. There was a heavy silence and my heart sank. If the vote was against us, I would be an unemployed layman again, facing the heavy task of convincing some other group of 'see' people that I should be treated as their equal. What's more, I had grown fond of these people and the thought of having to lose them as friends was very painful."

The minister was escorted to the platform, but Carole stayed at the back of the room. Then the president turned to Urich and said: "As president of this church it is my duty to inform you of the pleasure of this congregation in regard to your status as our pastor. We have tabulated the votes and we find that not one single vote has been cast against you. You are our pastor by unanimous acclaim."

The pastor got to his feet and controlling his voice with difficulty said: "You have given a blind man and his blind wife faith and happiness to a degree that you have no way of knowing. You are the kindest and most courageous people I have ever known. God grant that I serve you long with the full measure of love and humility that is in me."

A member of the congregation said, "I would never have believed before Pastor Urich came here, that blindness brings a special quality to a minister. He has a sense of understanding that could come only from downright wisdom. Isn't justice always pictured as blind? The way I feel, it is often the pastor who sees and it is we who are blind."

Another member said, "It is as if in his dark sensitive world he has acquired some special understanding of God's will, and of mercy and love and the other things he talks about."

A friend has said, "Pastor Urich's face is of a man who has found his place. It is the face of a man who need never walk alone again."

BLIND FROM BIRTH;
HAM OPERATOR AT FIFTEEN;
NOW ELECTRONICS ENGINEER;
ROBERT T. GUNDERSON

Of all enthusiastic interests which an amateur can develop and practice, radio for many American "hams" holds the highest rank. To be able to communicate through the air with almost countless persons in this country and throughout the world, without interruption, is a miraculous kind of pastime. The only qualification is that one be licensed by the government as an operator.

We do not know how many ham radio operators there are in this country who are handicapped in some way, but all are free spirits, and among them we do know there are more than 700 who can not see. Some of them undoubtedly retain their anonymity just for the fun of it and because of the independence they enjoy, for here is one of the activities in which blind and sighted are on an absolutely equal level, and may be known to each other only by their government license numbers—unless for some reason they wish to tell some one their names, and that they are blind. There is an ethical code among the ham operators and some of the radio publications by which they do not divulge the fact that an operator is blind without the latter's permission, because as W4 PMO put it, "Amateur Radio is the only major hobby I know of which a sightless person may enjoy on an equal footing with his seeing colleague. Won't you let us keep this feeling of equality? We're so proud of it!"

The subject of this sketch, Robert Gunderson, is W2 JIO, the call number assigned to him when he passed his examination and became probably the youngest ham operator of his day at fifteen years of age. Bobbie had always been blind. Now he is a successful electronics engineer, but he is best known for what he has done to teach radio to hundreds of blind boys and men and otherwise help them toward satisfying positions of independence and productiveness. For, as far back as he can remember he had a life aim, and that was, and still is, to convince other blind persons that they can make their way in life along with seeing folks; and he has done his part more through actions than words, although when words are appropriate he is very articulate.

In 1927 Robert Gunderson came to the New York Institute for the Education of the Blind as a pupil. He was then eight years old. Before his graduation he became a teacher, starting a class there in radio technology, probably the first of its kind ever available to blind persons. It was his boy pupils who named him "Mr. Gunn" and the affectionate appellation still holds with the younger generation whom he still teaches nights at the old school.

My first visit with this remarkable blind teacher of the blind was at the Institute on a Monday night recently, in old Schermerhorn Hall where perhaps twenty blind boys were working, from a very little one who was screwing down an apparatus which I didn't understand, to several youths making their own radio sets; all working toward the time when they would be in touch with amateur operators everywhere, and some of them on their way to responsible and remunerative positions in the expanding field of electronics. They know that this is a field in which Mr. Gunn can help, for on his recommendation many older blind fellows have found permanent positions.

Since 1937 Robert Gunderson has turned out of his school more than 200 blind radio technicians, including several World War II veterans, some of whom came to the Institute in serious states of mental depression. But no one around Bob Gunderson remains that way long. And what means so much to all his pupils is their teacher's concern for them not only in their work in the School, but in doing all he can to help them become established in work and life.

Two of several special achievements for which Robert Gunderson is responsible are his contribution to the literature of electronics in the form that blind persons can read, and the extraordinary preparation of a deaf-blind student to become a government-licensed amateur radio operator.

One of the first difficulties that the blind pioneers in radio encountered when they entered the field of training was that all instructions for building and operating radio sets were in printed form; practically none of this literature was in Braille. There were some instances in which volunteers had transcribed certain articles; but there had never been anything like a satisfactory quantity of material available. For a long time Bob Gunderson had been planning a radio and electronics magazine for the blind which would meet this and other needs. There were many obstacles in the way, but he said that obstacles were there to be overcome; and in 1950 an opportunity developed of which he took immediate advantage.

He appeared on the program of Ralph Edwards' "This Is Your Life" feature, with the result that the sponsors of the program financed the first issue of *The Braille Technical Press,* with Robert W. Gunderson as editor. Bob and his wife Lillian, equally devoted to the cause, have kept this publication going, at no small sacrifice, and it has become indispensable. Many of the blind hams take it and others have it sent them. The price is 60 cents a copy or $7.00 a year. Many sighted persons send in gift subscriptions.

There is no record of Bob Gunderson ever turning down a blind boy who aspired to become a ham operator, but there was once a time when, for a while, he thought he would have to. It was when Leo Sadowsky, a Brooklyn youth, studying at the New York Institute for the Blind and thrilled by what radio was doing for his blind classmates, asked "Mr. Gunn" if he could teach him. Leo was a very bright boy, advancing well in his studies, but he posed a problem which the young blind teacher of the blind had never encountered, nor had anyone in the history of radio; for Leo was both blind and deaf.

Leo had been born deaf, and an accident had destroyed the sight in his left eye when he was two years old. He learned to read, type, and converse with the manual sign language. But as he was a constant reader his right eye became overburdened and at sixteen he became totally blind. He was nineteen when he came from the deaf-blind department of the Institute and asked to learn radio. The teacher at first told him it seemed impossible; but the boy's heart was so set on it that Bob, who had learned the manual sign language that he might talk to the deaf boys at the Institute, told him, "We will try."

It took two years to work this problem out. Leo started with a crystal detector; then he built a superhet complete with detector. He learned the code through a low-frequency buzzer—felt through his finger tips. He received all his lectures through the manual alphabet.

After Leo had built and could operate his own transmitting and receiving outfit, came the application to the United States government for an amateur license in order that he could get on the air. Several reasons were advanced for why he could not take the examination. One was that the test must be taken aurally; Leo, being deaf, could not qualify. "But," his teacher now recalls, "I had spent two years in training this boy and I was not willing to give up so readily. Finding it useless to argue, I set to work on some new equipment. This time instead of the low-pitched buzzer, the translating device operated a 60-cycle source of a.c. the output of which was fed into a public address system. The output of this amplifier in turn operated a head set. I tried this new equipment out, and it worked perfectly after we had spent a week or two on it."

He then reapplied to the Commission and explained the new equipment and how it worked, arguing that even though Leo could not hear he could take the code with a pair of head phones on his ears and that was all that was required. Permission to take the examination was granted.

At the examination Gunderson transcribed the printed questions of the examination into Braille, Leo answered them in Braille, and Gunderson in turn rewrote the Braille on the typewriter. All diagrams were described in words. To ten pages of written problems and questions Leo submitted thirty pages of answers written by himself on a Braille typewriter; and Gunderson in turn translated these into regular typewritten form. The examination was supervised by Arthur Bachelor, chief radio inspector of the second F.C.C. District. Then the papers were sent to Washington.

There were long days of waiting for Leo and his teacher, but finally a telegram came from the F.C.C. announcing that Leo Sadowsky had passed his examination and number W2 OFU had been assigned to the first deaf-blind ham ever to receive a government license.

This was one, and a very outstanding one, of Robert Gunderson's great achievements in the radio field, and there is not space to record more. I might parenthetically add that one morning when I dropped in to see Bob to have him check up on my statements, he told me that the night before he had had a good long conversation with a friend at the South Pole, winding it up by telling him how he could reach his girl friend in Minnesota on the telephone. And Bob put him through. "Of course, I did not listen to the conversation," Bob explained, "but I think they must have had a good visit, for they talked for over an hour."

A SUCCESSFUL TEACHER WHO CAN NEITHER SEE NOR HEAR: RICHARD KINNEY

It was not an easy choice to select one blind teacher from the many throughout the length and breadth of our land; from kindergarten to college, from teachers in rural schools to a superintendent of county schools, and scores in special fields of knowledge in public, private schools and colleges; and last, but far from least, the many blind teachers of the blind. But I have chosen a teacher whom I believe to be one of the ablest, whose influence, geographically calculated, is perhaps the widest, and whose handicaps are among the greatest of those of many fine blind teachers I know.

The subject of this sketch is Richard Kinney, Assistant Director of the Hadley School for the Blind, of Winnetka, Illinois, the only correspondence school for the blind in the world, with pupils in many states and on every continent. The main purpose of the Hadley School is to reach the homebound or those who cannot get to other schools, and they do this without expense to their pupils wherever they may dwell. Mr. Kinney teaches American and English Literature and History and also the courses in physical geography and salesmanship. "My favorites," writes Mr. Kinney, "are probably verse writing, American and English literature, for grammar is technology, but literature is art. Whatever the subject, the chief interest is the student, and here I am lucky." And he shares a few of his experiences with us.

Richard Kinney was born in East Sparta, Ohio. When seven, he lost his sight through illness, after finishing first grade. Four years later he entered the Braille classes in The Waring School in Cleveland. Here he learned Braille and in one winter passed grades two, three, four, and five.

Next fall he entered the East Sparta School, though his hearing had begun to fail. His parents read his lessons to him evenings, and he worked hard, graduating from high school in 1942 as valedictorian of his class. During high school days he began to write.

In the fall of 1942 he entered Mount Union College at Alliance, Ohio, depending on a powerful hearing aid. He was active in college life, and was poetry editor of the college paper. In January of 1944 his hearing blanked out, and he went home. But after a few months he enrolled in the Hadley School's home study courses in short story and poetry writing. He did such outstanding work that Hadley instructors urged him to return to college.

In 1950 he received a Helen Keller scholarship, and with additional aid from the Ohio Rehabilitation Service entered Mount Union in the fall of 1952. A fellow student, Ron Smith, served as his guide, spelling classroom lectures into his hand through the "manual." In the spring of 1954, Kinney graduated Summa Cum Laude, with an average grade of 3.94 out of a possible 4.00. Again he was valedictorian of his class.

Then his home town, East Sparta, had a "Richard Kinney Day." Hundreds came to the high school auditorium, and, standing between his father and mother, he shook hands with everyone. Of his parents he said that afternoon, "They always walked with me through both the rain and the rainbows." Young people recited some of his poems, delegations were there representing proud groups, the people of the town presented him with a brief case and a purse of $350, and a portrait of him was unveiled. There were many speakers and many more who sent telegrams; among them, Ohio's governor, two senators, Helen Keller, and President

Eisenhower. When everything was over, Richard Kinney rose to his feet and said simply, "You just can't lose when your friends outnumber your problems."

The graduate of East Sparta High and Mount Union College was already an instructor at Hadley, but now he was to give full time, using his talents, his energy, and his good cheer to bring the chance of an education to hundreds of blind and deaf-blind homebound students throughout the world who could not have this opportunity any other way. Of some of these students he says:

"Surely the most colorful student with whom I have ever worked is Mr. V., a retired soldier of fortune, who earnestly assured me that he is now in a California prison because of 'politics and a woman's revenge.' Mr. V. learned Braille in his early eighties, is now studying writing in the hope of re-creating his real-life adventures in fiction form. He had a tale to tell, too, for he once hobnobbed with Jack London as a war correspondent and himself participated in four South American revolutions.

"Matteo is a learned Italian intellectual teaching in the school for the blind in Florence. He is studying American Literature with all the perceptivity and many-faceted allusions made possible by his background in classical studies. Once I explained to him my invention of a Braille 'smile mark,' a punctuation sign in which the Braille dots turn up at the corners, like a smiling mouth. Matteo was enthusiastic, assuring me he would present the mark to the 'Academy Grusca.' On being asked as to the exact nature of this august body, he explained to me, 'I think you would translate it, The Academy of Corn Meal.' (I'm still wondering about that one!)

"Jason is a young African living in Kenya. He has studied with Hadley for over four years, making remarkable progress. Jason, who is now married, has one child, and informed me he has been appointed a seventh-grade English teacher in a Salvation Army School for the Blind, an appointment he credits to his English studies with us. He has asked me to write special letters to his seventh-grade boys and girls, as of course I am delighted to. The young man has started a library in which blind Kenyans pool contributions to buy Braille books. They circulate among themselves, the first such library in Kenya. I feel we have a future leader in Jason. (Correction; he is obviously already a leader.)

"Nearer home, Eileen is a twenty-year-old Irish colleen, living in Chicago. She lost her sight at twelve, being unable to attend the school for the blind in Jacksonville because she must use crutches, and she has been until recently almost housebound. In the past three years, Eileen has mastered Braille and is making fine progress in her English studies. You will get some idea of her quality when I report that she has named her latest aluminum crutches 'Sputnik and Muttnik, because they are my little satellites.' At my suggestion she now is taking up our Hadley typing course in addition to her English. I have just had a chat with her on the tactaphone, where she has learned the Morse Code in order to answer me. Once, when I told her she was costing me a nickel a minute, she coded back, 'I am worth a quarter.' She is too.

"Well, the foregoing examples should be enough to show you why I like my job. I believe that teaching is a two-way relationship, for I certainly know that my students give as much to me as I to them. One Californian, studying American Literature, copies radio and TV news, analyzes in shorthand, works up full-blown transcripts in Braille for me to circulate among deaf-blind students and friends. The student is rare indeed who doesn't respond to a personal element in the study relationship. My task is not merely to correct the student's errors, but to awaken and encourage his desire to learn, his capacity to learn, his need to learn. I don't tell him that he has made three errors out of ten, but that he has seven right. And if he makes a perfect mess of something, I try to point out that this merely means that he has a wonderful opportunity to learn something he didn't previously know. The long and short of it is that I enjoy teaching, and so long as I am having a good time, so will the student.

"As to the mechanics of our teaching methods," Mr. Kinney says, "we send the student his textbook in Braille together with an assignment schedule. The student then submits his lessons typewritten or in Braille and we correct the lessons in Braille. We make our responses in the form of a letter, trying always to add a personal touch somewhere. This is not difficult for, to paraphrase Emily Post's observation about children, 'Students are people.'" Although Mr. Kinney's time schedule at Hadley's is from nine to five, and he has never been late getting to his desk, he is not an eight-hour man. He could not even do his school work which involves so much correspondence in that time, so he has his Braille and his regular typewriter and certain books and papers at home, an apartment where he lives alone, a short distance from the school. Here he does his own cooking, some of the housework, much of his "homework" from school, and entertains his friends.

"My culinary repertoire is still growing, that is to say, frozen foods of the 'heat 'em and eat 'em variety' are still multiplying, or is it that friends like Mrs. Jordan are still finding new ones to bring to my attention. Of course I am doing some genuine cooking in the raw now, such as frying pork chops, making tapioca pudding, cooking rice, and baking potatoes. I have always liked simple foods best, and thoroughly savor the bachelor's luxury of having just what I want, just when I want it. This morning I actually had Swiss steak for breakfast!

"I must admit, I am not fond of cleaning house, but this is something admirably taken care of by Mrs. Treeman, the colored maid who comes in every Thursday morning. Mrs. Treeman is wonderfully dependable, not having missed a single day in the year she has helped me. The intrepid carriers of the mail have shown no more blizzard-breasting powers than she has. I always leave a note for her on the tray in the living room, a sort of 'My Day' column to make up for the fact that I am rarely here to talk with her.

"When I first began living alone, a few people worried about falls or accidents. There was surprisingly little of this apprehension, however, and since Mr. Jordan's invention of the tactaphone, I am not really alone. Should you have questions about the tactaphone, by the way, I am sure Mr. and Mrs. Jordan would be able to answer them clearly. My own position is that of the grateful beneficiary of science, the man in the street (or in this case in the apartment), who reaps where a genius has sown."

Mr. and Mrs. Robert Jordan are members of the Hadley School family. Mr. Jordan is a volunteer consultant, and as an electronics engineer has contributed many services to the school, among them the invention of the tactaphone which Mr. Kinney uses. Mrs. Jordan is Assistant Director of Education, teaches English and Braille, has worked closely with Mr. Kinney in his five years at

Hadley and often communicates with him on the tactaphone through the use of the Morse code.

Persons who are simply blind can hear their doorbells as easily as anyone, and persons who are simply deaf know when the doorbell rings because certain lights flash on; but those who neither hear nor see must be "stirred" in another way, so the Paasche Airbrush Company has worked out a contraption by which, when Mr. Kinney's doorbell rings, a "fanfare," as Mr. Kinney describes it, takes place in every room, and this continues for forty-five seconds, and then automatically goes off. Mr. Kinney explains, "My friends know about this timing arrangement, and ring again if I do not answer. But bill collectors and peddlers don't; they give up when there is no response." Mr. Kinney also co-operates with his friends when he is at home, by placing a small "Welcome" mat just outside the apartment door.

Mr. Kinney's telephone, or "tactaphone," is simple and effective. When it rings, the fans begin to blow. The receiver looks like any other telephone receiver except that it has a small cell on which Mr. Kinney places the end of his finger and gets the vibrations of the Morse code, the message being spelled out in dots and dashes. The caller dials "1" for a dot—felt as a click by Mr. Kinney, and "4" for a dash, felt as a rattle; these are felt as plainly as he feels the Braille cell in his teletouch machine. Then he talks back as he would in any conversation, directing his voice into the telephone.

Mr. Kinney is about the "travelest" person I know, of those who work under the double handicap of neither seeing nor hearing. "Actually," he says, "I've never claimed independence in this field, preferring the phrase of our French friends about 'independence within interdependence.' The local taxi drivers who help me get around here on the North Shore have proved unfailingly obliging and considerate. For longer trips that must be made alone, I go by air. Summer before last I flew 'alone'—except for the crew and some seventy other passengers!—to San Francisco to visit friends, returning by plane afterward. The latter flight proved to be an exciting one, involving as it did an unscheduled return to the San Francisco airport because of motor trouble. It was fascinating to watch my own reactions as I realized that we were going down at a time when we should have been going up

—the deepened breathing, the quickened heart beat, the slightly suspect philosophical reflections! The incident did not spoil flying for me, however, and my aerial log now totals around twenty-five thousand miles, equivalent to once around the world."

In a recent letter, full of news about teaching, students and other things, Mr. Kinney concludes, "This letter is getting a trifle long, its architect a bit sleepy. My typewriter too has shown signs of impediment in its speech. Nevertheless, I want to add a few thoughts about beauty by touch:

"You are a pioneer in this field, a teacher who may often have to awaken a desire in those to whom you may bring tactile beauty. This may seem strange for it is generally assumed that blind or deaf-blind have a keen sense by way of compensation. In a sense they do have, but a keen touch, a utilitarian touch, is not the same as an appreciative touch. The consciousness of tactile beauty is a flower that will have an unusually rich soil in which to grow once the seed has been planted in a blind person's mind. The latent capacity is there. In our culture though, tactile beauty has been neglected and many blind people will not have realized the range of opportunities that touch offers for aesthetic experience. Your work will further the worthy goal of awakening our inner realization; that tactile beauty *does* exist and it is fruitful to cultivate; and I especially like your pointing up that people with normal eyesight can enjoy tactile beauty too!"

Mr. Kinney's poems and other writings have appeared in many magazines. Someone has said that his quatrain, "Sudden Strength," is symbolic of his remarkable life:

> He strove but could not lift the load,
> Then Fate unleashed her furious goad,
> And when he laid it down at last,
> Three milestones and a hill were past.

WILLIAM E. POWERS: FROM MILL WORKER THROUGH BLINDNESS TO SUPREME COURT JUDGE OF RHODE ISLAND

When in 1958 the state legislature of Rhode Island elected William E. Powers, blind for 32 years, to the position of Associate

Judge of the Supreme Court of the state, it was an act of official confirmation of the honor and trust in which the people of his native state had held him since they first elected him to their House of Representatives in 1938. Here he had served them for ten consecutive years. Then in 1948 they had elected him Attorney General of Rhode Island by the largest plurality ever cast for that position. And here he served continuously until 1958 when he resigned to accept this new honor and responsibility in the Supreme Court.

William E. Powers was born December 18, 1907, in Valley Falls in the Town of Cumberland, Rhode Island, in the house where his mother was born. His father was also a native of Rhode Island, his birthplace the neighboring city of Central Falls, then a part of the Town of Lincoln. William was the oldest of their seven children. When he was 14 years old his father died and he, being the only child old enough to work, became the wage earner for the family of eight. At first he worked in a small silk mill, then a very large silk mill, then in one of the largest cotton mills in the state, all in the Blackstone Valley. These changes in working places were due in the main to periods of seasonal unemployment, for the young wage earner could not afford the enforced vacation periods.

When about 19 years of age he found employment in the Potter and Johnson Machine Shop in Pawtucket. "There I started to learn my trade as a machinist and incidentally it was the only work that I did during these years that I actually enjoyed." But a slack season came at the machine shop and so the boy found work in the large Manville Jenks Company cotton mill at Pawtucket. And it was during this period when on April 2, 1927 he had the accident, at home, which resulted in his blindness. While attaching a wire from the battery to a radio he was struck in the eye by a loose wire and after seventeen months of hospitalization he sustained a complete loss of his sight through sympathetic opthalmia. He was then twenty-one years of age.

What should he do; what could he do? He decided to go back to school; to start in all over again, and follow an early dream. Judge Powers recalls: "My father, who was a house painter, considered the legal profession the height of attainable ambition, and this conviction must have been contagious. I can remember as far back as the second year in grammar school assuming that I would become a lawyer."

Then to the Perkins Institution at Watertown, Massachusetts. Here was the place to learn how to live and work as a blind man, and to study for the present and the future. William Powers studied at Perkins for three and a half years. Here he became acquainted with two persons who were to affect profoundly his future work and life. One was Jim Hannon, a fellow student; the other Esther Johnson, a teacher at Perkins.

"Jim Hannon was a senior at Perkins when I entered. We became close friends immediately. He attended three years at Boston University, College of Liberal Arts, while I finished Perkins and we entered Law School together. He is totally blind and has been since he was eight or nine years old. Born with normal vision, his eyes were exposed to a strong light without proper treatment and total blindness resulted gradually."

In 1932 at the age of twenty-five Mr. Powers and Mr. Hanlon entered the Law School at Boston University together, both finishing with honors. James E. Hannon ranked first and William Powers second in a class of 105 students. Powers was the class orator, and was associate editor of the Boston University Law Review. There were no other blind students in the class. As students and friends they were very close together in work and plans. Hannon is now a successful lawyer in Lee, Massachusetts. Justice Powers said:

"We concentrated a good deal more than the others I think. They did the required work, but they needed recreation. We spent that time studying and discussing the law."

Admitted to the practice of law in Massachusetts in 1935, he maintained a residence in his home town in Rhode Island, and in 1936 was appointed Probate Judge of the town of Cumberland which position he held until 1949. In 1946 he was admitted to the practice of the law in Rhode Island on motion and is now a member of the Federal Bar, including the Supreme Court of the United States. He holds a Doctor of Science degree in Business Administration conferred by Bryant College in 1951. In 1958 his alma mater, Boston University, gave him an honorary degree, Doctor of Laws.

Soon after graduation from Perkins, Mr. Powers and Miss Johnson were married, and Mrs. Powers did all the reading for him in law school. They have three children and five grand-children.

All of the four little brothers and the two sisters of William Powers who, at the age of fourteen went to work to earn the living for the family, are living; and all but one, the youngest sister, after William dropped out, worked in one textile mill or another in the Blackstone Valley of their native state.

A BLIND FRIEND OF THE INDIANS—
STILL WORKING FOR THEM
BERT (ALAMBERT E.) ROBINSON
OF ARIZONA

The part of Bert Robinson's life with which we are especially concerned here, begins with his purchase of a Pima Indian basket on a sidewalk of Phoenix, Arizona, in 1915. It was this symbol of the arts of the American Indian which opened a door for him to their life and culture which in time was to make him not only an authority in this field but one of the best and most effective friends the Indians of the Southwest and especially Arizona have ever had: an admirer of their culture, a conservator of their arts, and a champion of their cause wherever he could break a lance for them.

At this time he had come from his home in Missouri to satisfy a longing for "the wide open spaces of the West" and his first job was with the United States Reclamation Service, where he began a career in irrigation and land development that continued for thirty-five years and for which he was awarded a special Citation for Meritorious Service by the Department of the Interior in 1951. A part of this citation reads as follows:

"In 1921 he was appointed to the Bureau of Indian Affairs in Sacaton Arizona, where he remained until he retired in 1951 from the position of Superintendent of the Pima Indian Agency. In this capacity Mr. Robinson was responsible for the economic, educational and social progress of the Fort McDowell, Maricopa, Salt River and Gila River Indian Reservations, comprising his jurisdiction. Under his able direction extensive land subjugation and irrigation, administration of a good school system, rendering of excellent medical service, modern and scientific farming operations and many other benefits have accrued to the Indian people residing on these reservations, Beloved among the Indian families of his agency, Mr. Robinson widely counselled them in their economic and domestic difficulties. He is also an authority on Indian basket weaving among the Southwestern tribes. His personal collection of baskets is considered to be the best in the world. In recognition of his contribution to the welfare and development of the Indian people under his jurisdiction, and to an important phase of Indian arts and crafts, Mr. Robinson is deserving of the Meritorious Service Award of the Department of the Interior."

Signed

Oscar L. Chapman
Secretary of the Interior

What this splendid citation did not say was that eleven years before his retirement, in 1940, Bert Robinson had lost his sight entirely but continued his administrative work as effectively as ever; and his interest in, friendship for, and appreciation of the culture of the Indians, not only of his own reservations but of all Arizona, found fine and beautiful expression in his book, *The Basket Weavers of Arizona,* which he dictated and dedicated to his wife Estella; it was published by the University of New Mexico Press.

The Basket Weavers of Arizona is "much more than just another book—in a sense it is the life of a man—the author," writes a friend in the Foreword; and so it is, for the Indians have come to be his chief interest, and in addition to this beautiful and scholarly book which stands at the top of the publications dealing with the basketry art in which the Indians of our country have created the finest examples in the history of the human race, Bert Robinson had over the years used every means within his reach to make the arts and crafts of the Arizona Indians better known. The book was written, and much of his research done, after he became blind. As this is being written, he is giving much of his time to the schools and other educational institutions of Arizona to promote an interest in and a concern for the Indians. He writes, lectures, and exhibits selections from his great collection of baskets and other choice arts and crafts. And he writes, "Altogether I am very busy and very happy in the things that I can do."

Bert Robinson closes his book, covering every aspect of basket weaving in Arizona, with this tribute to The People of the Mesas; "He has built his culture in the face of hunger, drought, pestilence and aggression from the warring tribes that surround him. In spite of all these obstacles he has emerged strong, self reliant, and self sufficient.

"If you visit him today, you will find him friendly and gracious in the hospitality of his simple home. You will be seated in the best chair the home affords. You will be shown every courtesy by all members of his family. One thing you will notice is the large number of happy little youngsters whose respect and politeness toward their visitor is quite remarkable. When you depart, their shrill little cries of 'Goo bye' will follow you far down the winding trail toward the desert below. Then as you leave these enchanted mesas and watch them fade into the northern horizon, there is a hope—yes, a prayer in your heart that all this will never change, that this always will be the home of the Hopis."

DAVID BADGER'S FLOWER GARDEN

David Badger was sixty years old; he had cultivated his flower garden for six years, winning awards for its beauty and its contribution to community culture, when one day a news reporter for the Philadelphia *Bulletin* called on him for a story. Since David had been deaf and mute from infancy, and totally blinded at twenty-six, it was in sign language that he began to try to tell about his garden. But that seemed very slow, and in his eagerness to communicate he reached for the reporter's paper and pencil and wrote down in clear script as follows:

"I created my flower garden during May 1951, and bought top soil, cement, sand, some kinds of flower seeds, bulbs and plants.

"I have spent $725.50 on them since 1951. I have paid every cent myself.

"I have different kinds of daffodils, tulips, narcissus, squills, peonies, several colors of roses and honeysuckle vines, and day lily plants. Two coldframe beds are in my flower garden.

"I am a chair caner, a basket maker, and a leather crafter." And, to complete his side of the interview, he wrote out carefully, "I am registered in this district." And he signed his statement, "David W. Badger."

Not only was David Badger registered, but he voted. He had joined a church. He plays chess by correspondence, and with a look of pride on his animated face he says that he does not drink or smoke, but that he likes orangeade, lemonade, candy, and cookies.

There is more, back of the garden. Far back was the fact that before David lost his sight, as a deaf-mute boy he had learned to read and to write by hand and by typewriter at the Western Pennsylvania School for the Deaf. But when at twenty-six, through an accident on the farm, he lost his eyesight completely, he discontinued writing and all but the most primitive communication. When he was fifty-two, the Working Home for the Blind found him living in a church home, kindly cared for, but seemingly without incentive to do more than keep in fair physical health. Communication by now, with his triple handicap and his lack of activity, had become almost impossible.

However, given an opportunity to work with his hands in the shops of the Working Home, he became an excellent chair caner, and in six months was earning his own way and putting aside a little money regularly each month, in the hope, which he confided to his associates, of some day having a little plot of ground where he could raise flowers.

When this life ambition became known to his friends, they helped him find a plot across the street near where he lived. It was winter then, and during the long inclement months they all studied together every flower catalogue they could get hold of, and when spring came, David knew what he wanted and how to get it.

When the snow and ice melted, however, the new garden plot was far from ideal. It was a corner lot where two streets intersected, with a frontage of fifty feet on one and seventy-five feet on the other. The size was all right, but in the middle of the lot was a huge advertising signboard, and piled all over the ground were remnants of a former brick building, with clumped and broken bricks, broken glass, pieces of sewer pipe, and here and there small pyramids of coal ashes which neighbors had dumped on the premises after dark.

Permission to use the triangular lot came from the City Service Company which owned the billboard; the gardening could be done beneath and around it. And from a former neighbor of the Home, David got permission to use the part of the lot which lay behind the billboard.

David cleared and leveled the land himself. He carried the larger pieces of debris to a corner of the lot, and put the rest of the soil debris through a sieve. About twenty-seven loads of trash was transported to the dump, and David began to feel the base for his garden plot, then bought several loads of topsoil. These the truckmen dumped in the corner of the lot precisely on the piles of rubbish that were to be hauled away. The gardener patiently screened the new soil from the rubbish. The lot still contained many bricks, some single and some clinging together with mortar, but in time David separated the latter, cleaned them up, and used them all for low fence enclosures and other divisions of the garden. Other truckloads of topsoil were brought in, and then he began to dig and plant.

While he was digging, many old bricks came to the surface, all of which he garnered and used in some way for utilitarian and decorative purposes. In addition he built trellises against the brick wall of the neighboring building, which bounded the third side of the triangular plot, and on these he trained vines and other plants needing support, giving effective background to the annuals and perennials and shrubs.

Thousands of people have enjoyed the garden for its beauty and fragrance without knowing anything about the gardener. But the children of the neighborhood know him, and have ways of communicating—especially three or four who love to do errands for him, and have a proprietary feeling in sharing the wonder of the garden with him.

Although he has purchased most of his plants himself, in seed and bulb form, friends occasionally bring something they think he might like to include. Among these gifts, a favorite of the children is what is considered the most fragrant of all roses—the Christopher Stone, which an Irish neighbor lady gave him, and the neat white picket fence which now encloses the garden was a contribution from friends and neighbors who wished to have some part in this beautiful feature of their neighborhood.

His thorough tilling of the soil has, with the aid of the climate, kept the plot moist enough to support the many plants, but neighbors have made available a water pipe, to which he attaches his own hose and so is able to keep green such plants as need water during the long gray season. And sometimes a plant which is out of reach of the hose gets its drink through the co-operation of one of the children always waiting to do something to help the gardener out.

David's garden has received several awards in competition with others of the area, and for special plants which he has developed to perfection. To see him working in his garden, no one would think of him as lacking any of the senses of perception, except that on close inspection one would realize that the informally crooked walls and brick edgings for enclosing some special plant might have been laid by a child helper, or someone who could not see. These irregularities, however, augment, rather than detract from, the charm of the garden.

And, if one tarried long enough to watch David feeling different plants and flowers as if to measure the rate of their growth, or just to have the pleasure of feeling them, one gets a faint idea of the deep experience of knowing things by touch; an experience which can come to one who cannot see, hear, or speak.

A DOCTOR OF BABIES WHO IS BLIND
DR. ALBERT ANDRÉ NAST OF CHELLES, FRANCE

Dr. Albert André Nast of Chelles, in France, near Paris, was born in 1883. He was a young successful lawyer when, in 1913, his wife died in childbirth. This changed the whole pattern of his life and he resolved to give the remainder of it to helping mothers and their babies. Beginning at thirty to study at night he strained his not too strong eyes but was able to serve as an Army Surgeon from 1914 to 1918, and later opened his own maternity clinic at Chelles.

After ten years of practice and delivering hundreds of babies, he lost the sight of both eyes in 1931, when he was forty-six. Another turn in the road of life at first seemed inevitable. But on analyzing the situation and thinking out how much he had relied upon his senses of feeling and hearing in all his work at his clinic, and desiring more than anything else in the world to continue the work to which he had dedicated his life, he reorganized it and continued with his clinic and his practice.

He had married again and now was aided by his wife, his secretary, a midwife, and a nurse. He used his highly developed sense of hearing instead of the stethoscope, and his sense of touch became more and more acute as his practice enabled him almost to "see through his finger tips."

He had helped many a child to come into the world while he had his sight, and the fourteen beds of his rural clinic were quite as much in demand after he became blind. The photograph taken of Dr. Nast and the half-dozen babies which brought his total deliveries to 2,000 after he became blind, was taken by Stephane Tavoularis on September 25, 1954, in the modest but famous rural clinic which Dr. Nast established at Chelles, and where he continued to practice. He was seventy years old at the time this picture was taken.

Dr. Nast was a man of wide interests and great charm. He was an accomplished musician, a pianist and a singer with a fine baritone voice. As an author he wrote plays, novels, and poems, besides contributing to medical and legal works.

CHAPTER 4

THE COLLECTION OF OBJECTS OF BEAUTY
FOR THE SIGHTED AND THE BLIND

*When the sense of beauty is evoked in us by lovely
forms, textures or other stimulating qualities of objects
through the feeling hand, it may be as real, as satisfying
aesthetically, and as lasting as can come through any
other of our senses of perception.*—A.H.E.

THIS chapter, and the next, will tell something of the origin,
history, and use of the Collection of Objects of Beauty for
the Sighted and the Blind, around which much of this book is
written. It has been an experience of high value to those who have
shared in it. It has been a means of enjoyable and often inspiring
communication between those who see objects through their eyes
and those who perceive them through their other senses; it has
opened to both sighted and blind persons new sources of wonder
and beauty in the realm of what is usually regarded as visual
things; and it has helped to make everyone who has taken part
more conscious of the enrichment to daily life that may come
through the aesthetic development of all of the senses of perception.

Of the objects which are to be shared together in this collection,
the greatest number are handicrafts, things which people make
with their hands for their own use or pleasure, or to barter or sell.
If anyone chooses to classify these objects as minor arts, let him
do so; but although minor, many of them are nevertheless fine,
and behind them, in the artist or craftsman, is the same creative
impulse that has gone into the fine arts of all peoples. Our concern is with our enjoyment of them for the beauty and inspiration they bring. The objects range from prehistoric time to the

present, from tools and artifacts made long before man devised an alphabet for forming words or a calendar for dating events, up to the work of modern craftsmen.

When it had been decided to form a collection of objects of beauty to be shared together by those who would be seeing them and those who would be perceiving them in other ways, the first question to arise was what kind of things do the blind like? A little reason, plus some inquiries, established the fact that there is just as much variation in the tastes and the feelings of the blind as among those who see.

Inasmuch as this was to be a shared experience, and the initiative would have to be taken by the sighted, the first rule we adopted was that the objects chosen must first of all be beautiful to the one who selected them. They must therefore combine the elements of pleasant form, texture, and color. These are pleasure-giving qualities for which a sighted person looks, and so they presumably would be for a blind person, except that he could not experience color, a sensation that is reserved for the eye. The appreciation of color by blind persons is discussed elsewhere, but since pleasant color is essential to the enjoyment of most sighted persons, it was, as far as possible, considered in connection with all objects included in this collection. When color in an object adds to the enthusiasm of the sighted person for it, it will raise the quality of his interpretation of it to his blind friends; and quality of interpretation is a central consideration in this communication.

In forming any collection to be experienced by the blind, the size of the separate objects is of course very important; therefore the second rule was that the collection should include, as far as possible, objects that could be held comfortably either in one or both hands. The maximum sensation through the sense of touch, so physiologists and psychologists say, is through holding an object in both hands. There are, of course, practical gains also in having objects that can be easily handled and conveniently transported. The item of size, in its bearing on tactual perception, will be referred to often in these pages; suffice it is to say here, that experiments have brought out several surprises in the ability of some blind persons to get pleasure and accurate impressions from very small objects.

A third consideration for the inclusion of objects was determined by the fact that the objects would be handled over and over again and should be as fresh and pleasant to see and to feel for the late-coming person as for the early one. This resulted in the rule that the Collection would consist primarily of hard-surfaced objects.

And finally, it seemed best for reasons discussed elsewhere, to limit the inclusions in this Collection to the arts of man. If this worked out well, a separate collection of objects of beauty from the world of nature should follow. As will be seen in a later chapter, such a collection is now in work; moreover we have advocated and assisted slightly in carrying out at the Kansas Rehabilitation Center for the Blind at Topeka a plan for combining objects from nature and from the arts in one collection.

Having decided definitely that we would give the idea of a Collection of Objects of Beauty for the Sighted and the Blind a trial, and that we would include in the collection only objects which we ourselves liked, giving such consideration as we could to the qualities which we thought blind persons would respond favorably to, we began our treasure hunt. First at home, and then to a few of the many places in New York City where beautiful and interesting things abound; and then anywhere and everywhere, watching for objects for this purpose. The quest still continues.

The search, which at first was intermittent and quite haphazard, included Chinatown, the brass and copper shops on Allen Street, pawnshops, secondhand stores, antique dealers, galleries of the little arts, and shops which carried the work of the best craftsmen in our country and some of the countries of Europe. In those days there was not nearly the representation of the European countries that we have now; still fewer from Asia. Nor were there nearly so many craftsmen creating beautiful forms in varied materials in our country as there are today.

In a few months, the collection of many kinds of articles, each one intended to be in itself beautiful, interesting, and significant, began to take form and assume aspects of relatedness. We had, after visiting countless shops and sales places, decided that there were some desirable objects which we could not purchase, but which we might borrow from museums. In time, through the museums, our collection was greatly enriched with authentic objects.

Such a collection, like any growing live thing, is always changing. New objects float in, sometimes replacing an earlier one which may not have said quite so much, or said it so well, and sometimes adding an entirely new thought to the collection. The principle followed here has been to keep the number of objects down, but the quality of the collection high; and since it was planned to have a collection that could be portable, and yet one which blind persons could glance through in a reasonable period of time, say two or three hours, the number of items was tentatively fixed at about forty objects. The list as it stands now is approximately as follows, the order having no special significance:

Prehistoric hand tool of stone. Late Stone Age. France
Babylonian clay tablet, cuneiform inscription. Circa 1280 B.C. Mesopotamia
Boy's Copy Book. Ancient Sumeria Writing on Clay.
Small pitcher, blue and gray glaze; finger depression on sides instead of handles. Tennessee
Pomo Indian Ceremonial Basket of native grass and bird feathers. California
Spoon, or small ladle. From horn of mountain goat. Tlingit Indian, Alaska
"Otter and Young." Small Eskimo carving of walrus ivory
"Singing Frog." Carving from redwood burl. Cherokee Indian, Tennessee
Silver necklace, squash blossom design. Navajo Indian, New Mexico
Carved wood drinking cup. Kasai region. Belgian Congo, Africa
Carved ebony giraffe. Belgian Congo, Africa
Long, shallow mahogany hand-carved tray—15". United States
Toscanini baton. Birch, with cork handle, plastic decoration in coral and green. United States
Turned wood—small conical bowl of American ash. Prestini, United States
Turned wood bowl of African ebony. John May, New Hampshire
Turned walnut wood; covered container. Amish farmer, Pennsylvania

1. THE OLDEST OBJECT IN THE COLLECTION

This beautiful prehistoric hand tool from France, a fist-axe of the Late Stone Age, is a fine example of man's early skill as "a tool maker," marking one of his greatest steps in human culture. Possibly ten thousand years old. Easily perceived by sight or touch. See page 74.

2. AN EXAMPLE OF MAN'S EARLIEST HAND WRITING

This Sumerian or "Babylonian" tablet was written on clay about three thousand five hundred years ago, then fired and preserved for the long future. It is a fine example of calligraphy by an unknown but artistic scribe at the Temple, and it is a receipt to a farmer for 12 head of sheep. Translated by Professor Isaac Mendelsohn of Columbia University. See page 75.

3. A SCHOOL BOY'S "COPY BOOK" ABOUT 1700 B.C. *Exact size*

This is one of the oldest school boy's copy books in existence, preserved for us because it was written on, or rather "incised in" clay. The school master, or probably his assistant "big brother," set the copy and the boy (girls did not go to school then) did his lesson while the clay was soft. It afterward hardened or was fired and preserved indefinitely. Excavated at Nippur some sixty years ago by the University of Pennsylvania and translated by Professor Samuel Noah Kramer of the University Museum.

4. PITCHER WITHOUT HANDLE

While turning some dishes on his wheel one day a Tennessee potter, Kennedy McDonald, decided that there was no need of handles on his pitchers, so he just made some dents with thumb and fingers while the clay was soft. These "hand holts" as he calls them are liked by hundreds of people, both sighted and blind, and last longer than the "fancy ones." See page 75.

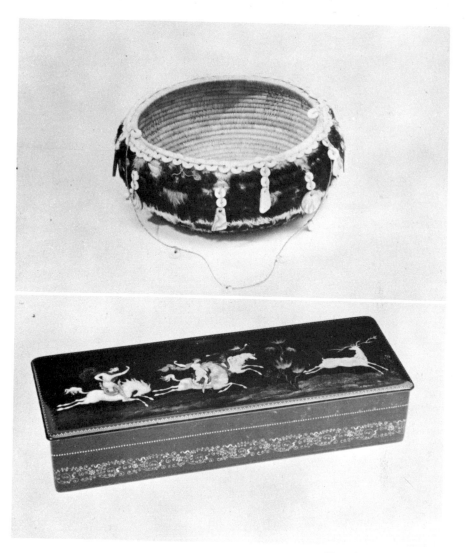

Photos by A. Burton Carnes

5. POMO, NORTH AMERICAN INDIAN BASKET

The American Indians have made the most beautiful baskets in the history of the human race. Probably no finer baskets have been made by any tribe than by the Pomos of California. See page 76.

5. A LACQUERED BOX FROM RUSSIA

Many times I had looked at this lacquered box from a little village of Russia, Palegh, and wished to share it with blind friends, but could never quite convince myself that it would be interesting to them. A blind friend who owned one something like it persuaded me to include it. See page 81.

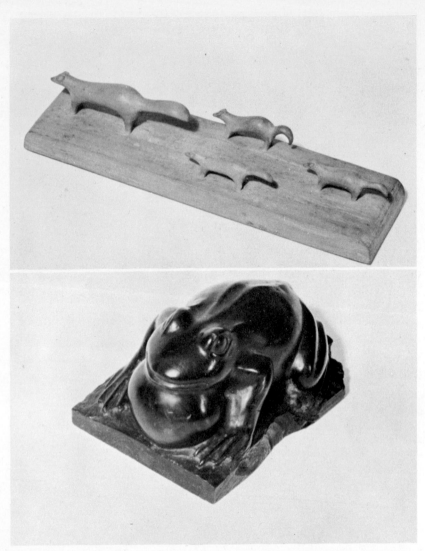

Photos by A. Burton Carnes

6. THE SKUNK FAMILY BY A MOUNTAIN WHITTLER

Perhaps this "Skunk Family" whittled out of a single piece of apple wood by a mountain man was the "conversation piece" of the collection. It was an excellent example of country whittling, but its chief service was to bring out individual experiences; it seems that most anybody is an authority on skunks.

6. WOOD CARVING "SINGING FROG" FROM CHEROKEE

The Cherokee Indians of Tennessee and North Carolina have a fine feeling for wood carving. This "Singing Frog" was carved by one of their best craftsmen, G. B. Chiltoskey, a member of the Southern Highland Handicraft Guild, from redwood burl sent him from California. The detail of the figure is easily perceived by touch.

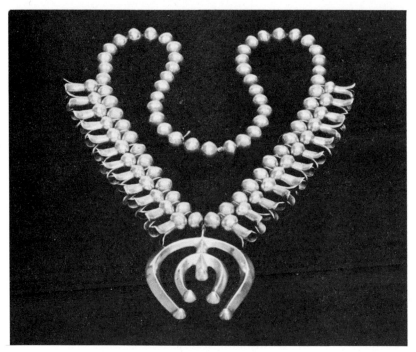

A. Burton Carnes

7. NAVAHO MAN'S NECKLACE, "SQUASH BLOSSOM" DESIGN

Silversmithing ranks high in the handicrafts of the Navaho Indians; especially skilled are the boys and men who make and wear much of the jewelry. Among the many valuable plant gifts of the American Indians to the white man are pumpkins and squashes; and the beautiful bell-shaped flowers of the latter are among the favorite designs of the Navaho craftsmen.

8. A DRINKING CUP FROM AFRICA

This drinking cup from the Belgian Congo was carved from a single piece of wood by an unknown craftsman of skill and taste. In both form and decoration it is equally perceivable to hand and eye. It is one of the first objects lent to our Collection by an American museum. See page 78.

Photos by A. Burton Carnes

9. WOOD TURNING, AN AGE OLD SKILL

Although the turning of wood is as old as Egypt, yet some of the finest achievements of this age old craft have been within the last twenty-five years. James Prestini who did this bowl of ash wood is one of the American pioneers in modern wood turning. See page 80.

9. THE NAUTICAL ART OF "SCRIMSHAW"

Since this Collection was to be seen by Americans especially, it seemed appropriate to include at least one example of that art of the sea, "Scrimshaw," to which the sailors and seamen of the United States have made some of the most outstanding contributions. For this purpose the tooth of a whale was procured and it was prepared and skillfully decorated with a typical whaling scene by a New Bedford craftsman.

10. A TURNED BOWL FROM AFRICAN EBONY

When John May of the New Hampshire League of Arts and Crafts took up wood-turning a few years ago it was his introduction to a study of the cabinet woods of the world. This bowl which he shaped from African Ebony has been a favorite "feeling piece" as well as a "seeing piece" for many sighted and blind persons who have shared the collection together. Incidentally, wood turning is a craft in which blind craftsmen have done excellent work. See page 80.

11. AMBER BEADS FROM GERMANY

The light yellow amber necklaces of natural forms but polished, was the lightest and warmest object in the Collection.

11. GLASS BOWL FROM FINLAND

One of man's greatest inventions, glass, can be blown, pressed, cast and cut into an almost infinite variety of forms. This utility bowl appealed equally to the eye and to the hand.

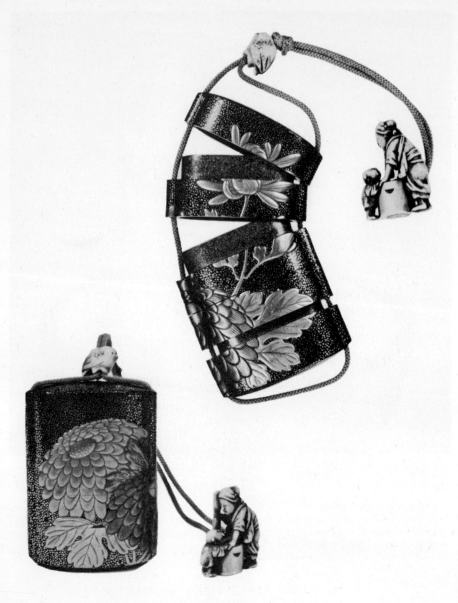

A. Burton Carnes

12. A LACQUER INRO FROM JAPAN

Wishing to have in our Collection at least one example of lacquer from Japan, for no other country in history has done as much with lacquer as these artists and craftsmen of the Far East, I found this beautiful inro which a museum generously lent. A practical series of receptacles for medicine or perfumes, and an object of beauty for the eye and for the hand, it has made a strong appeal to the many who have seen and felt it. See page 82.

A. Burton Carnes

13. A CRYSTAL SPHERE FROM NATURAL QUARTZ

Perhaps no man-made object is more impressive to both eye and hand than a perfect sphere cut from the clearest, the coolest and in many ways one of nature's most remarkable minerals, quartz. Of all the objects in the collection this was always the coldest to the touch. See page 83.

14. SCULPTURE IN MODERN PORCELAIN

This example of modern sculpture in Royal Copenhagen Porcelain from Denmark, entitled "Milk Maid and Her Calf," is probably the most complex object in the Collection, and yet it was one yielding much pleasure to the blind, especially to persons who had lived on the farm or who had experienced vacations in the country. It was one of the objects beautiful to the touch and fascinating hand exploration. See page 83.

A. Burton Carnes

15. OLD CHINESE PORCELAIN VASE

It seemed that at least one example of Chinese porcelain should be included in this Collection, for from China have come the oldest, the best and, to many sighted persons, the most beautiful porcelain ever made. This vase, traditional in form and texture, and in color a deep blue, is attributed to the 18th century. About eight and a half inches high to some who have held it long in their hands it has marked the beginning of a deep interest in one of man's most beautiful and enduring arts. For color see Frontispiece.

16. MOUNTAIN MADE DIPPER OF RHODODENDRON

This wooden dipper, one of the most beautiful feeling pieces in the 40 object collection, was made by a mountain craftsman of North Carolina who was inspired by "the gourd dipper at the spring." He made his own carving tools from discarded automobile springs, and "found him a bush of white rhododendron" from which he shaped a dipper as beautiful to feel as it is to see.

Set of 12 nested Russian dolls; turned wood, brilliantly enameled

Russian lacquer box with hinged cover. Palegh, Russia

Lacquer inro with compartments and netsuke. Japan

Crystal sphere; 2½ inch diameter. Hand carved from natural quartz. Japan.

"Baby Robin." Royal Copenhagen porcelain. Denmark

"Milkmaid and Calf." Royal Copenhagen porcelain. Denmark

Porcelain vase of deep blue glaze. 18th Century, China

"Mountain Dipper." White rhododendron wood. North Carolina

"Kobu." Natural maple tree root, polished. Japanese American. Rohrer, Arkansas

Singing cricket cage; gourd with incised decorations; pierced bone and ivory cover. China

Carved ivory spheres; 14 carved spheres within spheres. China

Life cast of Abraham Lincoln's Hands. Alva reproduction. Original in Smithsonian

Iron Teapot of 18th Century. Craftsman Unknown. Japan

Glass model many times enlarged of "Brilliant" cut of Diamond. Austria

Basket woven of palm leaves resembling Pennsylvania German weave. Circa 3200 years old. Egypt

"Scrimshaw" Carving on Whale's Tooth. Massachusetts

Necklace of natural amber nuggets polished. Germany

Small fan with frame of carved sandalwood. China

Plain heavy glass bowl. Finland

Folk carving in apple wood. A skunk family. North Carolina

Rosary Hand Carved from Quartz Crystal. Japan

Carved Walnut "Chicken Family" by a Country Craftsman, North Carolina

Rookwood pottery bowl. Matt glaze. Cincinnati, Ohio

Alabaster Carved Cosmetic Jar. Circa 2,000 B.C. Egypt

Boomerang. Carved wood. Australia

Among the reasons why this collection of objects has evoked a greater response from the blind persons who have seen it than was at first anticipated is, I believe, because of the many facets of interest which it holds for the average sighted person. Of more than a hundred exhibitions of one kind and another which I have planned and directed, including two of national scope, I feel that this small collection of about forty objects has been the greatest challenge to thinking, and in some ways the most fascinating. To describe it briefly as a unit may reveal some of the factors which have made it so interesting from a visual standpoint to me, and worthy to share with those who will experience it tactually and through other senses of perception.

One of the remarkable facets or elements of this collection of about forty objects was, and is, its "Time Span." It begins with a many-purpose hand tool of the late Stone Age—a fist axe, shaped, we know, by some human being at least six thousand, and maybe twelve thousand years ago; and it includes other objects made by man over many centuries, some as late as the years 1958 and 1959.

Another facet is the "Race Span." No one knows what the paleolithic craftsman who shaped the fist axe looked like, that is, the features of his face or the color of his skin; but later, much later, as man began more and more to distinguish things that are unlike, someone—some early ethnographer—classified the human race according to colors into five major divisions. The White Man to begin with; then the Black Man—that is, the Negro, wherever found; then the Yellow Man, of whom the Chinaman is the best-known symbol; then the Brown Man from so many places in Asia; and finally the Red Man, former proprietor of the country we live in, the American Indian. In this collection are beautiful examples of fine craftsmanship from men or women of all these primary human colors.

And if one wishes to classify the collection geographically into the "World-wide Span," he can see or feel at least one beautiful example of handicraft from every continent, beginning with North America, then South America, Europe, Asia, and Africa; and, for those who would include Australia as a continent, as a symbol for this largest of Earth's islands we have an ancient, authentic boomerang.

These objects from all our continents include a list of countries and states of origin which relate them still more closely to us. Beginning with the United States, there are objects from New York, Pennsylvania, Massachusetts, Maine, Illinois, Arkansas, California, Oregon, Alaska, and the District of Columbia.

Of the countries there are Austria, Canada, Peru, China, Japan, Finland, France, Germany, Denmark, Russia, Egypt, Iran, Mesopotamia and India.

It is not always easy to know what the roots of an aesthetic experience are, but it seems certain that every pleasant association with an object contributes to it. If we can, by seeing or feeling it, or otherwise experiencing it, carry away a pleasurable impression, we are aesthetically richer by the contact. And when to the knowledge we already have of an object we can learn something more of the When, Where, How, By Whom, and Why of it, we are building up our aesthetic feeling for it.

There was another element or property of great importance aesthetically, of which we were always conscious in collecting and selecting these objects, and that was the materials of which they were made. Nothing in the whole field of handicrafts is more fascinating than the endless variety of materials which the native people in every part of the world have adapted to their own use.

In these forty-one objects of our collection are stone, clay, wood (of eleven or twelve varieties, including maple, ebony, redwood, apple, walnut, poplar, pine, birch, sandalwood, dogwood, rhododendron), crystal, glass, grass, palm leaves, horn, lacquer, vellum, paper, silver, porcelain, cork, plastic, ivory (elephant, walrus and whale), amber, plaster, alabaster—altogether nineteen materials.

I have long felt that one of the roots of the aesthetic experience is the recognition of the material or materials of which an object is made. I never realized this as much as in the reception of this collection by the blind. A blind person will almost always wish to know, "What is it made of?" And if by feeling it, hefting it, tapping it, thumping it, or smelling it, he can recognize the material, he is happy in the discovery. He is at home, having the aesthetic experience of recognizing something which he knows and cares about. If one who is blind feels the material of which an object is made and it seems especially appropriate, I would almost say that because he experiences it so thoroughly through the sense of touch, without distractions, his appreciation of it is deeper than that of the average person who only sees it through his eyes.

After being strongly impressed by the pleasure-giving qualities of materials to the blind, I was happy to read that Santayana has written convincingly of the aesthetic value of the recognition of materials to those who see. He closes the discussion on "The Materials of Beauty" with these words: "The beauty of material is thus the groundwork of all higher beauty, both in the object, whose form and meaning have to be lodged in something sensible, and in the mind, where sensuous ideas, being the first to emerge, are the first that can arouse delight."

When we had brought together about a dozen objects of a quality and significance which would seem to justify their inclusion in the collection, I decided to bring them and some blind friends together, partly in the hope that they would give pleasure, but especially that I might learn from the experience whether we were on the right track.

It was possible to arrange for a small unoccupied room in the Russell Sage Foundation Building at 130 East Twenty-second Street, New York City. With a small table and some chairs and a table nearby upon which our collection of objects was placed, we were ready to proceed.

How to proceed was the first and most pressing problem. My thought had been that after a preliminary explanation of the purpose of the collection I would arrange to place each object in the hands of my blind friends or within easy reach, and leave the rest to him; but this method soon proved to be the wrong one. The right way was usually to give my friend as much information as he seemed to wish about the object, even before placing it in his hands, or within his reach.

There might, of course, be exceptions to this rule, but if so, the recipient's pleasure should determine them. To give a blind person an object without any interpretation is putting him to the guessing test, which could easily be embarrassing. Moreover, this is especially an experience in communication, and the easier and more direct it is, the better it will serve its end. So we must try, through spoken words, to supply something of the impressions a sighted person would get by glancing at the subject; and then add any intelligent observations which may enrich his impressions. On the impressions he has received orally he will build up his definite notions of the object as he explores it through his sense of touch.

Some instances of the usefulness of bringing an object to the hands of a blind person without any information or explanation concerning it, is given in the following chapter, but these are, as will be seen, definite exceptions to the best rule for sharing objects of beauty.

In all these early cases, most of the guests were new acquaintances, and I had therefore no knowledge of what their fields of interest might be, nor did I know when blindness had come to them, or whether they had always been blind. Some of these facts I could have had, but I somehow felt that it would be a better test of the general appeal of the idea at this stage if I did not know too much about the background of the guests. If the pleasurable communications could be naturally and spontaneously evoked for strangers by the objects brought together, that would be a good measure of the project's practicability, and, as I have stated, I never wished this project to be developed on what might be called a "professional level." It was really an experience in fine sociability, and the first important step was for us to get on easy terms with one another.

So I would introduce the subject by telling the guests that this idea of a collection of objects of beauty for the mutual enjoyment of the sighted and the blind was a new idea as far as I could find out, but it was based upon the assumption that there were many, indeed an unlimited number of things in both nature and in the arts which were beautiful to behold, whether perceived mainly through sight, or through touch and other senses. If experience proved this to be true, then we should do something about it for the gain it would be to both sighted and blind persons to have this fine and growing experience together.

I would then assure my guest, or guests, for sometimes there would be two or three, that I had personally chosen all the objects we were to see, and that each one was beautiful and significant to me; but that it must not trouble us if we did not find in this collection anything that seemed beautiful to them, for the experience of beauty is subjective, and cannot be other than an individual, a personal one for any of us. If we should not find something that they liked this time, perhaps if we tried again we would have better luck; or if there were any objects in their minds they would like to see, we might be able to get them for a later time.

I was explaining one day to a blind husband and wife, who had come in together, that when I go to an exhibition of painting, for instance, if I can find one out of twenty pictures that I really like, then the exhibition has been a success for me. For instance I said, "I am very fond of goats, and if I can find in an exhibit one good picture with a goat or goats in it, I am happy."

I did not get any further with my explanation. "You know," interrupted the husband, "I feel the same way about a cow. I don't know why it is, but I have always loved cows, and whenever I can, I touch them." "My favorite animal is a reindeer," his wife broke in, "Oh, I think it is the most beautiful creature in the world! I hope some day to see one." And so our conversation went, finding interests in common, then getting back to the objects they had come to see.

Where to begin? With such a collection, any place would do, but a natural place seemed to be at the beginning, with the oldest object then in the collection, a prehistoric stone hand tool from France.

One day, on a visit to the Canadian National Museum in Ottawa, the curator of the Department of Anthropology, to whom I had casually mentioned the project of Beauty for the Sighted and the Blind, on which I was then beginning to work, said, "I have something that I think ought to be in the collection, and if you agree, I would like to contribute it." And bringing from a storage chest an object which looked to me, at first, like a rather ordinary piece of rock with one end smoothed up, which anybody might do on a lapidary's grinding wheel, he explained, "This is a very old prehistoric hand tool, usually known to scientists as a 'fist-axe.' See how perfectly it fits in the hand when you grip it. It was found in France, and while possibly over ten thousand years old, it is a fine example of design and craftsmanship of its day. This beautifully rounded and blunt but very smooth chisel-shaped tool was probably used for many purposes—for cutting, pounding, mixing, smoothing, and possibly for skinning animals. It marked a great advancement over the crudely chipped hand tools which had been used for thousands of years before it, for this fine tool, a product of the late Stone Age, marked a new and very advanced era in craftsmanship; it clearly sets man apart as 'the great tool maker' of the animal family."

This tool was truly a fine example of the principle upon which much that is beautiful rests—utility, a first step to beauty. No sighted person would be happy just to look at it; he must take the object in his hand and experience it fully through the sense of touch.

Although, in viewing a collection of this kind, we may move from any object to another, and in any order that we choose, a next natural step, and a chronological one, was to an ancient Babylonian clay tablet, excavated near Ur of the Chaldees, Abraham's home town, on which was an inscription in cuneiform writing, done about four thousand years ago. In form this clay tablet is much like the mud pies that country children make playing with clay in a creek bed; only this mud pie was covered with incised characters, made with a small wedge-shaped stick, or stylus, and when the writing was finished, the clay tablet was baked in the sun or in a fire, thus giving the message enduring form, almost as hard as stone. Here we have an original dated written communication. It is in the characters of one of the first written languages invented by man, and it is as well preserved as though it had been written yesterday.

The first incised and inscribed messages to be discovered were excavated about a hundred years ago in old Mesopotamia, in the valley of the Euphrates River. Since then, and in recent years, many have been found, but they are mainly in the possession of museums; seldom can one get his hands on them. Therefore, having one in our hands is an impressive experience. The archaeologists are busily at work translating these writings, uncovering the story of the civilizations of several ancient lands, including those of the Bible—precious written records which we never could have known except for those enduring tablets in common clay.

The small tablet in our collection is an excellent example of ancient calligraphy; it is a receipt issued by the clerk of the temple at Uruk near Ur in Babylonia to a farmer who has just delivered to the temple twelve head of sheep. The name of the farmer is Ka-nin-u; or he may not have been a farmer but a donor of the sheep. In any case we know that twelve head of sheep were delivered in the year that King Shu-Sin built the west wall of the city.

From this artifact in clay we turn to a piece of modern work in clay, a small pitcher made by a young potter in the mountains of Tennessee, which in the color and quality of its clay is like much of that found throughout the continents of the Old World. We can make this comparison by examining the bottom, which is not entirely covered with the beautiful blue and gray glaze that gives it distinction.

The feature of this small pitcher which admits it to the collection, aside from its good shape and attractive glaze, is the fact that it has no handle. The mountain boy who shaped it on his wheel, as the ancient potter of the East might have done on his, when he got to the point of making a handle, instead pressed in the sides of the pliable clay with his thumb on one side and his forefinger on the other, making two large dents. Then he fired and glazed it, giving him a pitcher which he could take hold of easily and firmly, and pour from.

This original trick in clay was as pleasant a surprise for the blind as it was for me the first time I saw it. I had never known a potter to use it before, and I always delight in the inventions of these unknown craftsmen; but I did see later, in a collection of ancient Egyptian pottery, where a craftsman more than 3,000 years ago, in the same way had pinched in the sides of an old pouring vessel before he put it into his kiln to be fired for permanence.

Two of the most ancient and the most closely associated handicrafts are pottery and basketry. And both are widely practiced throughout the world in our day. The first example of basketry chosen for our collection was an Indian ceremonial basket from the Pomo tribe of southern California.

One reason for choosing a basket by an American Indian is that the finest baskets in the history of the human race have been made by our Indians, and some of them in the memory of people still living. This fact also was reason for giving both the sighted and the blind opportunities to see fine examples of Indian handicrafts, and to learn that the present standard of production among several tribes is better than it was twenty-five years ago. So a Pomo Indian ceremonial basket, possibly a gift for a bride, was selected for our collection.

It is a superb example of weaving of native grasses, with the small tips of brilliant bird feathers woven in. It is a pleasant size to hold in the hand or in both hands, and the texture, fine weaving inside, smooth, soft bird feathers on the outside, is lovely to feel.

The color of the basket is not perceivable to a blind person, but all the other elements are, and its beauty is deeply enjoyed, more, perhaps, because the absence of sight invites concentration on the form and textures, which are so impressive that there is no room to regret the missing element of color. The sighted companion will always describe the color of the object, if this is desired.

The practice of several of the old arts of the American Indians has disappeared, for too many reasons to go into here. However, one of them worth noting is that the materials once used are no longer available. A beautiful illustration of this in our collection is a spoon, or small ladle, made by the Tlingit Indians of Alaska from the horn of a young mountain goat. The spoon, beautifully designed for its purpose, and black as ebony, is a flowing line from the pointed tip of the handle through the bowl of the spoon, which is formed by splitting the horn at the base, flaring it out, then bending and molding it into shape while it is still wet; and when dry, polishing the complete ladle and the handle until it has the natural texture and sheen of the wild goat horn. The only material used other than the horn was abalone shell inlaid in the low carving of the handle. The shell was acquired in some way from the coast of Lower California, where in the old days there was considerable bartering for it by the Indians from the far North. Here is another Indian artifact which, to be enjoyed fully, has to be felt.

Without intending to show preference to any special group or nationality, we found we had included more things made by the Indians of America than from any other source. Among these were: a small carving in walrus ivory of an otter and her young, done by an Eskimo; a singing frog carved from a redwood burl by a Cherokee craftsman in Tennessee; and a silver necklace of squash-blossom design, done by an unknown craftsman of the Navajos. These few suggest eloquently the possibility of a future collection for the sighted and the blind which would focus interest on this beautiful and unique strain in present-day American culture—the arts of our own Indians. And it would give opportunity to bring out what too few of us know, our debt to the Indian for our present wealth. Of this, the squash-blossom necklace is a symbol; the squash and the pumpkin are gifts from the American Indians to civilization. Herbert J. Spinden, the eminent anthropologist, has estimated that over 52 per cent of the value of the agricultural products of our nation are from plants developed on this continent by the Indian. Among them, the most important are corn, potatoes, and tobacco, but the list of our debt is long and impressive, and it will always be to our credit if we acknowledge it. Our increasing knowledge and appreciation of the arts of the Indian will help keep alive a great original source of beauty in this Western world.

One of the first objects borrowed from a museum for our collection was a beautifully shaped drinking cup from the Kasai region of the Belgian Congo. It is carved, handle and all, from one piece of wood of a native tree, and decorated with incised geometric designs, which are almost as easy to make out through feeling as through seeing. This combination of fine design and craftsmanship in a utilitarian article, which everyone seemed to like, was an introduction to a people in whose culture woodcarving has been a strong element for centuries.

From a neighboring district in the Belgian Congo we acquired a carving of a giraffe in ebony. This, the most dramatic animal in our collection, and a typical example of the folk art of the region, compelled us to break our rule of twelve inches as a maximum measurement for an object, and extend it, in this case, to eighteen inches. All our blind friends say that this carving surely gives them a feeling of how very tall a giraffe is. And no one who sees it or feels it can doubt the ability of this native craftsman to say "giraffe" in wood.

It should be explained that among the reasons for keeping the size dimensions to twelve inches and under was to give the blind observer a maximum opportunity to feel the object quite completely without changing the position of his hands, the theory being that the most complete feeling experienced is when one can hold an object in both hands and get the benefit of the sensation, the message, traveling to the brain through each hand and arm. But when a rule is once broken, it is easier to do it next time; this rule we have broken three times so far.

Another exception (besides the giraffe) was a shallow mahogany tray, about fifteen inches long, very heavy, and of a flowing form almost like a boat, pointed at each end, shaped from a single piece of wood. Anyone looking at it would realize that even though the lines are very beautiful to see, the greater pleasure would come through feeling it; this was one object which could have been sensed quite thoroughly and most pleasantly by touch alone.

A third exception to our dimension rule came about in this way: a friend, a very skillful and sensitive woodworker, had turned out of a piece of walnut for me a small, delicate orchestra conductor's baton. It was less than ten inches long, exquisite in its slenderness, and I found myself picking it up time and again for the sheer pleasure of running it through my fingers. It seemed to say quietly, yet most pleasantly, "Form," or "Wood," or "Walnut" to both the eye and the hand. Maybe this should be in our collection, but was it significant enough? If it were a real, life-sized baton, one that had been used, perhaps it would be. Then the thought came: perhaps the great maestro, Toscanini, would have a baton he would lend us. It was worth trying, especially because of what it would mean to some of our blind friends so fond of music.

Omitting the details, Toscanini, although not well, was happy to send one of his batons for our collection, not as a loan, but as a gift. When it arrived, it had a very special interest for me because of its appearance. It was so simple compared to the different types of batons I had seen at close range in music stores, and sometimes at longer range in the hands of an orchestra conductor. This one, so plain and unpretentious, yet had something new for our collection. I have mentioned elsewhere the importance of materials, the aesthetic value of recognizing them, and our desire to include as many different materials as we could. Toscanini's baton added three new materials to our collection. The slender pointer was shaped from a piece of birch; the light handle was of cork; and the ferrules, or small bracelets supporting the cork handle, and giving the baton a little color, were of moss green and coral plastic.

I had never seen a baton like this, and I wrote a note to the conductor's son, Walter, asking if he could, at his convenience, tell me from what country it had come. He promptly wrote me that his father liked the feel, the weight, and the balance of this baton better than any he had been able to get elsewhere, and that it was made by Toscanini's personal physician, who was an amateur woodworker, and who fortunately had kept his father supplied wtih his favorite baton for the past twenty-five years. It is exactly twenty inches long, and weighs less than one ounce.

The mention of Toscanini's physician being an amateur woodworker reminds most any of us of some craftsman we know who has in the basement, the attic, an extra room of his house, or, if in the country, in the woodshed or the barn, a place where he can get off by himself, or in the good company of his dog or his cat, or with one—preferably only one at a time—of his children, and for a while work away on some simple thing, some device, or some contraption with his hands and his mind to his heart's delight. From such workshops are several objects in this collection. Among them come to mind some wooden bowls done on turning lathes. Possibly nothing is more natural for our purpose than a hand-turned wooden bowl.

Wood turning is a very old art. I do not know how old, but I have seen photographs of pieces of wood turning done in Egypt about 200 years before Christ, and it is scattered all along in the furniture making of European countries, finding its way to America very early through the adventures and the immigrants from Spain, England, France, Holland, Sweden, Germany, and other countries as they came along. But it is not the ancient history of wood turning that is so exciting to us in this collection; it is the modern things, especially the hand-turned bowls; and of these it can be truthfully said that no finer ones have ever been done in the long history of the wood-turning craft. And the best bowls of which I know have been made by American craftsmen.

I began looking for one by James Prestini, the son of an Italian stone carver, who mastered the science of curing wood and the art of turning, finishing his pieces with a delicacy that marked a new high in this ancient craft. The quest took me to his shop in Chicago, where I chose the beautiful, small, conical-shaped bowl of American ash, which is so pleasant to see and to feel that it still remains in the collection.

A few years later, I discovered in New Hampshire, at the annual Craftsman's Fair of the New Hampshire League of Arts and Crafts, a turner, John May, who, although he had been greatly influenced by Prestini's work, had developed a fine feeling of his own for woods from all parts of the world; he had, without knowing it, just turned a bowl of African ebony of the right size, color, and form for our collection.

Both these bowls were comparatively small and delicate, and I wished for a turned piece that would look and feel more rugged, one that would express the solidity of wood, its weight, its tree-like quality, and yet one that would be, as all turning should be, graceful in form.

This I found in Pennsylvania. It was a covered jar-like container, as graceful as a Greek vase in line, and yet rugged. It had been done by an Amish farmer who had turned it out of a piece of an American walnut tree that he had cut down on his farm some years ago, and saved. He had just recently learned wood turning. He was then eighty-four, and for seven years had been totally blind.

The Pennsylvania farmer's wood turning is the only object in the collection made by a blind person, and it is in because it meets all the requirements—that is, it is beautiful to see and to feel. But it also reminds us that wood turning is one of the handicrafts in which blind persons often excel.

There are other examples of wood turning in the collection, but of different types. One of these has given much pleasure to sight and to touch and manipulation. It is an old toy, in my family for years; we have always called it "our family of dolls," and it is from Russia. It consists of twelve dolls, all hand-turned out of soft wood resembling poplar, the dolls fitting inside each other so comfortably that when put together the complete nest is about nine inches high. The smallest doll is only about half an inch tall. This family of Russian dolls is enjoyed equally by sighted and blind, children and grownups, who delight in taking them apart and fitting them together again.

Another treasure from Russia is a lacquer box with traditional decoration, from one of the old Palegh villages. This was included as one of the early experiments, with doubt at the time as to how popular it might come to be. It has been so generally enjoyed that it remains in the collection. This box, with a hinged cover, is nearly ten inches long, about three and a half inches wide, and two inches high. Its size makes it pleasant to hold, and, being lacquered inside and out, there is not a part but that is agreeable to the touch.

The entire box is lacquered in jet black, the best possible background for the gold and color of the painted decoration on the cover and the golden bands of finely wrought conventional plant forms that encircle the box. The decoration is a hunting scene, full of grace and movement and charm; both drawing and coloring suggest slightly the miniature painting of India, but upon closer examination it is beautifully and uniquely Russian.

This work is done by descendants of families who for centuries did the icons and other religious subjects for prince and peasant, and who, shaken by the Revolution, realized gradually that they would have to find other ways to employ their talents if their exquisite craftsmanship was to be preserved. So they turned to the decoration of small utilitarian objects, especially boxes of many shapes, and released their old techniques and talents through new outlets for a new world.

One day, when showing some of the objects in our collection to an American, a blind woman now working with the blind in the Orient, she said, "There is one thing I wish you had in this collection, for it is one of the loveliest that I possess, that is, an example of Russian lacquer." And when she had finished describing her piece, it could be nothing else than a box from Palegh, Russia. I told her that I had a lacquer box from the same place, and now that she, who could not see, felt her own to be so beautiful, I would include mine in the collection. She was very happy about it, and gave me a silk scarf to wrap it in.

The inclusion of the Russian box carries an important lesson. We sighted people should be careful not to allow visual preference in any object to crowd out or to subordinate other qualities which, perceived in other ways, might appeal strongly to blind persons. There will always be a great number of objects beautiful to the blind yet to be discovered and interpreted by the sighted, and mutually enjoyed.

The mention of lacquer carries the thoughts to several countries, but most often to Japan, where lacquer has had its finest and widest use in any country or in any time. One of the objects from Japan in the collection is a fine lacquer inro, a small closed receptacle, or set of receptacles, to hold medicine or perfume; an inro is usually carried by a cord suspended from the belt. They vary in size from tiny ones to those two or three inches wide, or even five or six inches high, with anywhere from one to six or eight compartments. But the average, and that includes the one in our collection, has five compartments, is about four inches high, and at the end of the cord which holds the compartments together, is a miniature carving called a "netsuke," a kind of button, with which every inro is furnished.

The inros are among the most beautifully designed and decorated small utilities ever made, the decorations running the gamut of many materials, from simple wood carvings to the most elaborately inlaid and encrusted jewels. If one were limited to the choice of but one object as a symbol of Japanese imagination, taste, and craftsmanship, it might well be an inro.

For the purpose of this collection, an inro is a natural, designed to fit in the hand. In addition, the small lacquer surfaces and the raised decorations are delightful to touch. The compartments fit with exactness into each other, and are held together with a cord running through eyes, or channels, on each side; altogether the perfect miniature craftsmanship is an invitation to the person holding one to open and close the compartments over and over again; one can almost believe that inros were made for people to enjoy without looking!

One of the objects most wished for, and one which took longest to acquire, was a two-and-a-half-inch crystal sphere, carved from natural quartz; lovely to see, lovely to feel, and it proved to be one of the most perfect objects for this collection. It too was made in Japan by a Japanese craftsman. The Chinese have also made them. I have known of only one made in America, and that by an amateur mineralogist who, when I asked him how he happened to make it replied, "It's nothing. What man has done, man can do."

Those who have seen, but never touched, a sphere of real crystal have only partly experienced it. I think of nothing in nature or in art which, to me, has such exquisite form, and to its appearance and feel is added—and this is especially pleasant on a summer day —the lowest temperature of any object in our collection.

Probably never so cold, but always pleasantly cool to the touch are two examples of the most famous decorative porcelain of our time, the Royal Copenhagen porcelain of Denmark. Both pieces are excellent examples of small sculpture, one quite simple, "Baby Robin," about life-size, that can be held in one hand; the other a much more elaborate example, "Milkmaid and Her Calf," a realistic rural subject of a girl feeding a hungry, thirsty calf from a pail of milk.

The robin is almost streamlined in its modeling, and the very smooth texture of the porcelain and its size makes it one of the pleasantest objects to hold and explore. And because the robin's song is known to almost everyone in our country, this piece calls up one of the pleasantest sound associations.

The girl feeding her calf is especially enjoyed by blind adults who have lived in the country, and who have helped with the farm chores. It is a delicate piece, but no parts of it too fragile for careful handling. There are varying opinions concerning the enjoyment of sculpture by the blind, the generalizations about it are likely to be misleading, but this storytelling piece, which can be quite completely explored with the fingers, was interesting to all, and fascinating to some. The usual rule for presenting any new object to a blind person is to interpret it quite fully before turning it over for his tactile examination. But in connection with "Milkmaid and Her Calf" a new experiment was worked out with a number of individuals.

The only explanation given to the person was, "This is a good example of sculpture in a fine modern porcelain. It is a typical farm scene. Perhaps you would like to figure it out for yourself." The procedure was fascinating to follow. There was very little in the figure of the milkmaid that could serve as a clue to the composition, as her long skirt was massed against the calf's body, but the exploring fingers soon discovered that the key to the puzzle was the animal. Then followed the search for identification.

One who talked as he explored showed what was going on in his mind. As his fingers discerned the arched tail of the calf, he said, "It is an elephant—but no—an elephant wouldn't be on a farm. It's a horse." Then, gathering the supporting evidence, he ran his sensitive fingers down the leg of the supposed horse to the ground, and discovering the cloven hoof he declared, "No, I am mistaken. It's a cow or a bull—I know by its divided hoof,—or —it could be a sheep or a pig." But in another instant he felt the calf's outspread ears, and following the nose to the pail with the milk in it, he knew the rest.

While it took considerable time for some to figure it out, each one declared that it was a real pleasure to do so. As one said, "What I can make out for myself seems better than what some-one else can figure out for me." Everyone was impressed by the beautiful feeling of the porcelain and the skill of the sculptor, and much interested to learn that porcelain was in reality just the highest form of pottery.

It seemed to me that we should have at least one example of Chinese porcelain also, because, over the centuries, it is from China that many of our finest porcelains have come. So it was a real event for our collection of arts and crafts from everywhere when we acquired a beautiful Chinese vase, deep blue and of a traditional form, and with the signature of an eighteenth-century potter. It was an acquisition possibly as satisfying to the touch of the hand as it could be to the sight.

If there is any pleasure that rises a little higher than another for me in the quest for objects of beauty for both the sighted and the blind, it is to discover an article that seems to have been made for our purpose, though unconsciously, by some unknown and heretofore unrecognized craftsman. It was such an experience at the 1956 Craftsman's Fair of the Southern Highlands Handicraft Guild at Asheville, North Carolina, that brought us one of the most beautiful pieces of woodwork to see and feel that has ever come into our collection. We will call this object a "mountain dipper"—some would call it a hand sculpture, others an abstract, perhaps, others a pure example of folk art; but it would be difficult to imagine anyone, sighted or blind, who would not be moved by its form, texture, and color.

The traditional garden-gourd dipper of the Southern Highlands, which this wooden dipper immediately suggests, is often a very attractive container, but its weak point is its fragility; it will crack or break in time with rough use, or it will otherwise wear out. But this prototype, shaped by hand from a choice piece of the rare white rhododendron wood, will never wear out, and you wonder what tools could have been used to cut out the beautiful cup or bowl and shape the graceful handle; and you learn that this craftsman's cutting tools were designed by him just for this purpose, and fashioned by hand from scrap steel, a junked automobile spring. To see this mountain dipper is only partly to experience it; you must take it into your two hands to feel it completely, and you will do this again and again; and you will likely share the quiet pride of the mountain craftsman, who explained, "I don't reckon anybody ever did make a dipper just like this anywhere before— anyway, not from a rhododendron bush."

As to the "feel of wood," probably no single piece has been more enjoyed than a "kobu," a gift from a Japanese American from the War Relocation Camps in Rohrer, Arkansas. A kobu is an unusual growth of wood in a tree, chosen for its interesting form and texture, and after the piece is freed from deadwood, or over-growth, it is rubbed and polished by hand to perfect finished smoothness. And because of its attractive shape and exquisite texture, anyone taking it into his hands will wish to feel it over and over again.

The kobu in our collection is a kind of swirling knot from the root of a maple tree which had been cut down to make way for the building of barracks. The only mark of a tool is where a saw was used to sever it from the tree; these marks have been softened by what appear to be many rubbings of sandpaper, or possibly sand itself, and into the polished surface where the knot has been severed is delicately engraved the date and the name of the "artist" who saved this beautiful wood form, so different from anything that had ever grown before, or would ever grow again.

Of all the objects from foreign lands, possibly the quaintest and most surprising is an old cricket cage from China. Nearly every-one knew the chirp of crickets and many were fond of them, but no one had ever heard of the custom in China and Japan of making miniature cages for singing crickets. That they might have the charm of their music, the owners would bring them into their houses and gardens, and sometimes carry them around with them wherever they went. Our cage, one of the first loans to the col-lection, is from the Museum of Natural History in New York. Made from a garden gourd, it has a beautiful cover of pierced ivory and bone.

In both China and Japan there are elaborate cages, some of them costing hundreds of dollars, for both singing and fighting crickets, with miniature feeding and sleeping quarters and other accessories, of the finest materials and most perfect craftsmanship. Probably the most extraordinary collection of cricket cages in America is at the Chicago Museum of Natural History. Our cage, while very attractive to see and also to feel, for it fits comfortably into one's hand, was not expensive or pretentious, but has a beauty of its own. The gourd itself is almost pear-shaped; it has a patina finish of straw color and it is covered with floral decorations in low relief, which were achieved in a most original and ingenious way.

The craftsman made a plaster mold in exactly the size and shape he wished his prospective cricket cage to be, and on the inside of the mold he carefully incised the design, a plant motif, which he wanted ultimately to impress upon it. Then he took this mold into the garden, and finding a small growing gourd, he tied the mold onto the vine, suspending the gourd within it. The gourd grew until it filled the mold completely, taking on the incised design. All who heard this description were intrigued; some of them grew gourds, and most of them knew gourds well enough to understand the process.

One day, when I was showing the cage to some friends in North Carolina, one of the women in the group, who had always been blind, said with a thrill of excitement, "I had singing crickets when I was a little girl in Pennsylvania." All of us urged her to tell the story. This is about as she told it:

"We lived on a farm, and my brothers would sometimes let me help carry wood from the yard to the kitchen and put it into the woodbox near the big cookstove. In the evening, when the kitchen began to warm up, I would hear a cricket chirp, and going to the woodbox I would listen, and with my hands making a little tent, I would finally capture him. Then I would put him in a fruit jar and take him to my room and have music, sometimes far into the night."

The life cast of Abraham Lincoln's hands was of deep interest to many who saw them or felt them, and their effect was heightened by the account which the eminent American sculptor Leonard Volk of Chicago left of his experience, and to which his son Douglas Volk the painter, my friend, added in our visits together. The sculptor went to Springfield shortly after Mr. Lincoln was nominated for the Presidency and arranged to make these casts of the candidate's hands, and arrange for other material which would help him in the full length statue which he was planning to make. He had previously made the cast of Lincoln's face in his Chicago studio.

Lincoln set aside Sunday for the undertaking and invited the sculptor to his home in Springfield, the house which thousands of people from all over the world visit each year and which is preserved much as it was when the Lincoln family lived there.

The sculptor first cast the left hand in a relaxed pose; then, wishing to get a different effect, he asked Mr. Lincoln if he had something that he could hold in his right hand. Mr. Lincoln looked around but seeing nothing suitable disappeared through a side door. In a moment the sculptor heard the bucksaw going in the woodshed and presently Mr. Lincoln appeared with a short round stick in his hand which he had cut from a brown handle. He was trimming, with his pocket knife, the rough edges the saw had made. Mr. Volk assured him that the stick was all right as it was, but Mr. Lincoln said, "While we are about it we might as well make it nice."

On seeing or feeling the cast of the right hand one may notice that it seems somewhat larger than the left. And this, the sculptor tells us, is true; for the night before, a Saturday night, a public reception had been held in Springfield in celebration of his nomination, where he had shaken hands with hundreds of his neighbors and countrymen, and the swelling of his right hand had not entirely subsided when the cast was made.

Daniel Chester French, who did the great statue in the Lincoln Memorial in Washington, told me that, helpful as many photographs of the President had been to later sculptors, by far the greatest help had been these exact castings of Lincoln's face and hands. And it is almost a miracle that we have them. The sculptor, in his plan to do a full length figure of "our next President", as he put it, on that Sunday in Springfield, had assembled in his Chicago studio a number of Lincoln props and photographs to be used later. But that summer Mr. Volk turned the key of his studio door and went to Rome. While he was away the great Chicago fire came and burned the studio and everything in it; but fortunately the sculptor had taken these casts of Lincoln's face and hands to Europe with him, and thus they were saved.

Finally we come to the most extraordinary examples of crafts-manship that I know of. This incomparable object is a unit collection of fourteen carved ivory spheres within spheres, each one moving separately, and all carved from a single block of ivory about the size of a billiard ball. The outside sphere, to protect the inner spheres, is carved in rather high relief (about one quarter of an inch thick), with detailed figures of dragons and other traditional themes. But each of the inner spheres is very thin—about the thickness of a goose-egg shell; and each one is pierced with hundreds of fine precise patterns, which one would think could only be produced by the most accurate of dies. Then it dawns on one that they could only have been fashioned by the most delicate of tools manipulated by that most miraculous of all instruments—the human hand; and with a skill and incredible patience which we of the Western world do not know; but which we must believe, for here it is.

These then, are some of the arts of man which have gone into this pioneer collection, which we have called, "Objects of Beauty for the Sighted and the Blind." They and the experiences already had with them suggest that there are no limits, excepting those which we ourselves make, to the knowledge, the pleasure, and the inspiration which both the sighted and the blind may have through sharing together the beauty of our world.

CHAPTER 5

THE INTERPRETATION OF OBJECTS
OF BEAUTY TO BLIND PERSONS

*Imagination is not the talent of some men
but the health of every man.*—EMERSON

THE objects referred to in the previous chapter, about forty
in all, represent the collection about as it stands at the time
of this writing, and quite in contrast to the handful of ten or a
dozen objects which a few persons were invited to see in the early
days of the experiment at the Russell Sage Foundation. But ten
or a dozen carefully chosen things were quite enough to prove
what it was desired to prove, namely, that the world is filled with
objects of a character, quality, and beauty that can be mutually
enjoyed by sighted and blind persons, just as by two sighted persons, or by two blind persons, if ways can be found to bring the
experience about.

The experiences recorded here have been over a broken period,
in which the longest interruption was between the conception of
the idea, as already roughly described in the Introduction, and the
period of renewal and continuous activity beginning in 1955.
However, in that long period of comparative inactivity when
other work had to be done, time was not entirely lost, for I had
an opportunity to become acquainted with much of the literature
by and about the blind, make new acquaintances and friends of
blind persons, including several who could neither see nor hear,
and see many objects from which I found an occasional one to
add to the original collection, feeling that these objects might
serve a definite purpose in the future.

Returning briefly to the Russell Sage Foundation, this first
collection of a few objects could neither be housed nor shown

in the quite fully occupied office space then available, so an un-occupied room was arranged for. At a still later date a larger room was provided, which also served as a private exhibition room for the Russell Sage Foundation staff. But it is the earlier room which merits a little attention here, because it was, as far as I know, the first art gallery for the sighted and the blind, and could serve as a model for anyone wishing to carry on similar experiments.

This room was small—about twelve by fourteen feet in size. The furniture consisted of one table, thirty-two inches wide by five feet long, one end against the wall, and with a five-foot bench on each side; a smaller table on which the objects were placed, usually in the corner of the room for the safety of the objects and for convenient reach; and two plain chairs. The table was covered with a handspun and handwoven cloth of a cotton which grows yellow instead of white, a plant which the Acadian women of Louisiana have cultivated in their little home plots for over a hundred years solely for domestic uses; this cloth is pleasant to the touch and to the sight, and interesting to know about. That was all, except for three prints on the wall which I liked, and which I was to learn later some of my blind friends liked to know about. This simple equipment served well the one, or sometimes two blind visitors who, occasionally with sighted companions, came to see the small collection. Later, when the need arose in other locations to present the objects to larger numbers, sometimes to groups of both sighted and blind, techniques of showing had to be modified and developed.

In presenting the project to a sighted audience with perhaps three or four blind members in it, the task of course begins with the description of the objects, which the sighted ones can get almost at a glance, but which the blind have little notion of, until descriptions of such features as color, shape, dimensions, etc., are given. These descriptions, so obvious to the sighted, are apt to be boring to them, yet if such details are not given to the mixed audience, the impressions for the blind are inadequate.

In these mixed groups two possibilities are open, neither too satisfying. One is to pass the objects through the audience, after they have been briefly described, the blind members receiving them in their turn and passing them on to others. This method of passing things around the audience is bad in any case, even with a sighted audience, because it interferes with the reception of what the speaker is saying. It is therefore better not to pass the objects, especially in a large audience, but to have the speaker stop in plenty of time to let those who wish, come up and take them into their hands, giving the blind persons the first opportunity.

But, if the audience consists of blind persons only, or predominantly, it is necessary to pass the objects from one to another, and to this method the speaker must adjust his conversation. In this case, if there is to be no time for examining the objects afterward, it will help if the blind persons are grouped together. Then sighted assistants can see that the objects go directly to them. In this procedure, the blind persons might well be seated around a table together with enough sighted ones to help in passing the objects.

But the showing of the objects and their interpretation will be most satisfactory when the audience is limited to blind persons only, with of course an occasional sighted companion or assistant. In such cases the difficulties of presentation will be about in proportion to the numbers served. The speaker should be well enough informed about every object to make his interpretation informing and interesting while the object is going around.

If there are four to six persons, they can be seated at either a round or oblong table, and the object passed from right to left, beginning with the speaker and coming back to him. If all are blind persons, they can, with a little explanation as to position, pass the object from one to another, but it is very helpful if a seeing companion or guide will help around the table, thus leaving the hands of the blind persons free for examining the object, and relieving him of the responsibility of placing it where it is convenient for the next one. Questions, unless they are very short ones, had usually better wait until all the objects have gone around and each blind individual has had an opportunity to feel the objects under discussion.

If the number of persons does not exceed twenty, longer tables can be used and the same order followed, that is, the objects passed one at a time from right to left; the speaker can follow the object with his eye at all times, and assist in its return if it is taking too long. Twenty is a large number to see the objects within a reasonable time; if there are more than that number, one can only do the best he can in the time at his disposal.

Once in North Carolina, after we had shown the collection at the Rehabilitation Center at Butner, Mr. H. A. Wood, executive secretary for the North Carolina State Commission for the Blind, asked if we could also spend an evening in Raleigh, where he would like to have a few of the home people see some of these things. We held the meeting in a large room at the headquarters of Services for the Blind, where I had previously met his staff. I arrived early in the evening to arrange the setup, but a few blind folks, some by themselves and some with guides, were already there, and Mr. Wood was scouting around in his car for those living some distance away.

Others kept dropping in; Mr. Wood brought one load and went out for more, and when the appointed hour arrived we had about fifty people, a new high, and a new problem. There were more than we had tables for, or even chairs. More chairs were collected from other rooms, and finally everyone was seated, and everybody comfortable but me. I was wondering how we were going to do it—how, when I released an object, it would get around, and how and when it would get back, for the seating arrangement was quite informal, some having naturally arranged their chairs in little island groups of their own choice.

But we did have two long unbroken lines of chairs around the tables, which we had placed end to end. Everyone seemed comfortable, and attention was excellent as soon as I began to speak; and with the shortest preliminary talk on record, we started the objects, not around in the usual routine, but out in the several directions of our expectant guests. It was at once apparent that we could not keep those who first saw the object waiting until all had felt it, and it was even more apparent that I could not keep talking about it until it had returned; so there was nothing to do but release other objects, with a minimum of explanation, and leave it to Mr. Wood and some of his pinch-hitting assistants to launch each object where, at the moment, it seemed best. We few sighted people followed them up and answered questions as best we could, going from one part of the room to another to accomplish this. Everyone seemed interested and occupied, as my assistants carried the objects from place to place, often guided by requests to see this or that, or to show something that was a favorite to someone who had missed it when it first went around or who had not had time enough to see it. For more than two hours there was entertainment for everyone; and I felt reasonably sure that a good time was had by all.

As always when it came time to go home, some remained behind to be sure that they had seen everything, or to look at some special object again, or ask some question which didn't get answered in the preliminary explanation, or that had arisen from the examination of the object; and several to say that they had always wanted to know what such and such a thing looked like. A few suggested some things which we might want to include in the collection sometime; and many expressed their appreciation of an opportunity to see so many beautiful things, hoping that this kind of an experience could be extended to blind persons in other places. No one had come dressed up, and we did not have refreshments, but it was a party nevertheless, differing from any I had ever attended before, with a high level of interest and enthusiasm which was proof of the entertaining and knowledge-giving values which blind persons recognize in objects sighted people regard as beautiful.

Two other experiences threw light on this problem of presentation: one at the annual Craftsman's Fair of the Southern Highland Handicraft Guild at Asheville, North Carolina, and the other at the State Rehabilitation Center for the Blind, Topeka, Kansas.

One day when Mrs. Marjorie McCune, herself blind, who has charge of the visiting teachers of the blind for Buncombe County, of which Asheville is the county seat, and a mutual friend, Miss Patricia Stone, and I were looking over some favorite objects together from our collection, the question came up of showing some of them at the Craftsman's Fair.

It so happened that I was giving a talk each morning at the opening of the Fair in the Asheville Auditorium, and the manager of the Southern Highland Handicraft Guild, Miss Louise Pitman, at once approved the idea of inviting two groups of six to eight blind persons each to come to the Auditorium at nine in the morning, an hour before the official opening time.

This gave us an opportunity to gather around a table in the

middle of the main exhibition hall and see some of the exhibits of the Craftsman's Fair without the interruption of the visiting crowds. I collected from the main exhibit a dozen carefully chosen objects, which in that quiet, uninterrupted hour we were able to see quite at our leisure. Some of the guests had companions, and there were always three or four members or friends of the Guild ready to help. After we had spent an hour together looking at the objects I had selected, these helpers guided our guests through other parts of the building to see the many demonstrations by mountain craftsmen.

Our setup was a long table around which the guests sat near enough to each other to pass the objects; I stood at the end of the table within easy reach of the things they were to see. After an explanation to our guests of where we were located in the middle of the main exhibition hall, I told them something of the Guild, with its great variety of exhibits characteristic of the Highland country, and of the many craftsmen at work from the mountain areas of eight southeastern states, and that we were having a privilege, not accorded to the general public, of seeing with our hands some of the choicest handicrafts from this extraordinary regional show.

We would usually begin our inspection of the exhibitions with things made of wood, because in the Southern Highlands is to be found the widest variety of native hardwoods in America. We would, for instance, look at a handsome walnut bowl turned on a lathe, then at some domestic animal, bird, or other figure, maybe an angel for a Christmas crèche whittled out of a piece of holly wood. Then two good examples of pottery, shaped by hand, or turned on a kick-wheel in Kentucky—in a place where they had made pottery continuously for over a hundred years; a hand-woven shopping bag or purse, done by one of a family of six girl weavers near Gatlinburg, Tennessee (where there are more hand weavers than anywhere else in the United States); an egg basket of white oak splints, shaped to carry eggs on horse- or mule-back from far in the mountains to the country store; a child's chair of maple and hickory put together, as had been done for generations, without nails, screws, or glue; a small angel with outstretched wings, made of cornhusks for a Christmas-tree decoration; a dipping ladle of hard wood—a beautiful form to feel, the shape suggested by a gourd dipper; a graceful fox, or a dancing bear cub, of native cherry, with the most natural lines and the smoothest hand polish, done by a Cherokee Indian member of the Guild; and finally, perhaps, a mountain "dulcimore," that plaintive graceful instrument known only in the southern mountains, this one made by a fine young craftsman whose folks had lived there for generations. And I would tell them: "Take this dulcimer in your hands and thrum the three strings, so you will know what it looks like when you hear Jean Ritchie play it, as she sings the mountain ballads with the music makers and the folk dancers in the next hour," and maybe add, "Jean is the youngest of fourteen children of a Kentucky mountain family, and she sings more folk songs than anyone you'll ever know. The whole family, a little while back, before the children began to scatter, all sixteen of them, including the father and mother, on Christmas Eve used to go from cabin to cabin in the little village of Viper, Kentucky, singing old English carols to their neighbors."

Something like this would usually end the hour of seeing things together, except that always through the thoughtfulness of one of the Craftsman's Fair volunteers, we were each given a generous handful of sweet-smelling rose geranium leaves, or perhaps lemon verbena, to take home. One of the blind women, with a specially green thumb, reported that last year she had, from these slips of her favorite geranium, started enough new plants to give one to each of her neighbors. There was time in this hour for the guests to feel a dozen objects quite thoroughly, to ask any questions they wished and, best of all, to express their thoughts and feelings about some of the objects. Then they would usually stay long enough at the Fair, or come again later, to meet some of the craftsmen who were very thoughtful in giving them opportunities to try making something by hand.

Occasionally, I would arrange for some interested craftsmen to sit quietly at a distance and observe what happened during the hour when the guests were looking at their handicrafts. I shall long remember the surprise of one craftswoman on seeing the pleasure a blind person got through feeling an object in the round. A country woman wood carver, whose representation of a rooster, hen, and little chickens so intrigued me that I selected it as one of the objects for the blind to see, sat one day watching, and as she saw the sensitive fingers of the blind visitor gradually discovering what the figures were, the discovery reflected in a smile of recognition, the carver said, "I surely never thought a whittling of mine could ever do so much." The whittling of this mountain woman became such a favorite that it is now in our collection.

The experiences of beauty with the blind to which I owe most, because they were more controlled and had continuity over a period of more than two years, were carried on with the splendid co-operation of the staff of the Kansas Rehabilitation Center for the Blind at Topeka. The result of this co-operation has been the acceptance of the principles of the project as a vital part of their own rehabilitation program. As they have expressed it: "Rehabilitation of the individual, without aesthetic experience, is only partial rehabilitation."

When the Federal Office of Vocational Rehabilitation of the U.S. Department of Health, Education and Welfare made it possible to develop this work through co-operation with some state agency, the Kansas Center was selected as a base for concentration because of its initial interest in the principles involved. They were already pioneering with a project in musical therapy, and this experiment in another branch of the arts, with definite aesthetic content, offered them another opportunity to implement their program. William Dauterman, director of the Center, expressed their attitude as follows: "We continue to be impressed with the necessity of being alert and sensitive to all the areas of human experience to which our clients may have been exposed in the past, to which they might possibly wish to be exposed, and through which valuable and aesthetic educational experiences might be available, and through which vital therapeutic relationships may be established for use in achieving a specific treatment or rehabilitation goal."

The first visit to the Topeka Center was exploratory, and was valuable for two reasons, even if it should go no further. It provided an opportunity to find out how another group of blind persons would respond to the collection of objects; and it was, for me, a new and important lesson in the technique of presentation.

Although there was no preliminary announcement of the kind of things we were to see, there was a general expectation among the dozen or more clients at the showing. Presentation to a group of a dozen was new to me; the only experience I had had which was at all comparable was with the much smaller group at the Craftsman's Fair in North Carolina. But here the case was quite different. I had for Kansas forty or fifty objects, instead of ten or a dozen as at the Fair; this was a far more varied collection with, I hoped, something to interest every staff member and every client. I felt too the importance of this occasion, in which we were all part of a pioneer experience.

My desire to have them all feel its importance as much as I did, made my introduction too long, as I realized when, at my request, the clients were invited to give their frank opinions on how the presentation could be improved, for some thought too much time was taken up in preliminary explanation when everyone was anxious to get his hands on the objects. But, in spite of the rather long delay in starting, we were busy with the objects for about three hours, and no one seemed to want to stop when we did, sometime after eleven o'clock. Several of the clients expressed their wish for more time.

From then on there was no room to doubt the appeal this collection held for the average rehabilitation client. But the strong desire shown by some of the clients to see everything that evening, and by some to see the objects in rapid order, was evidence that the technique of presentation was faulty, at least for some of the more deliberate ones; and I sought for ways to improve it.

Good suggestions came from members of the staff, and from several very interested clients. From this first meeting with clients, and related conferences with staff members, it was decided that I should bring the collection back for new clients as they came in, on an average of every three months, and the staff resolved to begin building a collection of objects of their own for the Center's use, expressing the hope that I could give them a little help on it from time to time. This I was glad to do, especially as the two men most directly concerned, William Dauterman, Supervisor, and Jerry Dunham, Chief Counselor of the Center, were both blind persons and would give the undertaking special significance. I hoped there would be ways I could be of help to them; I knew that their experience in building a collection would be of interest and help to me.

The members of the staff did not, I think, know at this time that it was in my mind not so much to help them acquire objects similar to those I had brought to Topeka, but rather to encourage them in directions of their own choices and those of their clients. The value of this point of view to them and to me, has already been shown in the work we have done together in the early stages of the development of their collection, with which I have kept in continuous touch. Reference will be made to this co-operation in later pages.

The keen interest shown by the different groups of clients in our original collection of objects, and the decision and implementing action of the staff in forming a collection of their own, were sources of real satisfaction to me, and to this was added the genuine concern for the project and the continuous co-operation of Mr. Harry E. Hayes, State Director of Services for the Blind in Kansas.

Through all the experiences at the Topeka Center the question has been how to present the collection so that clients could get the most out of it at a single preliminary showing. I used every opportunity while at the Center to get opinions from staff and clients, and I continued this with some of them by correspondence after leaving.

An important suggestion came from a client who said, "I would have liked, after seeing the objects in the evening, that we could have had all of the next day to see them again, selecting at our leisure those we were most interested in, and seeing them without hurry, interference, or competition."

This helped determine our future procedure. We had the general showing to clients in the evening, as formerly, and on the next day, an hour-or-two appointment with each one, leaving the door open for even more time if any desired it, to see the objects at their leisure. Some clients came back two or three times.

This arrangment did not answer all the questions as to how best to handle a single showing to a number of clients, but by degrees we worked these details out. One improvement was not to show too many objects in a single meeting; perhaps twenty at most, instead of thirty-five, as we had done in the general eagerness of that first night. It is important, if a smaller number of objects is to be shown, that the clients not be informed that this is only a half or part of the collection, for some will always prefer to see everything, even if only at a glance, than to take a chance on missing something.

Another mistake made with the best intentions on that first evening, was to ask the clients at the beginning if there was anything special that any of them would like to see first. I put the question twice, and the same answer came back in a chorus, "We want to see everything." I was reminded later by one of the clients at that meeting, that it was impossible for them to express a preference, for there was really no way of knowing what there was to see! This led to a new suggestion, which thus far I have had no opportunity to carry out, that it might be helpful if some description of the objects could be sent to the clients in advance of my coming, either in Braille or by a letter which could be read to them. Such a description need not be long, nor need it include every item; only enough, perhaps, to create some interest and curiosity in advance, and enable them to express a preference for the objects they would like to see, anticipation being one of the most satisfying experiences.

When there is time, the best technique is to have a general showing, followed reasonably soon, perhaps the next day, with opportunities for those who wish to see again the objects in which they were most interested, with time to observe them thoroughly and ask all the questions they like. Always we have to remember that the blind client or guest can not come up, as we sighted persons can, and survey something he wants to see. It must be placed in his hands or within his reach before he can begin to comprehend it. Also the time which he takes to see an object must be multiplied by the number of persons who are yet to see it. Obviously it requires some careful calculating to give a group of blind persons the opportunity they desire and deserve, to see a small collection of beautiful objects; someone has roughly calculated this as about fifteen times what a sighted person would require.

In all the showings of our collection I can recall no single instance in which there was a lack of interest after the clients had an opportunity to get the objects in their hands; and always in the smallest groups the majority were enthusiastic about several of the things. Most of the clients had positive preferences. Perhaps one out of twenty found an object or two that he did not

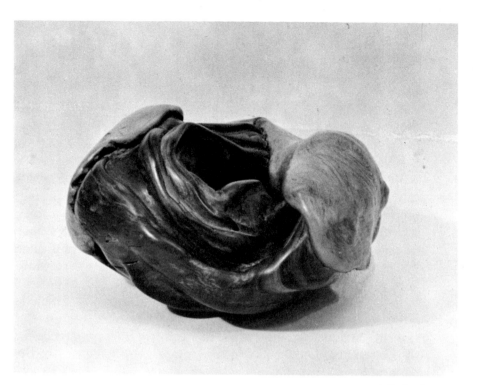

A. Burton Carnes

17. A JAPANESE "KOBU" FROM A WAR RELOCATION CAMP

During World War II our people of Japanese ancestry wrote one of the finest chapters in the long history of the human arts. Detained behind barbed wire, and cut off from communication with the outside world, hundreds of them, not in one camp, but in all ten of the camps, set about to make beautiful things from almost nothing. One form of their creative activity was to discover interesting growths of wood in the roots and trunks of trees, and by separating them, after rubbing them by hand to satin smoothness, thus preserving the grain of the wood, the end result would often be as beautiful to feel as to see. These pieces they called "Kobus" and they collected and shaped hundreds of them from trees that were cut down for roads or to make room for building barracks.

A. Burton Carnes

18. A SINGING CRICKET CAGE FROM CHINA

To many Americans the song of the cricket is a most welcome sound. In parts of China and Japan it is so prized that cages are made that the people may bring the cricket's song into the garden or into the house; and sometimes they carry their little musicians wherever they go. Some of the cages are very beautiful and elaborate, selling for hundreds of dollars each; the one in our collection is modest, though quite beautiful; it is made from a garden gourd. See page 86.

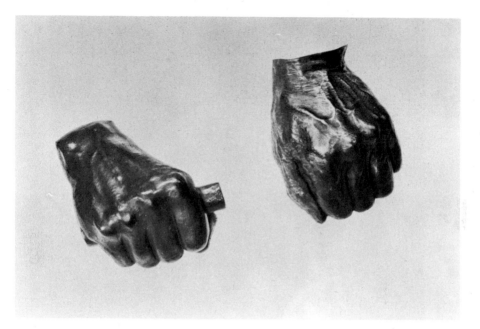

19. LINCOLN'S HANDS FROM A LIFE CAST

On a Sunday in June 1860 after Abraham Lincoln had been nominated for President, Leonard Volk, the American sculptor, visited him at his home in Springfield, Illinois and made a cast of both hands, preparatory to a contemplated statue of the "President to be" as the sculptor correctly guessed. The replicas in our Collection were cast directly from the originals in the Smithsonian Institution by Alva Studios. See page 87.

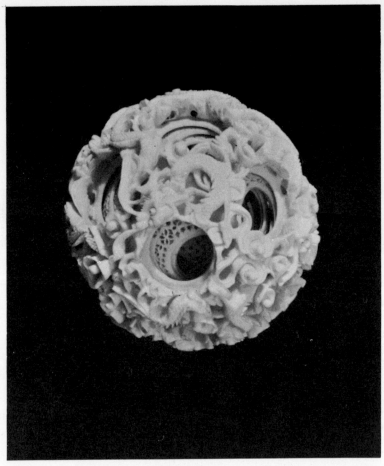

20. IVORY SPHERES FROM CHINA

By far the most extraordinary example of craftsmanship in the Collection of objects is the twelve spheres carved from one piece of ivory one within the other and each with such precision that they move about each other freely without friction. The outer sphere is rugged and a protection for all the others which are almost as thin as a goose eggshell, each pierced with perfect accuracy hundreds of times, too delicate to be touched except with great care. However, blind persons can often get a clear notion of this wonderful achievement in craftsmanship in ivory, if given the opportunity to explore it carefully, as they can be entrusted to do.

A. Burton Carnes

21. EGYPTIAN BASKET MORE THAN 3000 YEARS OLD

Basketry and Pottery, two of the oldest of man's handicrafts, of which writers are ever debating which is the older, were both widely made in Egypt. We were very fortunate to have this ancient basket, probably of coiled palm leaf, handed down to us in such perfect condition.

A. Burton Carnes

22. "THE BRILLIANT CUT" OF A DIAMOND

This great enlargement in glass of the traditional 58 facet cut of the engagement ring diamond was made in Austria to show the eye the way in which our most precious stone is often cut. The model is about 2½ inches across, and the facets or sides are easily perceivable to the finger tips. It has answered satisfactorily the eager wish of a blind friend to know what a cut diamond is like; and it has led him and others, who could see only through touch, to a wider knowledge of the great diamonds of the world. See page 101.

A. Burton Carnes

23. A RURAL WOOD CARVING, "THE CHICKEN FAMILY"

This excellent presentation of a rooster, hen and little chickens was carved in native walnut by a neighbor of The John C. Campbell Folk School of Brasstown, North Carolina. It was a favorite especially with the rural people who saw it with their hands and could explore it until they made out all the members of the barnyard family. The country woman who carved it was self taught. When she made up her mind to learn how to whittle she bought her a jackknife, caught her a rooster and tied him to a porch post, and stayed with her carving "until anybody could tell it was a rooster"; and then went on to carve other inhabitants of the barnyard. She is now one of the most skillful carvers of the Folk School community.

care for. Most clients, when given an opportunity to see the objects at their leisure, welcomed it, and frequently expressed the wish that some friend or member of the family could see this or that.

There were several instances in which sighted neighbors, hearing of the collection through clients, asked to see it, and one evening friends and neighbors of the community were invited to the Topeka Center. While this was not an intended result, neighbors then began to bring gifts to help build up the Center's new collection.

It came to be our standard practice to show and interpret the whole collection at a preliminary session, and afterward to give the clients, as individuals, an opportunity to see thoroughly the objects they were most interested in. In these cases I tried to find out if there were other objects they would like to see, thinking I might help in obtaining them. This often led to the discovery of a personal interest or hobby, and one thing I always tried to find out was the client's favorite material—wood, metal, clay, stone, plastic, or what. I believe that the majority, especially the men clients, preferred wood, next, perhaps, was metal, and the least liked seemed to be plastic.

One day one of the men, a blind member of the staff, said, "I have a strong preference for stone as a material." My mind went at once to some of the semiprecious stones and mineral crystals, so beautiful in form, and I asked, "Is there anything in stone which you would like to see? Maybe we could find it." "Yes, there is," was the prompt answer. "If you could find somewhere a model of a brilliant cut diamond in wood or pasteboard or plastic, or any material, big enough so I could feel the facets and see what a diamond looks like when it is cut for a ring to bring out its beauty, I would rather see that than anything I can think of just now." I promised I would look around next time I had a chance.

Later I found in New York a large model of a cut diamond in glass. It was about two and a quarter inches across and maybe two inches high, with what I learned was the standard "brilliant cut" for engagement rings of fifty-eight facets. The model was made in Austria, with every facet easy to feel. It was a great treat for the staff member, but it proved equally fascinating to several clients; and when an opportunity came for the Center to acquire a group of glass models of twelve famous diamonds which were exact facsimiles in size, cut, and color, the vote was unanimous to include them. These replicas show that each of these famous diamonds is cut differently, one containing over a hundred facets; some clients spent an hour or two in exploring and comparing them.

One of the glass replicas was of the Kohinoor, the only great diamond to have been cut twice, and replicas of both cuts were included. The smallest of the great gems was the Hope diamond, which everyone was surprised to learn was blue; and finally there was the largest diamond ever found, the Cullinan, cut into several stones, the largest of which is I believe still the largest cut diamond in existence, and is part of the British Crown jewels, in the Queen's scepter. The original can be seen—but not felt—in the Tower of London. This interest for the blind had never occurred to me, so this discovery was a new and pleasant lesson, and it created my first interest in diamonds too. But why should not everyone, sighted or blind, be interested in the hardest gem, the rarest, the most expensive, the most famous of all earth's minerals, the diamond? I not only left the model of the beautiful "brilliant cut" with them, but I added a replica of it to our original collection where it soon became a favorite.

Because of the desire to learn as much as possible about the uses of our collection and its influence, and to improve the technique of presentation as well as to measure its aftereffects, it has not been shown in many places, and the greatest concentration has been on the three periodic visits to Kansas, all within the range of about a year and a half. Many letters of remembrance have come to me, in addition to the regular responses which the Center collected more or less methodically from former clients, all deeply appreciative of the opportunity the writers had had of seeing things which had broadened their horizons and given them some fine experiences. After the Kansas Center had begun their collection, the clients were especially interested; everyone who wrote approved the idea, and some sent to the Center objects to be considered for inclusion; others, unsolicited, sent in small money contributions. I quote from a few of the letters from clients of the Center:

"I want to express my personal gratitude for the work you are doing for the blind. The exhibit was of interest to me and to the whole group. The best part of all was the opportunity the things gave to talk to you in a private interview. The articles that have stood in mind longest have been the cast of Lincoln's hand, the cutting stone from prehistoric times, and the hand turned bowl of African ebony. They caught my fancy and stayed with me. I urge you to keep on with the work. You have started one fire with your sparks, and I am sure that others will catch the fire also."

A former teacher writes: "These things are important in several ways. They give clients new avenues of interest in things they have known little of before, and more appreciation of things they have overlooked. A collection gives more feeling about things than one gets in writing. Writing may seem vague in the mind's eye, but actually handling them brings them into definite form, feel, and they have meaning."

A radio mechanic wrote: "I wish I could see all of the objects again. Most of them were entirely new to me. Among my favorites were Toscanini's baton because of its origin and profound history, and the ancient Babylonian clay tablet, because it represents a survival of the earliest known written language."

A deaf-blind client wrote: "These objects will always leave a memory of beauty. Almost all of the objects I saw for the first time."

Another wrote: "I have seen the collection twice and I would like to see them all again. I recall them often. I like best the primitive objects and those made of wood; I have always been fond of wood."

An elderly client who saw the collection in a leisurely way and welcomed the opportunity to see some of the things again, wrote: "I liked many of the things [and she named ten]. Noah's Ark was a pleasure; I had never seen anything like it before. It was a big thrill to look inside and find all the animals, and part of the thrill was to be able to recognize some of them—I was very much interested in the rooster and the hen carving because of the shape of them and the little chicks alongside of the hen. This reminded me of how nice it is to feel a live chick, even though the wood did not have that texture. . . . The fine piece of [Egyptian] linen reminded me of the pleasure I once took in sewing fine materials. It was really educational for me, since I have never seen anything like that collection before—I have been to the museum in 1920 [about thirty-six years ago] but could not touch anything, only could look, and I felt this experience was more satisfying. It was a very unusual experience for me and one I won't soon forget."

The Kansas Center collection of objects is not limited to the works of man, but includes also beautiful or significant objects from nature, thus giving it a wide scope especially designed for a Center where there is room to care for many inclusions, and where the size of the objects is not the problem it is for collections that are often transported. In starting with nothing and throwing out their net for whatever might be in the sea, they collected more objects that were different from those in my original collection than things that were like them. Therefore it was a pleasure for me to find something which they had and I had not, to build on. Studying their collection one day I came across a Korean cowbell of clay—nothing very striking, perhaps, but because it was different from anything I had included or thought of including, I decided to try building on it; maybe to help them carry the bell, as a symbol of their originality, to a somewhat higher aesthetic level.

Why I had never thought of including a bell in the original selection of objects for the sighted and the blind, I do not know, for it is a "natural" for such a collection. There are many beautiful forms and sizes of bells that are pleasant to feel; some of them fit the hand perfectly. Several materials, from wood and clay to metal, and glass, porcelain, and what not, are used, and some collections have bells with very special and intriguing sounds. But with all this and more, I had never thought of including bells until after the Kansas Center discovered it. I must, I thought, do something in recognition of their inclusion of the rather homely little Korean cowbell.

In New York again, my first discovery was a small string of three brass bells of different but harmonious sounds, which upon reading the attached labels I found were "Bells of Sarna." The sounds were very pleasant, but what was the meaning of the word Sarna? I found out by going to a salesroom of that name in the city, where there were many other bells, singly and in groups, and all from India. A boy from India by the name of Sarna once came to the United States to go to school, and in working his way through, he sold a few bells from his native land and learned enough about America to lead him later to develop a business of importing Indian bells and other metal handicrafts. And to my surprise he had returned to the United States, had become a citizen, and was still importing bells.

Here was my chance, maybe, to learn something about bells, for if I should carry out my thoughts to find one or two worthy of the Kansas collection, I must know quite a little more about them. So I found Mr. Sarna on the telephone and told him of my problem, with which he was immediately sympathetic, and he anticipated my wishes by asking me to meet him at the place where he kept his stock of bells from India. I found that instead of acquiring one or two bells, I could offer the Kansas Center collectors, if they liked them, a slightly wider selection. After looking at, feeling of, and listening to all the hand-size bells in Mr. Sarna's store bins, I felt that there were at least ten which I ought to take to show the Kansas people and give them a chance to make their own selection.

I asked Mr. Sarna if I could take these ten I had selected with the privilege of returning most of them within thirty days. "Of course," said Mr. Sarna. But none of them ever got back. They are, by the choice of the Kansas Center staff and clients, the nucleus of a bell collection from which I prophesy we will hear more some day.

I confess that before leaving home for Topeka, after rounding up the "ten sample bells," I became quite bell-conscious, and thought of things to do that I couldn't get around to. One was to get some musical records of bell compositions. At the Center, after I had unpacked and arranged the bells to be seen, felt, and heard by staff and clients, I expressed my disappointment at this omission to Mrs. Beatrice Worthington, who was directing the project in music therapy there. She responded immediately, "We have some bell records, and we can have a bell session Thursday night, when we try to have some special musical program for our clients." And so we did, relating these musical records to our bell collection, and as a part of it, Mrs. Worthington gave an informal talk on the percussion instruments of an orchestra.

At one point she explained to the clients that they could make practically all of these percussion instruments used in an orchestra but one—the cymbals. This was a very special instrument, made by a few experts, and they were very expensive. One of the clients, a boy from the country, broke in, "I know how to make cymbals, Mrs. Worthington, and they are not very expensive." Invited to explain his achievements, he told us that a pair of cymbals made out of the disks of an old farm plow, or disk harrow, made the best and loudest noise of anything for a country charivari, and immediately one or two other clients from rural areas confirmed his high opinion of these homemade instruments.

So the next day all the clients, crowding into a truck, went in a body to the local junk dealer, returning to the Center workshops in the evening with four great disks from an old plow for cymbals, a carload of metals in various forms for bells and other percussion instruments, and their minds filled with plans they could carry out to make Topeka not only the most musical, but on certain special occasions the noisiest Rehabilitation Center to be found in the country.

The members of the Kansas Rehabilitation Center Staff were continuously reminding each other of the great importance of discovering an interest, a preference, in the individual client on which they could build and to which they could relate their rehabilitation program. I have simply tried to apply that principle in the "bells of Kansas" matter.

In assisting with their collection I tried to build, especially in the case of the bells, on an interest which they had established, using the opportunities open to me to help further what came to be a mutual interest of considerable importance. From this experience I have personally gained a considerable knowledge of bells and of bell music, of which I had known little before. My appreciation has been greatly increased in the part that bells have played in the life and culture of so many people; and this finally led me to membership in the American Bell Association, a new and cherished link with a group of congenial fellow Americans. I gladly acknowledge my debt for this new and fascinating interest to the Kansas Rehabilitation Center for the Blind, and their modest little Korean cowbell of clay.

CHAPTER 6

INDIVIDUALS SIGHTED AND BLIND
SHARING WONDER AND BEAUTY
TOGETHER

It takes two of us to discover truth; one to utter it, the other to understand it.—KAHLIL GIBRAN

EVERY person who is blessed with sight has, by virtue of that fact, the essential equipment for initiating aesthetic communication with a blind person if he has the will to make the effort. He has one of two courses open: to find objects, which he thinks of sufficient beauty and significance, to share with his blind friend, or to discover some subject which his blind friend is genuinely interested in and try to find objects and information which will contribute to the growth of that interest. If he will do one, or both, he is quite certain to make a real contribution to the cause he seeks to promote—a happy communication between them, better understanding of each other, and mutual growth.

To one who is in continuous touch with blind persons, verbal communication is so natural and so taken for granted that he may not be conscious of the fact that he has this great additional opportunity to do something that the blind associate could not do for himself, to take the initiative in locating objects and bringing them within their mutual reach. A sighted person can with little effort bring within the reach of his blind friend objects of special importance to him. An instance of this kind can be illustrated by an experience with a blind member of the staff of the American Foundation for the Blind in New York City, although in this case it was the blind friend who was responsible for the first move.

He usually had some object on his desk which he wanted to show me whenever I dropped in, and this time he was holding in his hand a miniature model in metal of a llama which someone, returning from a vacation in Peru, had brought his secretary. It was a figure about three inches long by three inches high and half an inch thick. "What a noble little animal," he observed as his sensitive fingers followed its contour and he held it for me to see. He told me some new things he had learned about llamas and incidentally mentioned that he was always glad to get his hands on any representation of an animal like this which would increase his acquaintance with it.

I was of course much interested in the information about the llama. It had been a symbol to me of that fascinating country, Peru, which I had never visited; but my greater interest that afternoon was in the fact that a person who could not see was getting useful impressions from a metal image too small, I would have thought, to have any meaning for him; and certainly of a texture quite in contrast to the soft, almost downy llama's coat. When I asked him if he had ever had an opportunity to feel a llama's fur, he replied, "No, but I would like that best of anything."

This was something new to me, that to some blind person at least (and I was afterward to learn of many) a very small object is sufficient, especially with the aid of conversation, to give very satisfying and often quite accurate impressions.

As our conversation continued, my thoughts were much on llamas and the prospect of visiting the zoo with special permission for him—and I hoped for both of us—to pat the real llama just once. But nothing came of this because another idea crowded it out. His comprehension and enjoyment of the small figure had encouraged me in a direction I had not thought of going, further than my experiences had thus far traveled. I had not realized what small models might mean to many blind persons. So I asked, "Is there any other animal you would like to see in a small model?" "Yes," he answered, "there is one but I don't suppose there are any models of the animal that I am most interested in." "Well, name it anyway," I said, "and maybe we can see." He laughed as he told me," "The animal family that I am most interested in and know most about is the dinosaur. I have read everything I could find in Braille on them, which unfortunately isn't much, and I've had someone read to me whatever we could find in print, including the wonderful exploration of Roy Chapman Andrews in the

Gobi Desert where he found the nest of dinosaur eggs; and I know there are dinosaur skeletons but I never heard of any small models of dinosaurs."

I said, as casually as I could, "I'll inquire about this model business sometime." And as I left the Foundation building instead of going east to keep an appointment, I canceled it to turn west for the subway that I hoped would get me to the American Museum of Natural History before closing time, where my eye had once caught a glimpse of a small model of a dinosaur.

I remembered it pleasantly because of its bronze-green color, though this curious form made no special appeal to me. Somehow I had never been introduced to a dinosaur so the extent of my knowledge was the recollection of the little model and, of course, of passing many times the huge skeleton of the Brontosaurus dinosaur in the great hall of vertebrates. But I had given him only a passing thought—as a matter of fact his footprints had made more of an impression on me than anything else; they seemed to be the nearest link tying us together. But now that a blind friend showed such interest in this extinct animal, almost chortling over the bits of knowledge he had gained about it, I was really excited about the possibility of getting the little green model for him, and maybe to enjoy it myself. Sure enough, it was in the showcase where I had glimpsed it, and as soon as the slow, though obliging, clerk could hand it to me and tell me the price I said, "You needn't wrap it up," and I was on my way to the fifth floor of the museum to ask the Librarian of Vertebrate Paleontology, an old-time friend who wouldn't mind my ignorance, if this model was fairly accurate and to gather a few facts so that when I took it to my friend the next day I wouldn't appear as ignorant as I really was.

Well, the little model, on which I had staked everything, I never took to my friend at the Foundation, and he doesn't know to this day that I ever had it in my possession, for when I arrived at the Library of Vertebrate Paleontology, the librarian was not there, and when the temporary assistant asked if there was anything she could do for me, I had to say that I didn't know. But, feeling that she really wished to co-operate, I took the little bronze creature out of my pocket and meekly asked, "Would you say that this is a good, reliable representation of a dinosaur?" "I wouldn't know," she assured me. "I am in another field." "So am I," I rejoined. "But," she said, "Dr. Barnum Brown, the greatest authority on dinosaurs we have, is in his office next to the library and I'm sure he would be glad to tell you."

He did tell me. When, after explaining that I was getting it for a blind friend, I finally pulled the innocent little model out of my pocket, the great authority on dinosaurs threw up his hands and said, "By no means should you show such a model as this, even to a blind man. It is only an artist's conception without any respect for a single exact measurement." Before I could recover he went on, "Now you and your friend come up to the museum whenever you can, and Rachel and I [Rachel was the missing librarian] will have exact models of several types of dinosaurs which you can see and he can feel, and you will both know just what dinosaurs looked like."

When, a few days afterward, I arrived at the museum a few minutes late, my blind friend and his secretary and Dr. Barnum Brown and Rachel were already gathered around a table in the library with several exact models of dinosaurs within reach. And the poor innocent little model that had led up to this was far away, where I had left it, in my attic. That afternoon I listened to the most fascinating conversation I can remember about extinct creatures. Toward the end, thinking I ought to participate in some way, I asked Dr. Brown, "About how many different types of dinosaurs were there in their day?" thinking that there might have been ten or a dozen. "We do not of course know exactly how many," he replied, "but we have already found more than five thousand different types," which was far more about dinosaurs than I had ever expected to know.

This is the reciprocal side of sharing an interest with blind persons, and I could add many more instances of how blind friends opened my eyes to wonders and beauties new to me or reminded me of qualities of objects which I had only partly seen with my eyes.

Incidentally Dr. Barnum Brown in his eighty-fourth year is planning three new dinosaur hunts. He has discovered and recovered probably more dinosaur skeletons than any specialist who has ever lived, and he has mounted or supervised the mounting of most of the specimens now to be seen in the American Museum of Natural History in New York.

When Dr. Brown learned of the collection of objects of beauty for the sighted and the blind which consisted entirely of the artifacts of man, he was very much interested; but more so when I told him of my plan to form another collection of objects from nature. He said he would like to offer one item to the new collection. I assured him that any item of his choice would be welcome, but "What will it be?" I asked. "It is a dinosaur's gizzard stone or, if you prefer, a gastrolith," he replied; and soon this new prize was in my possession.

Even now while the objects from nature are being assembled, I still carry this stone, from a dinosaur Dr. Brown dug up in an old creek bed in southwestern Wyoming, in my pocket. Once in a while I try it out on somebody. Rural people who have extracted similar but smaller stones from gizzards of chickens, preparatory to cooking them, are usually interested; but those who are unfamiliar with gizzards of either little birds, chickens, or dinosaurs, do not feel so much at home with it. But I have never shown it to a blind person who was not extremely interested, and I should add that while a very pretty stone to see, a kind of agate, it is even more attractive to the touch. It is very like an abstract finger piece I once saw that had been carved from a piece of old ivory by a Japanese craftsman of great sensitivity, not only to be looked at but particularly to be felt of; I saw it and felt it one memorable day in the shop of a New York art connoisseur. I had long wanted the ivory carving for our collection but could not afford it; here, however, was more than its counterpart, a gift from nature which a dinosaur had shined up for me millions of years ago.

Any of us can encourage our blind friends to make collections of objects and gather information about any tangible subject of special interest; and as a part of that encouragement to take an interest in the hobby which is being built up and otherwise developed. Individuals can also, with all-around gain, encourage small groups of blind persons in schools, camps, or other centers to discover in the immediate environment whatever they can find that they think to be beautiful or especially meaningful and share these enthusiasms with their associates. If this seems more like a suggestion for children than for adults, it may be remembered that we are all children though of different ages. No one can know when exposure to an object of interest may strike a special age level, but whenever it does it will be a life gain.

No one should infer that hobbies for the blind is a new idea. An excellent monograph, *Hobbies for the Blind,* has been written by Charles E. Ritter of the staff of the American Foundation for the Blind and published by the Foundation. Mr. Ritter has full qualifications for this new contribution he has made to the literature of the blind. Although sighted himself he knows the blind and cares about them, and he has probably learned more about their hobbies than anyone else.

But what is known is only a small part of what should be known to sighted and blind alike, and those whose privilege it is to work with or be associated with blind persons should help bring this information and knowledge from its many hiding places for the guidance and inspiration of us all. This is an invitation to any blind person with a hobby to communicate with the writer.

A most pleasant instance of happiness given by a sighted person to his blind friends occurred recently at the Kansas Rehabilitation Center in Topeka. The Kansas Center, in addition to building up a collection of objects of its own, is also in other ways putting into practice, in its growing rehabilitation program, its conviction of the importance of aesthetic experiences and environment. One of their plans is to make every part of the large living room in which the clients spend much of their time, interesting and attractive by the occasional inclusion of something choice enough to become part of the Center's permanent physical and mental furniture.

We had talked a good deal of what the first acquisition should be; small monetary contributions had been made in case it should turn out to be something to be purchased. The idea of a piece of sculpture was considered and it was generally agreed that portrait sculpture, which often appealed to the sighted, would probably not appeal to most of the clients, but that something in round form could be found which would be generally liked. It probably ought to be in wood or stone. One day someone reported seeing some interesting stone carving by an emerging sculptor in Utica, New York, Henry di Spirito, who was born in Italy, but had come to America as an immigrant boy and learned to lay brick and to cut stone for a living. He was still doing it, but in spare time was working to become a sculptor. The National Institute of Arts and Letters had discovered him and given him a grant that would enable him to give more time to his art. He was most interested in the suggestion of nature forms—a flower, bird, animal, or insect partly released from the stone, and it was always a field or river stone, which by its form and texture suggested the subject to him.

In Henry di Spirito's type of sculpture there might be something which would prove a "natural" for the living room in the Kansas Rehabilitation Center. But what would the subject be? A letter to the sculptor asked what subjects he had done, and gave some of the points which would need to be considered, and invited suggestions of his own.

The sculptor's prompt reply was that he had gone down to his garage studio, looked over all his collection and had selected, temporarily, a "Baby Rabbit" that he had recently carved from a stone he had found in the bed of Sterling Creek about seven miles east of Utica. The figure was about nine inches long by four wide and five inches high, and, he said, if the clients enjoyed the feeling of this as much as he had enjoyed the carving of it, he wanted to present it to his "unknown friends." But he made it clear that the carving was on trial, and if it did not meet all requirements it should be returned.

When the baby rabbit came everyone agreed that it should never go back. It was perfect in every way. It took many hours for everyone to see it, and there were long waits for a few, because someone would take the rabbit home at lunchtime for the family to see, but of course bring it right back again; or another would take it to keep overnight but always to be returned early in the morning. By the time I left the Center everyone on the staff, all the clients, and several friends and neighbors had seen it, and it had settled down for keeps. It is quite certain that those who saw the "Baby Rabbit" through their eyes, or through their hands and finger tips, or both, will never forget the little creature.

CHAPTER 7

A COLLECTION OF OBJECTS OF WONDER
AND BEAUTY FROM THE GREAT
STOREHOUSE OF NATURE

And this our life, exempt from public haunt,
finds tongues in trees, books in the running brooks,
sermons in stones, and good in everything.
—SHAKESPEARE, *"As You Like It"*

IT IS from the great storehouse of nature that we shall always
draw the largest number of beautiful objects and also the
deepest wonder.

This natural beauty is the heritage of every human being who
will claim it. Probably the naturalists have the most unforgettable
glimpses of nature, and as there is something of the naturalist in
each of us, we have our glimpses too. Many a layman understands what the adoring student of the natural world, George
Washington Carver, felt and meant when, contemplating an opening bud on a sapling tree, he said: "He who has not felt the
wonder and beauty of an opening bud in springtime has not really
lived."

The works of nature, as the works of man, may seem at first to
be the special possession of those who can see, but, direct and
immediate as is the sense of sight, "the eye is not all of a man,"
or nearly all, and as we begin to explore the million treasures of
the natural world we come to realize that many of them, an unlimited number, can be more definitely and satisfactorily explored
by touch than by any other sense of perception.

We can begin our study of nature, or our collection of objects
to symbolize nature, at any point and wherever we happen to be.
The one requirement is that we start with something in which we

114

are genuinely interested, or of which we have enough knowledge to lead us on to the point where the object has meaning; seeking to find in it, as in our collection of man-made objects, something that evokes our wonder, our sense of beauty, or that suggests its great usefulness. As children, our inquiring minds reach out in many directions; as adults we feel the need, sometimes the necessity, of choosing a few things carefully. But choose we must, if we are to continue to grow; and to keep on growing is the most important thing in life.

We might begin our collection with a starfish; this beautiful one from Florida. The dictionary defines the starfish as "Any of the numerous echiderms constituting the class Asteroidea; having a body of radially disposed arms or rays of triangular outline and more or less flattened cross section, coalescing at the center to form a disk, on the lower surface of which is the mouth—" all of which is undoubtedly true, but this description does not excite us as much as some facts learned from an old fossil bed, with a little help from a geologist, which proved that the starfish has been with us now for more than 300 million years. We will pick him up again in our story, for he is a fascinating creature; but perhaps we should start our collection at another and more appropriate point. Instead of beginning a long way off in time, let us begin a long way off in space.

Where then shall we begin? It will be as far from where we are now as we can imagine; with the outermost space of which we know or from which we have ever had a message or a messenger that we can see and feel. And so we take into our hands a small object, a fragment of a meteor which has come to earth from a distance we cannot calculate with certainty; we can only say billions of miles away. It is a grain of dust from a shooting star—a meteorite.

This object from the farthest distance out is made up of iron, nickel, and other minerals which we know because we have found them in the crust of our planet. We know almost nothing of the history of this meteorite, where it came from or when. We do know that it "dropped" into the part of the United States which we call Arizona; that it is a fragment of the meteorite that made the largest pit in the earth ever made by a falling meteor, as far as man's knowledge goes. So this fragment of a star which we can hold in one hand will be the first object in our collection.

Some of us have seen and some have felt a few of the largest and most famous meteors in the world, because they are now in our country. I think of three of which I know a little, perhaps enough to make someone else wish to see them too.

The largest meteorite anywhere, called Ahnighito, meaning "The Tent," is in the American Museum of Natural History in New York City. It weighs 68,085 pounds—a little more than thirty-four tons. A special scale was built to weigh it. This meteorite, a great mass of almost pure nickel iron, struck the earth thousands of years ago near Cape York, Greenland.

The fourth largest meteor, about one half the size of Ahnighito and weighing fourteen tons, is more interesting to feel because it has many pits. It is also in the American Museum of Natural History in New York. It is called "The Willamette" because it came from the Willamette Valley in my native state of Oregon.

If one visits Washington, D.C., he can see in the Smithsonian Institution the eighth meteor in size, which also fell within the boundaries of the United States. It is called "The Drum Mountain Meteorite." It was discovered in Utah, not far from one of the War Relocation Camps where our people of Japanese ancestry were detained during a part of World War II. This discovery was made in 1944 by two residents of Camp Topaz who came across a rock on Drum Mountain that seemed different, for, on being struck with a hammer, it gave off a metallic ring. It created great excitement in the camp and what to do with it was finally decided by the discoverers themselves, who presented it to the Smithsonian Institution.

Quite the largest element in all meteors is iron and this gives us an opportunity to connect a meteor with our earth, for one of the four main components of the earth, the innermost, so scientists assure us, is iron. Encasing this iron core is an inner shell of olivine 2,000 miles thick. On top of this olivine is basalt, ten to twenty miles thick, on which "float" the continents of granite. Each of these materials, granite, basalt, and olivine, is lighter than the mineral or metal below it.

We seldom find these materials in the pure state, for within the last two to four and a half billion years most areas of the earth's crust have probably been shifted many times by warping or bending, by the moving of masses by glaciers, or by erosion; and in these processes materials have become mixed, fused, and chemically changed. But we do find each of these four basic elements of the earth in a sufficiently pure or original form to be recognized; and so they go into our collection. They make the base of it, and are the beginnings of our small personal collection of minerals. At a later point we shall include more minerals.

Closely bound up with the minerals of the earth are the metals. These produce magnetism, a great force which pervades space. We can not see this force but we can feel it pulling together and pushing apart, as in this horseshoe magnet which came from the Five and Ten store. Another way to feel this magnetic force is through a compass, an instrument which sailors, explorers, and travelers have used for many years. The magnetic needle of the compass always points north, unless some nearby magnet or metal diverts it. There are now compasses made especially for the blind, and blind persons who have been lost have found their way home by them.

All of these elements which existed long before the beginning of any kind of life on the earth, we still have today; and we think of them and their many modifications of form as the land, that part of the earth on which we stand and move from one place to another, for man, so far, is a land animal; the water, which covers the largest surface of the earth; and the air, which envelops all of it.

We shall be especially concerned here with water and land, for from these most of the objects in our collection will come. But before we consider either of them, we can well make a note or two about the air, or atmosphere which envelops everything animate and inanimate we know about. Moreover, it envelops the earth for a distance of several hundred miles. We are apt to take air for granted, but it has wonders of its own.

Air is comparatively invisible and intangible, that is, we cannot see it, nor can we pick up a handful of it as we can these minerals; but we can comprehend some of its qualities, at least two of them —its great weight and its fluidity. Its fluidity we feel in the winds. We cannot feel its weight, as we can that of a stone or any other object, for the air pressure and fluids within our bodies offset it. But its weight is there and we can discover and demonstrate it by filling a glass partly full of water, holding a sheet of paper across the top, and then turning the glass upside down. The weight of the air outside will hold the paper against the rim of the glass. It is said that the whole weight of the atmosphere surrounding the earth is equal to a one-half-mile-thick slab of granite 2,000 miles long by 1,000 miles wide.

Water is one of the two great tangible items of which the earth is made up. A good deal might be said about water, much that is beautiful has been said, but we will have space here only to note that there is quite a lot of it on this globe of ours. The deepest water we know is east of the Philippine Islands; it measures 34,000 feet. If we could drop the highest mountain in the world, Mount Everest, into it, the water would cover its summit by more than 5,000 feet, or almost a mile. Our purpose in speaking of water before land is to remind us that all life, both plant and animal, we believe *started* in the water.

It is these two forms of life, plant and animal, with which we will be mainly concerned from this point on in building up our collection, a few samples of which we shall see and feel. All of these plant and animal forms came after eons of time and ages of change and development.

Life on this planet is comparatively young, only 500 million years as compared to the earth's possible age of five billion years, or one tenth of conceivable time. Here again we ask the question: Where shall we begin with these plant and animal forms for our collection? It should be with the single-cell plant form out of which scientists quite generally believe all our plant and animal forms evolved; but we cannot begin there because there are no tangible shapes or forms of these microscopic organisms available which we can take into our hands, or whose qualities we can sense. But the time will come when we will approximate this experience through the use of enlarged models. However, for our present purpose we will have to choose actual objects from nature which are at present available and which we can take into our hands, examine for themselves, and relate to other things we know in nature, and sometimes to the arts of man.

So, for another starting place in our collection, while all plant and animal life is still in the water and long before there is any evidence of life on land, we come around again to our starfish; and we are lucky to have it, for this is a tangible form we can take into our hands readily and explore as far as we like. One of its wonders is its adaptability: while it appeared in the sea some 300 million years ago, it still survives and is in every ocean on our globe.

This particular starfish came from Florida. It is a typical five-point star although they sometimes have as many as thirty points or rays. In his living form he is somewhat fleshy with a soft shell. At another time we might well concentrate on the starfish as a subject for a special collection, for he is such a remarkable link between the past and the present, and his many colors and forms and often beautiful markings, and his marvelous adaptation, make him one of the most interesting and remarkable creatures of the sea.

We leave the starfish in the water to look for what we can find on the land to add to our collection. Here the seeds of plants are among the most inviting objects. It was the coming into being of the seeds of plants that made life on the land possible, independent of water. Seeds are easy to find, and a few of them should be in every amateur collection of nature forms, some for their beauty, some for sheer wonder, some for both.

From hundreds, yes thousands of seeds in our own country we select three; an acorn from the live oak; a cone-bearing seed of the largest (and until recently believed to be the oldest) living tree, the Sequoia Gigantea; and an ear of yellow dent corn. From outside this country, from the Orient, a lotus seed one thousand years old.

It is already apparent in selecting these few seeds, that seeds alone would be one of the most fascinating collections of nature forms that we could make. Here we have selected an acorn not only because "great oaks from little acorns grow," but because the live oak is one of the most beautiful trees we shall ever see. It is a story-book tree, wonderful to see, to feel, and to sit in; especially the varieties that grow in our southeastern states along the Atlantic Ocean and the Gulf of Mexico.

This little cone, bearing the seeds of the largest tree in the world and the largest that has ever grown on earth, the Sequoia Gigantea, "the big tree of California," is, because of its small size, the most surprising cone we could find. This one is less than 2 inches long and about half as wide; but the fingers can easily explore its form. The Sequoia Gigantea has for a long time been known as our oldest tree, some attaining an age of over four thousand years, but scientists have recently found a specimen of the Bristle Cone Pine, also a native of the mountains of California, which lived to be over five thousand years old.

Among the many reasons for including the beautiful ear of yellow dent corn is that corn or maize is one of the great contributions of the Indians of South and Central America to the world. Until the voyagers and explorers from Europe came across it, after Columbus had discovered America, it was not known in any Eastern country, but now, in addition to being one of the greatest food crops in the United States, it is cultivated in some form in practically every country in the Temperate Zone, and in some tropical lands. It is one of the most beautiful growing crops that man has ever cultivated.

Probably we could find no single seed, unless it would be rice, that would be a better symbol of plant life in the Far East than this small lotus seed. The lotus plant with its roots in the mud and slime and its beautiful flower above the water surface in the air, has for ages been a symbol of human life to the people of India, China, Japan, and other countries of the Orient. The artists and the artisans have painted it, and carved it in wood, stone, ivory, and gems, since before recorded history. This particular seed, resembling a small olive in form, has a history of its own; it is one of a cache of seeds found far under the ground in Siberia and reckoned by scientists to be about 1000 years old. From this batch of seeds in 1922, was germinated the "oldest living flower." It was planted and tended by a young Japanese studying in this country at the time. I was fortunate enough to know him and he gave me this seed for my "children's museum." A few years ago, a story in *Life,* from Japan, pictured a lovely pink lotus in blossom from a seed reckoned by scientists to be about 2,000 years old. The gardener with the green thumb who brought it into blossom was my old friend, Dr. Ichiro Ohga, now known in Japan as "Dr. Lotus."

For us amateur collectors of objects of wonder and beauty in nature, it is easy to turn from any one thing to another, as it might not be possible for the scientist to do. He would naturally follow a system, but children and amateurs are not so restrained; it is not ignorance, however, but eagerness and a kind of intuition which leads us on from one interesting thought or object to another, just for the pleasure of it. If we had to defend ourselves, as happily we do not, we would claim that learning pleasantly acquired is good learning—moreover, it is likely to be remembered.

An easy and pleasant step for the amateur in collecting natural objects is from trees and plants and their seeds, to birds, their eggs and their feathers. The collecting of birds' eggs is not so popular with adults today as it was with boys when I was one in the country on a western farm. But since our collecting is now done partly in the city we will seek help from the museums, and try to persuade one of them to lend us just two birds' eggs, one of the largest now to be found, an ostrich egg, wonderful to behold by sight or touch; and, just as wonderful in its way and somehow more appealing, the littlest egg in the bird world—that of the hummingbird.

These two eggs, which we can never forget once we have held them in our hands, will send us off into research in many directions; to the home of the ostrich in Africa where her egg supplies not only food but also storage jar and water carrier for a Bushman family. And the hummingbird, one of the most beautiful and delicate creatures of the bird world, we are to learn makes an annual trip from North to South America, flying without a stop across the Gulf of Mexico to spend the minter months, and returning in the spring.

We also have as a symbol of the egg-laying family, a turtle shell, since the turtle, being so well adapted to both water and land, has remained almost without change for about 200 million years. Turtles range in size from tiny vest-pocket ones to a fossilized tortoise from India weighing about one ton. Some existing turtles live to be over 150 years old.

The first feathered creature appeared on earth at about the time of the turtle, the geologists specializing in fossils tell us, or about 200 million years ago. He did not much resemble any bird we have now. But in time the Canada Goose, that we do know today, came along, about 75 million years ago, and he is still with us. A flock of twenty-one flew over our house this morning about six o'clock, led by "Akka," whose honk we heard in time to see them before they disappeared in the west. As far as we know the Canada Goose hasn't changed any in these 75 million years that he has been on the North American continent, but while he has been flying around in the air, several very great changes have taken place in what we now call the United States. Camels were here at the time of the Canada Goose; so were elephants, tigers, and the rhinoceros, and the horse was only beginning to evolve from a little four-toed creature about the size of a terrier dog. We do not have room in our hand-size collection for any of the fossil skeletons of these long extinct animals, or even a Canada Goose; but we do have room for this turtle shell from North Carolina about the size of my hand. The turtle to which this shell belongs has a life expectancy of a hundred years.

We can not leave the bird world without gathering for our collection one or two of the loveliest objects of sight, and certainly of touch, in all creation, the feathers of certain birds. Ornithologists divide all bird feathers into three groups; one, feathers of flight in the tail and wings; two, feathers of contour, covering the bodies of the bird; and three, down, one of the softest of substances, which serves as temperature insulation.

Just to be fabulous we will choose for our collection of wonderful and beautiful things a full wing if we can get it, but if we can not, a single feather from the wing of the Arctic tern. Not because he is one of the farthest north of any birds we know, but because he holds the world's record for the longest annual bird flight in history. The Arctic tern, not one bird but thousands of them, journey every year from near the North Pole, way south to seas skirting the Antarctic Continent, a distance of at least 11,000 miles, and back again the same year.

For our second choice of feathers we will get, if we can, the down from an eider duck, for it is probably the lightest and softest to the touch of anything we can imagine. But the down from any duck or goose will do; also the fur of northern animals, especially rabbits, which have for ages contributed to man's comfort. We shall try to include some examples of animal fur and fleece in our collection, but nothing we can find will quite equal in softness and delicacy of touch, the down of an eider duck.

For examples of the plant world we will choose from the largest plants that grow, the trees. And because lumber has been and still is one of the chief sources of shelter for man, as well as for his countless forms of construction, we shall choose two small pieces of lumber. These will be two cubes each about four inches square; one from the lightest known wood in the world, the balsa of Central and South America (Ecuador); the other the lignum vitae from North America. These woods, the lightest and the heaviest in the world, are so different in density and weight that we can only sense this difference by feeling and lifting them. One who had this experience said, "I lifted the lignum vitae first; when I took the balsa block in my hands I felt as though it would lift itself and me to the ceiling."

To the woods of our collection we must add one more, which the botanists tell us really isn't a wood but a grass—the bamboo. But when you see it growing more than a hundred feet high, it is hard to think of it as a grass. The botanists' dictionary definition of grass reads: "Grass is any graminaceous plant with hollow jointed stems and sheathing leaves, including all the common cereals as wheat, rye, oats, barley, maize and sugar cane." This doesn't include bamboo; but if we turn back to the definition of bamboo it says in so many words, "Bamboo a tall tree-like or shrubby grass." So we can't do anything about the definition, but we admire the wood of the grass as we see the hundreds of useful and beautiful purposes to which the people of the Orient, especially the Japanese, have put it.

We will include two examples of this grass; one a beautiful slender handle for a writing and painting brush; the other a bucket for carrying liquids, a "pail," if one prefers. I prefer "bucket" and it is the only one I know that is, in the main, shaped by nature and not by the hand of man; for the hollow stem of the bamboo, which is sometimes six inches wide, has in the joint a natural watertight bottom for a bucket, wanting only a bail or handle to complete it.

If we are a long time in finding a bamboo bucket we can take as a substitute a holder for Japanese paint and writing brushes; for a joint of this remarkable grass is the commonest and most acceptable brush holder of Oriental artists. When it is filled with his tools we shall have a unique bouquet of paint and writing brushes.

For many years the closest connection which I as a western

farm boy had with the culture of the Orient was through my bamboo fishing pole which I could buy for ten cents. I was yet to learn of the many uses the ingenious people of the East had made of this most wonderful of all grasses. Someone has written, "Bamboo is one of the most wonderful and most beautiful productions of the tropics, and one of Nature's most valuable gifts to uncivilized man."

It is with regret that in this initial collection of nature forms we can give no more space to grass and grass seeds. But sometime we shall be more inclusive, especially in the collection of grass seeds, for the seeds and stems of grasses have, for ages, been the chief support of human life; and of much animal and bird life as well.

While at first thought one might not include the seeds of grasses as among things in nature which would be readily sensed and enjoyed both by sight and by touch, on second thought, they are a natural. As I look back to my days as a farm boy, I recall seeing many plant seeds, and sowing a good many of them too; but no experience is remembered with more pleasure than the running of seeds through my hands just for the pleasure of it. There is something about the flow of seeds through one's hands which to me was nothing short of beautiful when as a very small boy, and older too, I would dip my hand into the bins and boxes of my grandfather's wonderful granary, picking up sometimes a double handful of wheat, millet, vetch, or clover seed and running it through my fingers—not like water, not like sand, but like seed. There is no other experience quite like it.

For our collection we can not bring back the bins from the old granary, but there are other ways that take up little room which would be practical: bags, jars, bottles, and bowls would do it. And just recently I have seen one batch of seed which thrilled me, and from which we might hope for a loan. What I saw was a large pottery jar, holding several quarts, more than half full of Mentbelia (blazing star) seed, which was left in Cordova Cave, New Mexico, by the Indians about 200 A.D. It is described by Paul Martin in his book, *Digging Into History*, published by the Chicago Natural History Museum in 1959. Dr. Martin records that, two thousand years ago, the Indians parched, ground, and ate the blazing star seeds.

From the vegetable kingdom we turn to the vast and beautiful, though much hidden, treasures of the mineral kingdom. And here we find what some mineralogists have described as the most marvelous flowers in existence: mineral and metal crystal flowers which are in blossom not for the day, the month, or the season, but for all time. To those who explore the wonders of the natural world mainly through touch, the crystal flowers of the minerals and metals make a special appeal.

Much of the wonder and beauty of the crystals is perceivable through the hand; many of these forms are as vivid to the touch as to the sight, and some more so because of their texture, temperature, smoothness, weight, and other properties which the eye can not discern as well as the hand can. Also, many of the crystals of minerals are of a size and character easily explorable by the fingers and encompassable by the hand. As form is a basic element of aesthetic experience for both sighted and blind, one finds in these permanent crystals a field of happy mutual exploration.

A third reason which makes the field inviting is its growing popularity. Mineralogy is now one of the most popular hobbies for both young people and adults. The "rock hounds," as they, half in fun and half in affection call themselves, are all over the place; they have clubs and meetings almost everywhere and their literature is widely read. This is all a good sign for the amateur collector, for it means that more specialists are writing, lecturing, and demonstrating in this field, increasing knowledge and broadening appreciation.

Every mineral has its characteristic crystal shape ranging from the simple cube or square of table salt to garnets with sometimes as many as thirty-two clear-cut sides. Although in the case of many minerals the crystals are not perfect in form because of mixture with other substances or distortions brought about by pressures, yet very many near-perfect ones are to be had and because of their indestructibility can be handled over and over again without risk of damage. A collection of minerals could last forever.

One crystal carefully studied is a key to this fascinating and stimulating world; and although crystals vary in size from the tiniest forms too small to be discerned by the eye to others weighing hundreds of pounds, yet large numbers are to be had of most convenient size for hand exploration, and in ideal form. Like fingerprints, however, no two of them are exactly alike and the acquiring of just the right specimen is worth a long and careful search.

For this, perhaps the first amateur collection of mineral crystals to be shared by the sighted and the blind together, our first choice should surely be some form of quartz, "the most interesting of all minerals" and for most of us beginners the most beautiful. It was with this fabulous nature form, quartz, that the study of mineral crystallography began, and some collectors have spent their lives and their fortunes on it, alone and in its infinite combinations with other minerals. Two great American authorities, George Letchworth English and David E. Jensen, in their superior book, *Getting Acquainted with Minerals,* say of quartz: "It has a large number of distinct varieties and there are wider differences between them than in the varieties of any other mineral. . . . There are few places in the whole world where it would be possible to walk a mile and not see some quartz." For our purpose we choose some twin crystals of ice-clear quartz from Joplin, Missouri.

Other minerals which we will include for their crystal form will be fluorite, a quite perfect specimen from southern Illinois which is an octahedron and amethyst in color. This is the form that the diamond takes when it crystallizes perfectly, which is very seldom. We will add one more crystal because of its many sides and angles, the garnet. We are choosing one of the commonest varieties of garnet, almandite, which is usually a deep red in color, opaque, and with sometimes as many as thirty-two facets or sides, often all easily perceived. This specimen comes from Gore Mountain, New York.

One more form of mineral we will include, a stone which is partly man-made or at least man-formed, rather than one of nature's minerals. It is a core from the boring of a deep oil well. In these borings for oil, man has gone farther toward the earth's center than has ever been done in any other way. These cores bring not only the most distant stone to us, the deepest, this one from almost four miles deep in Texas, and some cores contain fossils and forms of carbon which have pushed back the date of life on earth millions of years.

From the land with its trees, grasses, rocks, and gems, we go to the vast area of water, the oceans and the seas with their shells, corals, and myriad forms of marine life. Of all nature forms none are more wonderful or more beautiful to see and to feel than the shells of the sea. Many of them are of a size comfortable to fit into the waiting hand; they are strong and rugged to the touch, some with surfaces of lovely smoothness. They are easy to carry around, to see and to feel and to share with people, and are readily cleansed when they catch the dust. A small collection of shells is ideal for anyone.

We can include only a few of the hundreds of shells which sighted and blind may enjoy together. The reader, especially the American reader, has probably guessed that the first one chosen will be the chambered nautilus from the Pacific or the Indian Ocean. The nautilus is famous as an architect and a builder of his own house, and since he keeps the inside of his house concealed from public view we will have one shell sawn open in the middle so that anyone may see and feel the rooms he builds for himself, one at a time, beginning with a tiny one and gradually enlarging them with an architecture as beautiful as has ever been achieved. Beginning with a room so small the sensitive finger can hardly perceive its form, he widens the room each year, its walls strengthen as the spiral grows, until the walls can easily be traced, and the blind person can get a fair idea of what the first little rooms, which he cannot see or feel, look like.

There is another form produced by a nautilus, not so well known but with an architectural exterior even more beautiful, which though fragile we must include, for its wonder and its beauty seem to exceed the imagination. This is the cradle of the argonaut or paper nautilus. It is an eggshell-like structure built by the mother for the purpose of carrying her eggs until they are hatched. Shortly afterward the little squids abandon it, leaving the empty exquisite cradle for the shell collector. It is as delicate as an eggshell and its form more easily damaged, so when perfectly recovered it commands a high price. But as an object of natural beauty it is worth it.

From this point on, all the shells are so sturdy that no one need feel hesitant about examining them with thoroughness and submitting them to every test. They are the oyster shell with a pearl forming inside, the abalone shell, the turban shell, the helmet shell, and the queen conch.

The lustrous inner shell of the abalone is used now for jewelry and buttons, but much earlier it was important with the Indians of the North and of Alaska for inlaying their wood, horn, and other artifacts. The natural form of the abalone shells makes them immediately useful for dishes and dipping vessels.

The turban shell, scattered the seas over, was a favorite drinking cup for royalty in early days; because of their many beautiful bright colors they are used now for jewelry and personal ornamentation. The shape of the shell is among the finest of all forms and one of the loveliest to hold in the hand and to listen to the music of the sea.

The helmet shells are the favorites of cameo cutters. Our selection here is the red helmet of the Mediterranean and the Red Sea: beautiful in color and perfect in size, form, and texture for exploring through touch.

A middle-sized queen conch is included, because the full-grown is too large and heavy for the pleasantest handling, being a foot long and weighing about five pounds. Semiprecious pearls are sometimes found in this conch; the shells are so hard the natives of the West Indies make tools of them. They are used for making porcelain and cameos, and are used as horns in Barbados by fishermen coming in from the sea, to announce their homecoming and their catch.

We cannot leave the sea without examining at least one type of coral. Coral is a marine skeleton found in all the seas, but from this great family we have selected one which lives only in the sunlit equatorial waters, the star coral, that is mainly responsible for the "greatest single edifice ever raised by a living creature," the Great Barrier Reef off the northeast coast of Australia, 1260 miles long and enclosing approximately 80,000 square miles of water.

Coral was in the sea 150 million years before the insects came, among the first of which was the dragonfly, a giant to begin with, so fossil remains tell us, with a nearly two-and-a-half-foot wing-spread. From the more than 650,000 insect species in the world today we shall see the beautiful cocoon of the silkworm. Silk culture was started by order of the Emperor of China about 2600 B.C. The silkworm, which would probably not have survived had it not been for man's care and nurture, is now one of the most useful insects, supplying us with silk filament of unsurpassed quality.

The basis for all the estimates of scientists as to prehistoric animals and plant life have been fossil remains, or imprints in stone, mud, asphalt, and amber. Here, for example, is a fossil of the leaf of a ginkgo tree. This tree, living today and a favorite in many parks and gardens, is called "the fossil tree," because it is the survival of the one which the fossil tells us was on earth in many places as far back as the dinosaurs. The tree as we know it today is said to have survived in Asia only through the care of man. Trees have been imported from the Far East, but fossils of the ginkgo leaf have been found in several parts of the United States. This one is from the Columbia River Gorge in Oregon.

As we close these pages of suggestions for objects of wonder and beauty from nature which sighted and blind can share together, we realize that we are just beginning rather than ending. But it is hoped that enough has been set down and suggested, to encourage us to give objects from the natural world a trial with sight and touch similar to those we have given the arts of man.

CHAPTER 8

BEAUTY FOR THOSE WHO CAN NEITHER SEE NOR HEAR: THE DEAF-BLIND

We can only be alive when our hearts are conscious of their treasures.—THORNTON WILDER

THE last of the blind to be reached, but when reached often the most responsive, are those persons who can neither see nor hear, but who because of the very absence of these two major senses give us glimpses of the human mind and soul that we could not get in any other way. They seem to bring us clearly the supreme fact that with the gift of life comes to all of us a small, tightly but delicately wrapped package of unknown human potentialities, inherited not only through our mothers and our fathers, our grandmothers and our grandfathers, but through all our forebears; potentialities that we, with help from family, teachers, neighbors, and society, may unfold and refold into minds of normal and useful human beings—with possibilities beyond the power of anyone to foretell.

When these doubly handicapped persons who can neither see an image nor hear a sound are reached by goodness, truth, or beauty, the response is often of a quality and an intensity not matched by us who have the full equipment of perceiving senses. Perhaps there is an appreciation, a degree of gratitude, which can come only to those living without the senses of seeing and hearing, by which they are able to know better than others could the worth of that indispensable messenger to the brain, the great sense of touch. "What I can touch and feel," said one of them, "that I know, as well, I believe, as ever I could had I both sight and hearing; it may not give me the same notion which you have, or which I would have had if I had seen and heard; but it is my best notion and I am certain it is good."

130

And who can doubt the words of Helen Keller who wrote, in *The World I Live In*, "My hand is to me what your hearing and your sight together are to you. In large measure we travel the same highways, read the same books, speak the same language, yet our experiences are different."

A deaf-blind friend, a man of fifty years, after we had spent nearly two hours looking at ten or a dozen objects from our collection, said: "This has been one of the finest days of my life. Such an experience will mean even more to some who are deaf and blind because of their utter isolation and their very few opportunities to sense the fine things around them. Remember you can see much of the world that is around you; they cannot see any part of it. Remember too that you can hear much that surrounds you; they can not hear a sound of it to either guide them or refresh them. Most of the world they get must be through their remaining sense of touch. But touch is enough because it opens the mind to the meaning, and even to the appearance of an object of beauty, if the object is interpreted and brought within the reach of their hands."

More than once it has been said here that the blind are just like other persons only they do not see. Of the deaf-blind it is quite as true to say that they are just like anyone else except that they cannot see or hear; and what has been said of blindness is true of deafness, or of both when joined, that there is nothing in this great affliction which in any way harms the "personality." With opportunity there are no limits to the mental and spiritual growth which deaf-blind individuals may attain.

But what a different and varying factor opportunity is to those who can take advantage of it through sight and through hearing and those who can take advantage of it only through touch. I do not believe that anyone who is not blind and deaf can fully understand or imagine what it is to be thus doubly handicapped, but we can grasp enough of its meaning to know some things that can be done—and that we can help to get done—to bring opportunity literally "within reach." One of the greatest needs of deaf-blind persons is human communication and companionship. The purpose of this chapter is, in part, to suggest one of the ways toward this communication and companionship by sharing a very small yet very choice part of our world of the five senses with them, through objects which we now know will, if adequately interpreted and brought within the reach of their perceiving hands, evoke delight.

Communication must come to the deaf and blind person in one of two ways: either by way of a manual alphabet, that is by spelling things out with the hands by letter and symbols with the fingers of the transmitter, and received usually by some part of the hand of the recipient; or through mechanical devices, one of which is the wonderful machine "tellatouch," developed by and now made available through the American Foundation for the Blind.

By the "tellatouch," which looks like a small portable typewriter, one who wishes to speak to a deaf-blind person will write his letters out just as he would on an ordinary typewriting machine, except more slowly, while the recipient, holding the tip of his finger on a single round cell at the back of the machine, gets simultaneously in Braille letters what is being spelled out. The communication is almost without loss of time; but the recipient must be able to read Braille. This machine is the medium which has been used most in the interpretation of objects of beauty to the deaf-blind. For them the title of the project might be extended to read: "Beauty for the Sighted and the Blind and the Deaf-Blind," but the shorter and simpler title seems adequate.

The difficulty of reaching the deaf-blind with descriptions and interpretations will be realized at once, when it is known that every message must be given and received letter by letter without sight and without the helpful sound of the human voice. And even after this slow transmission of thought in words and through words into sentences, the completion of this experience must wait until the recipient can leave his machine and take the object in his or her hands. We are completely and thoroughly dependent here on the human hands; first through the playing of the thought on the keyboard with the fingers, then through the recognition of the Braille letters by the recipient, and finally through our handing the object to him to complete the experience of communication. One of the results, a by-product of this long but necessary way of seeing objects, is that it makes the showing of them to the blind only, where the human voice comes in, seem so easy and so simple.

24. JAPANESE IRON TEAPOT

One of the objectives of this Collection was to bring in examples of the different materials from which man has shaped his arts, and this old teapot of the 18th century was chosen to give the feeling for iron. A photograph can hardly do justice to this useful and beautiful container, sand cast in a mold with a delicate ship design as a decoration on the body, and a cover of cloisonné. Japanese artists and craftsmen have specialized in iron teapots for centuries, making some of the most beautiful in the world. This fine one, about 7 inches tall, is very pleasant to feel, especially when filled with very warm water.

25. NOAH'S ARK

Although this Noah's Ark was not in the Collection of Objects, it was often shown to clients or guests because it has long been an enchanting toy to children the world over, and it is today fondly remembered by many grown-up Americans. It could probably be classified as an example of folk art, this and similar arks and animals coming out of Old Germany, probably from the Black Forest where many of them were once made by the peasants and shipped everywhere. Because it was—and still is—my favorite of all toys, it was a pleasure to share it with friends who could not see them but who got much pleasure from feeling and playing with the animals.

26. A BOOK IN BRAILLE

The greatest of gifts to the blind was the invention by Louis Braille of the Alphabet of raised points. Slow as was its acceptance in his own country, and even slower in England and the United States, it is now in universal use. The points corresponding to our printed Roman letters, are always within a certain size cell. And each letter or set of points come within the dimensions of the discerning finger tips. The reading hands of Richard Kinney of the Hadley School for the Blind, Winnetka, Illinois.

27. A BRAILLE BIBLE: PUBLISHED BY THE AMERICAN BIBLE SOCIETY

Miss Pauline Nodhturft with her Bible which is in twenty volumes, each about 11½ inches high by 12 inches wide from 2½ inches to about 4 inches thick. The pages are single spaced and completely filled on both sides, with margins only about ¼ inch wide, except on the binding side which is less than an inch. The Braille volume upright on the floor is the Book of Psalms, the small black volume is a complete pocket edition of the Holy Bible. It is 3¼ inches wide by 5 inches high and ⅜ of an inch thick.

Chas. E. Donnelly

28. A BLIND MAN BUILDS HIS FAMILY
A HOUSE

Francis Burnett, once a jeweler, after complete blindness, designed and built this 8-room house in New Jersey doing everything himself except the concrete foundation and brick chimney. See Story, page 32.

29. A SUCCESSFUL AND HAPPY BLIND FARMER

Joseph McDonagh, "The Blind Farmer of the Catskills," New York, at the door of his barn, with his cows and calf and his dog Bozo. See Story, page 36.

The Evening Bulletin, Philadelphia

30. A SUCCESSFUL DEAF-BLIND FLOWER GARDENER

Richard Badger, deaf, blind and mute gardener, preparing his flower garden on a vacant city lot in Philadelphia, Pennsylvania, where he later won awards for its beauty and the quality of its plants. Note the wall he has just built of discarded bricks. See Story, page 60.

31. A MINISTER OF A CITY CHURCH

John Urich, the blind boy who wanted to be a minister, administering sacrament to his parishioners in Grace and St. Paul's Church, Lutheran, in New York City. See Story, page 39.

Marshall Berman, Jr.

32. A DEAF-BLIND TEACHER IN A CORRESPONDENCE SCHOOL

Richard Kinney, deaf and blind teacher and Assistant Director of the Hadley School for the Blind in Winnetka, Illinois, the only correspondence school for the blind in the world. Mr. Kinney teaches pupils by Braille in many foreign countries. He is here using the "tactaphone" through which he can communicate by telephone with anyone who can use the Morse code. See Story, page 49.

33. A BLIND CHAMPION OF THE INDIANS

Alambert E. "Bert" Robinson, a blind but understanding administrator and friend of the Indians of Arizona, and an interpreter of their culture. He is here shown with a few of his collection of Indian baskets, one of the finest in the world. See Story, page 58.

34. A PIONEER IN ELECTRONICS FOR THE BLIND

Robert T. Gunderson, blind from birth, a "ham operator" at fifteen, now an electronics engineer; but above all an inspirer of blind persons to become self-supporting citizens. See Story, page 45.

35. FROM MILL BOY TO SUPREME JUDGE

William E. Powers, entirely blind, was elected by the State Legislature in 1958 to the position of Associate Justice of the Supreme Court of Rhode Island. He had served this State for five terms in the House of Representatives and was elected five times as State Attorney General. See Story, page 55.

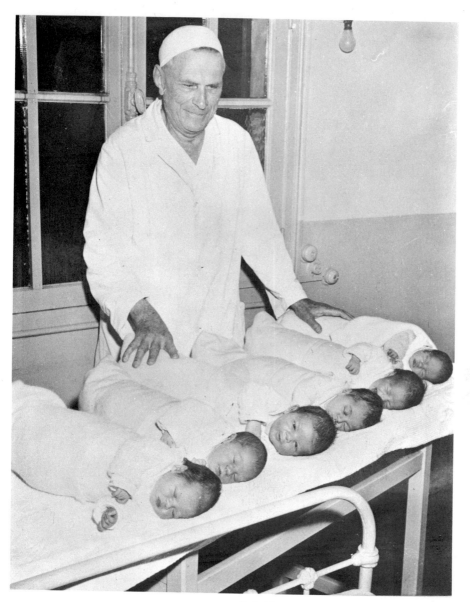

36. A LAWYER BECOMES A GREAT BLIND DOCTOR

Dr. Albert Nast, in his rural clinic at Chelles, France (a village near Paris), blind for 23 years, "looks" at the six babies he delivered within 36 hours in September 1954, bringing his total deliveries to 2,000. See Story, page 63.

Doris Day

37. A BLIND FARMER LEARNS WOOD TURNING AT 84

John Hess, an Amish farmer of Pennsylvania who, after being blind seven years, at 84 learned the craft of wood turning, becoming both expert and artistic. The rose jar (he does not use tobacco) in upper right, he turned from a fallen walnut tree on his farm, having saved the wood for 10 years for "something nice."

38. A BLIND FORESTER

A. Robinson, a forester and farmer near Moscow, Idaho, makes his skilled hands do the work of his eyes. He is totally blind, and his only assistant in felling a tree is the voice of his wife. She stands where the tree should fall, or be felled, and calls out to him thus giving him the direction, so that other trees in their forest preserve will not be injured in the felling.

39. SCULPTURE SUGGESTED BY FIELD AND RIVER STONES

This "Baby Rabbit," a gift to the Kansas Rehabilitation Center for the Blind at Topeka, was carved from a river stone which shape suggested the subject, by the Sculptor Henry di Spirito of Utica, New York. He found the stone in the bed of Sterling Creek about seven miles from his home. See Story, page 112.

But if our communication to the client seems slow and tedious, the playback is not so, for whether the message goes to him by hand or by machine, the sighted person is usually surprised at the speed with which it is interpreted and the conversation completed. The deaf-blind client, often, by an anticipation which is extraordinary, gets the message long before it is fully spelled out, and repeats it back in rapid-fire words to the sender; almost always revealing a mind alert, alive, and eager for any further communication which the situation will produce.

The deaf-blind are the members of society of whom we know least, the ones with whom we have the minimum of communication. Many are hidden away in remote and unknown places, no one knows how many there are. The United States Census of 1920 noted 169 blind-deaf persons in this country. Ten years later, in 1930, after a most painstaking search by private individuals, 665 were located in the United States and Canada combined. But there was one who knew there must be many more, one who was herself hidden away in the earliest years of her life but who will now go down in history as having done more than any other human being to help reach and to alleviate the deaf-blind of her country and the world. Helen Keller tells us that we have knowledge now of about 3,000 persons with this double handicap in the United States alone.

If any minority in our country has the right to complain of its state it surely is those who can neither see the world nor hear a single sound; yet they are the least complaining. If it is a good world, how can they know? But they do know, better than many of us, for they discover so much that is good, and proclaim it.

Their voices are so few among the many that we do not hear them, but they are here; and some day we shall have more time to listen. This month my mail has brought four messages from deaf-blind persons, and because few have the good fortune to know even one person who neither sees nor hears, I would share these messages with my readers. The first is a copy of *Touch and Go*, a monthly publication edited by Sam Chermak, himself a deaf-blind man, and published in both Braille and mimeograph print. *Touch and Go* meets a real need, since deaf-blind people are starved for every bit of news of human interest, news which comes to others easily through the air waves and newspapers. My copy is in mimeograph and it is so full of human-interest events from everywhere that I always read it myself, and sometimes to my family.

The second communication is a letter from a friend in North Carolina who tells me of one of her clients, deaf and blind, who is eighty years of age but who told my friend, "I do not feel my years, because I am so happy." One of the reasons, maybe, is that she "cuts and sews all her own dresses, usually measuring them by other dresses and quite frequently does not use a pattern. She threads her needle by using a needle-threader, which is one with a split eye through which the thread can easily pass when stretched across the top." Other blind seamstresses have threaded their needles with their tongues.

The third communication was written on a typewriter by a deaf-blind person and signed by her hand; it is her annual appeal for support of the work of the blind overseas. It is a letter such as no one else in the world could write except Helen Keller. A few lines of this letter are printed here because they reflect so clearly the life, the work, the hard-earned gifts and gratitude of one of America's best-known and most-loved citizens.

"Amid the happy labors that crowd my life I offer each day a humble prayer of thankfulness for the blessed years of devoted love given to me by my teacher, Anne Sullivan. She, it was, who came to me in my silent darkness and led me into the radiant light of learning and usefulness.

"It was one of my darling teacher's earnest wishes that through me the United States should hold up a torch of friendship and enlightenment for the blind of the world. Thus, I have traveled far and worked unceasingly in recent years as Counselor for the American Foundation for Overseas Blind so that her fervent wish might be realized. In every continent of the world I have talked with blind and deaf-blind children who dwell in ignorance and isolation because of the lack of those trained teachers who could unlock the doors of wisdom for them. Ever conscious of the bounteous providence that brought me Teacher I am filled with the recognition of the urgency for sustaining the flow of understanding aid from the people of America to their cousins across the sea."

The fourth communication, which I have just received, is a letter from a deaf-blind friend in Topeka, Kansas, giving me much news of the Rehabilitation Center for the Blind in which I am so interested, and most welcome is the good report of the writer herself, Miss Fern Chapman, who was the first deaf-blind person ever to see the Collection of Objects of Beauty for the Sighted and the Blind. She had written her letter on a portable typewriter.

It was on my first visit to the Kansas Center in 1956 that I met Miss Chapman. She did not come to the meeting where the blind clients on the evening of our presentation "saw" the collection, because she could not hear. This session was naturally for those who could both hear and feel; but next morning, when I was busy with some of the clients who had come back to see some of the things again and to ask if there was anything more to see, Jerry Dunham, of the teaching staff of the Center, was seated at a nearby table showing some of these objects to Miss Chapman. Mr. Dunham is himself blind, but hearing my voice, called me over and introduced us; and they went on looking at the things together. Mr. Dunham had come to know the objects through touch and through our conversation, but how could he tell his client, who could neither hear nor see, about them?

It was by means of the almost magic little machine to which I have referred, the tellatouch, which turns Roman letters into Braille. The keys were on the front of the machine, as on a typewriter, where the letters of the message were spelled out one letter at a time, and at the back was a small cell-like aperture where appeared, to the tip of the waiting finger, the same letter in Braille.

Fern had her favorite objects as did all the other clients, and when a year later a questionnaire was sent asking if they remembered any of the objects that had been brought to the Center, her reply was, "Yes, they will always leave a memory of beauty." And her account of what she then saw and liked was an accurate recollection and a fond memory second to none of those who had heard about and felt the objects a year ago. Through the silentest of communications, touch, she had gained a solid, accurate, and satisfying experience of things lovely to her, not only for the time being, but to look back upon always.

If there is anyone anywhere who longs for human communication and companionship more than another, it is he who cannot see or hear you but with whom you can communicate through the magic sense of touch. He knows better than anyone can who reads these lines, what human communication means, its presence and its absence. It was one of the deaf-blind, Richard Kinney, who said, "The human being will break through any barrier to reach other human minds."

Above the door of an old but understanding Institution for the Blind is printed in large letters for visitors to read, "Do not pity the blind." It should be amended by adding these words, "or the deaf-blind." They do not need or want pity. Their need is communication with, and interpretation of, the world which they cannot see, which they cannot hear, but which they can, if they are reached, understand. Let us not pity them, but rather rejoice with them, that they are living in the best world that there has ever been. No matter what we who call ourselves normal may think of it, in its relation to ourselves, this country is, beyond all doubt, the best century for the blind and the deaf-blind so far in human history. And what is better, the last half of the present century holds the best promise for the deaf-blind that we or they have ever known. Because of its relation to this new promise, I would mention here a recent event which those who know the field well consider an historical milestone in the lives of the deaf-blind.

This epochal event was opened with an international forum on the evening of Tuesday, July 9, 1957, as a part of the program of the annual meeting of the American Association of Workers for the Blind at the La Salle Hotel in Chicago. It was followed by a one-week conference of the participants at the Industrial Home for the Blind in Brooklyn, New York, and visits by them to other cities, including one to President Eisenhower and to the Office of Vocational Rehabilitation of the Department of Health, Education, and Welfare in Washington.

The subject of this meeting was "A Forum on Communications for the Deaf-Blind." It would have been notable if only for the fact that nine of the eleven speakers on the panel were blind persons, but what was more remarkable, something which never had happened in any meeting before, was that four of the main speakers were both totally deaf and totally blind. Yet all knew what was taking place and what each speaker was saying, through a form of communication too silent for any of us who were looking and listening to understand, but so effective was their communication that each of the deaf-blind guests knew immediately what was going on through the hands and nimble fingers of their companions and interpreters.

It is the spectacle of the meeting to the sighted audience, rather than its content, that I would picture briefly. The content will eventually be available to any reader, but the spectacle never before enacted, will, I think, never be forgotten by those who witnessed it.

The forum was sponsored by the Committee of Services for the Deaf-Blind of the World Council for the Welfare of the Blind, and the Chairman was Peter J. Salmon (blind) who is Executive Director of the Industrial Home for the Blind in Brooklyn, New York. The panel's speakers and their interpreting companions were seated at a long table, the deaf-blind speakers sitting two on each side of the center toward the ends of the table with their interpreters. They stood up to speak but remained at their respective positions with their individual microphones suspended, resting lightly on their chests.

The address of welcome was given by Colonel E. A. Baker (blind), President of the World Council for the Welfare of the Blind, and Managing Director of the Canadian Institute for the Blind, Toronto, Canada.

Moderator for the evening was Miss Annette Dinsmore (blind), who also spoke on "A Nation-wide Picture of the Education of the Deaf-Blind Child." Miss Dinsmore is the Consultant for the Department for the Deaf-Blind of the American Foundation for the Blind.

The two seeing speakers on the program were Edward Evans, M.P., President of the National Deaf-Blind Helpers League of Peterburough, England, who brought greetings to the convention from the United Kingdom, and Dr. W. L. van der Pool, Chief Engineer of Research of the Netherlands Telephone and Telegraph Services Laboratories, the Hague, Holland. He also interpreted the meeting to Dr. Gerrit van der May of The Hague, Holland.

An accidental, but to the audience astonishing, feature of this program was that each deaf-blind person in this panel used what appeared to be a different type of manual communication.

The order of the deaf-blind speakers, three of whom were Members of the Committee on Services for the Deaf-Blind, was as follows: Richard Kinney, Instructor at the Hadley International School for the Blind, Winnetka, Illinois, who spoke on "Adventuring Alone with Communication"; Mrs. Robert Jordan interpreted the proceedings of the meeting to him through the one-hand manual alphabet in which the words and symbols were spelled out in the open palm of the recipient. This required that the recipient hold his open hand firmly to receive the commentary of the interpreter accurately.

Next spoke Arthur R. Sculthorpe, M.B.E., General Secretary of the National Deaf-Blind Helper's League of Peterborough, England, whose subject was "The League and Its Work in England." He listened to the proceedings of the evening by having the words printed out on the palm of his hand in capital letters by Miss Peggy Hogge, who came as his interpreter from England. This method is one which anyone who knows the alphabet and can spell fairly well could use.

The third speaker was Gerrit van der May who is Programmer for Electrical Computers, Netherlands Telephone and Telegraph Services Laboratories. His subject was "The Lorm Alphabet," which his seeing and hearing interpreter of proceedings used with him during the evening. How simple and quiet it looked; just a series of light taps on the back of the hand.

The Lorm Alphabet was not only quiet and direct but was, in a later conversation between Mr. and Mrs. van der May, one of the most beautiful plays of hand expressions that I have ever seen. Mrs. van der May, who had been sitting in the audience, arose quietly, near the close of the program, to speak with her husband. His interpreter, Dr. van der Pool, seeing her approach, with a tap or two on the back of Dr. van der May's hand, informed him; and in response he extended his arm, his palm resting easily on the table, the back of his hand ready for the message.

No one who saw that picture is likely to forget it. Her fingers were playing as lightly and as gracefully as on a harp, only more gently, and of course on only a small area. When she had finished, she placed her hand beside his and in a few masculine taps, but gently, the conversation was closed. Dr. van der May, in his paper, had mentioned that one advantage of the Lorm Alphabet was that it was easy to use anywhere, even on a stroll, where the persons could walk and talk together. He did not say what I learned later from a mutual friend, that he and Mrs. van der May converse by Lorm while riding a tandem bicycle together.

The last of these very personal conversations, the content of which only those who took part will ever know (and I guessed from the occasional expression on their faces that sometimes their conversation may have been about something other than the speeches going on), was the ingenious and almost unbelievable accuracy of the one-hand manual alphabet achieved through the palm of Robert Smithdas, as he held his hand on the top of the back of the half-closed hand of his interpreter, David Windrow. The opening and closing fingers of the interpreter would usually be pointing toward the floor, as he spelled out the words or indicated the symbols through a vigorous movement of the fingers, literally in the air. Thus their meaning would travel through the back of his hand up to the palm of Mr. Smithdas and somehow from there to his brain with amazing speed, possibly swifter than spoken letters and signs would have traveled if the recipient could have heard them. The title of the address given by Mr. Robert Smithdas, M.A. was "The One-Hand Manual Alphabet."

It was a revelation unprecedented, to see these several hand languages demonstrated there; but I was to learn that there were several more manual alphabets, perhaps many more, because sighted and blind and deaf companions often develop their own special codes. A dear one was used by a boy and his deaf-blind father, both baseball fans. As they sat together in the bleachers, the boy would see the game for them both. With his arm over his father's shoulder, in a code pretty much of their own invention, the son would tap out on the father's back all the main plays of the game.

Seeing so many different methods of communicating with the hands was in a sense discouraging to one who did not know how to use any of them. How could one know which alphabet or code to learn? This complexity of means of manual communication had probably discouraged many from trying any one of them. It had been a great comfort to me to find the tellatouch machine which would change my Roman letters to Braille, but then I found that many blind persons do not read Braille. Moreover, few people have these magic machines; and those who have can not always carry them everywhere with them.

It was with great relief that we learned that in the week of concentrated exchanging of opinions in Brooklyn, which immediately followed the Chicago forum, a great forward step in communication was taken by adopting as standard for the future the method of spelling with the capital letters of our alphabet into the palm of the hand of the recipient. This is just as anyone who knew the alphabet would print it out in large letters with pen or pencil, except that the index finger would be the tool or instrument used. This is a slow but sure method; it does not require a reading knowledge of Braille; or anything other than an elementary knowledge of our ABC's, and how to spell with them. Nor does it require the possession or use of a machine; for all the tools, the instruments, and wherewith are present within the human hand.

The results of the conferences at the Industrial Home for the Blind in Brooklyn have enabled Peter Salmon, Chairman of the Committee on Services for the Deaf-Blind of the World Council for the Welfare of the Blind, to make his report which is printed in book form. It offers suggestions for the establishment of minimum services for the deaf-blind, and it was presented to the World's Council for the Deaf Blind in July 1959 at its meeting in Rome by Richard Kinney, a member of the original committee.

Incidentally two deaf-blind persons are included in the life and work sketches of blind persons in Chapter 3 on Some Abilities and Achievements of Blind Persons. These are Richard Kinney, a teacher who is deaf and blind, and Richard Badger, a gardener, who is deaf, blind and mute.

It is believed that the Chicago meeting, the week in Brooklyn, the exchange of thoughts and the ideas projected, promise the greatest advancement for the rank and file of the deaf-blind that we have yet known; and that the last half of the present century will mark the highest points yet to be attained for those who live with this double and severe human handicap.

Of several hundred blind persons who have seen the Collection of Objects of Beauty for the Sighted and the Blind, only a few are deaf-blind, but in every case their response has been proof of their longing for beauty, and their power to enjoy it; many of these objects bring them that happiness and sense of well-being which are components of aesthetic experiences. The sense of touch brings far more than knowledge to the mind; it can and does bring, often as clearly as sight could, the notion of an object which can evoke pleasure and delight.

None of us can know quite what is in the mind of another person, much less what may be in the mind of one who can neither see nor hear that which we see and hear; but two wonderful revealments of the human spirit have come to those whose privilege it is to know those valiant ones who, although seeing not and hearing not, yet extract from life some of the finest experiences. One is, that we know their power to enjoy beauty; the other, that we know their power to be more grateful for what they have than regretful for what they have not. Who could be clearer, more convincing, more comforting on these points than the eloquent deaf-blind Counselor of the Brooklyn Industrial Home for the Blind, Robert Smithdas, as he speaks to us of his joy in life and work:

> "Pity not that light no longer fills
> These eyes with shapes of suns and moons and stars,
> And crisp young blossoms from an April field;
> Nor that the birds no longer sing to me
> Their gay cascades of gladness from blue heights,
> Where all the voices of the winds are hushed.
> I know the joys of full and active days—
> The task well done, the goal I sought attained;
> The keen delight of knowing that my deeds
> Span future years, and bring to those who share
> The desire for fuller living I have known,
> The strength of faith, bright hopes for happiness."

CHAPTER 9

MUSEUMS AND THEIR POSSIBLE SERVICE
TO THE BLIND

*Next to the grace of God is the power to distin-
guish things that are different.*—ANONYMOUS

PROBABLY no country in the world has ever experienced in a
short period such a remarkable growth in museum building
and service as did our own United States in the first half of the
present century. It is probably not an exaggeration to say that if
one person wished to visit all the art museums of our country,
giving a single day to each, he could not make the rounds in a
year's time. A hundred years ago he could have covered them
all in a week, with such traveling facilities as we have now.

Yet the art museums constitute only a fraction of the museums,
for there are the museums of natural history, of human history,
of industry, and many collections of various kinds, and if we include those in the schools and institutions, the count will rise
into many hundreds. And the great advances made recently in
building design, in arrangement of space, and in perfection of
installation give many of these various museums a high rank
architecturally and aesthetically.

It is not, however, this unparalleled physical and material
growth which has meant most to our people, but rather the
splendid services the museums have developed in the educational
field for both children and adults, bringing them cultural advantages and aesthetic experiences never before enjoyed to such
an extent by the average citizen.

It may therefore seem strange, in view of this unparalleled
growth and development, that no art museum has yet developed
a sustained program to meet the needs of the blind, of whom it is
estimated there are at least 350,000 in our country.

142

This can undoubtedly be attributed largely to the age-long belief, even now almost universal, that the blind can not enjoy beauty, that is, the beauty of the visual world. It is hoped that the experiences recorded in this book will help correct this great error, an error which is general and by no means confined to museums. And the museums can be, and it is a reasonable hope that they will be, one of the strongest possible influences in correcting this error as they bring within the reach of the blind many of the privileges of aesthetic enjoyment now so generously extended to the sighted.

There are two other factors in the situation which should help all who are now working to bring these cultural advantages to the blind, to understand the problem and be patient about its solution. One is that the American museums, which have had their almost phenomenal growth in little more than half a hundred years, since the return of the century, have had to expend a large measure of their energy, invention, and wisdom in meeting the needs of our seeing people.

The other explanation for this lag lies in the fact that the blind and those working for the blind have not pressed the museums for this special service. It has so happened that the greatest advancement in the growth of general services for the blind in America has taken place in the same half century as the museums' growth; and in this time the individuals and organizations trying to help improve the social and living conditions of the blind have had more than they could do to meet what have seemed to them the most pressings needs. Because of the concentrated efforts of each of these two social forces to meet their separate obligations there has not until now been the opportunity to join in a mutual effort.

Although the organizations working for the blind have never pressed the museums to add another class to their visitors and members, a few museums have extended some help as requested by teachers and others, and have often shown a real concern for the blind and a desire to share their treasures with them. The time and the condition for a sustained continuous program for the blind seems now to have arrived, and the need of co-operation between those working with the blind and those in charge of our museums is clear. But it is equally clear that the initiative and responsibility for this great cultural service to those who must reach art and beauty mainly through their sense of touch, rests upon the museums, as it does in their general service to the sighted. The great urge now is an awakening of the whole museum world to the need of the blind for knowledge and for beauty, and an all-out commitment to help satisfy this need.

It must not be inferred that museums here and elsewhere have been insensitive to the needs of the blind. There have been a number of efforts especially here and in England in the last twenty to forty years, notably in natural history museums, to reach blind people, a few of them very promising; but they have been temporary, and not integrated into the ongoing program of the museums. And in cases where some service has been given, it has been touch as a way to knowledge which has been recognized, and not touch as also a way to beauty and the aesthetic experience.

The progress which has been made by a few museums in bringing knowledge to the blind has depended largely upon personalities behind the activities, or on the favorable attitudes of special museum directors. What has been lacking has been the element of continuity and growth that can only come when a museum resolves to make services for the blind as important, though of course not so extensive, as service for those who see.

The literature on museums and their services to the blind is meager and scattered, but a valuable study and report has been made by Nelson Coon, Librarian and Curator of the Museum at Perkins Institution and Massachusetts School for the Blind, entitled "The Place of the Museum in the Education of the Blind," published by the American Foundation for the Blind in its series on Educational Theories. It is especially recommended, for it gives in one publication the most comprehensive study which has been made in recent years on the services of museums to the blind in the United States and Europe. Perkins was the first institution for the blind in the United States to establish a museum for its own use, and this is probably still the most important such institutional museum in our country. The author gives many excellent suggestions for materials, especially in the field of natural history.

In his report Mr. Coon mentions several public museums which at various times have given some attention to the blind. Replies from each of these museums, in answer to a letter of inquiry sent them in 1958, revealed that while some have responded to requests for a limited service, not a single American museum has yet developed a continuous and sustained program for the blind.

It is hoped that the experience gained through the Collection of Objects of Beauty for the Sighted and the Blind will be useful to the museums which in the future may develop programs and services. The choosing of these objects, the showing and interpreting of them, and some reactions to them are to be found in several chapters, but much of this information is in Chapter 4, "The Collection of Objects of Beauty for the Sighted and the Blind"; in Chapter 5, "The Interpretation of the Objects to Blind Persons"; in Chapter 6, "Individuals, Sighted and Blind Sharing Objects of Beauty Together"; and in Chapter 8, "Beauty for Those Who Neither See Nor Hear: The Deaf-Blind." In the last chapter, "A Glance Back and a Look Forward," a recent experience in sculpture with a few blind persons in The Hall of Man in the Chicago Natural History Museum will be briefly described.

What has been said here about the lack of a sustained program for the blind by our museums, is not to overlook or underestimate the excellent services a few of them have from time to time given blind individuals, especially children. Nor can we forget instances in which some sympathetic member of a museum staff has given very special attention to an eager blind child who happened to come to his attention.

One of the ablest and most interesting blind men I know has told me of his everlasting debt to a member of the staff of one of our great natural history museums. His parents, striving to bring the best that could be had to their small son who had been born blind, prevailed upon a kind friend on the museum staff to show the boy everything in the museum he could "get his hands on." Describing this experience, the now grown man explained that they began by giving him a chance to feel dinosaurs and fossils, thinking them safe to entrust to his unguided hands; but in time, when they learned there was no risk to run, they let him feel the butterflies! It is to help extend to many blind boys and girls some of the privileges of that fortunate child, and also to reach the many blind adults who are hungry for knowledge, that we must encourage the great effort to provide sustained and expanding programs in all our museums in order that those who can see the world about them only through touch, shall have as good a break as we who see with our eyes can give them.

While in any adequate museum service for the blind, many of the provisions and procedures that have been developed for the sighted public will apply, yet because of the fundamental differences inherent in the seeing and the touching processes, some entirely new and different methods must be devised. Therefore new problems are posed for museum inventiveness.

Seeing things with the eyes, although always an individual experience, may also be, as in an audience, a collective or mass experience; many sighted persons can have it at one time, and instantaneously. But this is not possible for the blind, because their perceiving must be mainly by the hands; they can "see" but one object or a part of one object at a time, and they can not perceive anything else at that instant. Even if the hand had the quick glance of the eye, it would take a blind audience of a hundred persons, one hundred times as long to see an object as it would take a sighted audience of the same number.

The basic difference in arranging for this experience for the sighted and the blind is that with the former, objects must be placed so that they can be looked at, while with the latter they must be placed where they can be felt of. Everyone who thinks about it will realize the advantage of seeing things with the eye. It is the quickest way, it is the easiest and generally the most convenient. It has many obvious advantages; objects can be shown to one or to many sighted persons at one time, lights can be flooded on the subject, flashed on or off or diminished or increased to give different values at will; backgrounds and associated objects can be included; objects can be seen and understood without verbal interpretation in silence; color, form, and texture can be quickly perceived; things that are near can be seen, also things that are distant, and some, like the stars, can be seen millions of miles away; and it can be arranged so that one or thousands, or even millions of sighted persons can view the same spectacle at the same time; and beyond all this one can see two or more objects at the same instant and he can distinguish and even compare them; and there is much more.

But not so with the blind person where the hand must be substituted for the eye. Almost all the ways of imparting information by sight must be forgotten, when it comes to those who can not see with their eyes. All but one, the sense of hearing. Both sighted and blind can often get quite definite notions of objects, things, scenes when they are adequately described orally or in written communication; but the nearest equivalent that a blind person can have to the experience of one who sees an object through his eyes is to get the object in his hands, with time and opportunity to explore it. It may be a cliché, but it is worth remembering that, as a blind person has said, "Tactuality is actuality."

And for these experiences the museum must prepare the way. It will not be enough to open the doors and let the blind visitor find his way around; it will not be practical to allow the sighted companions of blind visitors tactual access to exhibits kept in cabinets and cases. There are, of course, a few fully exposed objects in most museums which anyone could touch, but most things to be adequately examined must, by arrangement, be brought to the blind visitor or the visitor brought to the object and the latter placed within his hands or within hand reach. It will, in the case of most museums, be impractical or undesirable, and of course unnecessary, to have more than a small per cent of their treasures made available for the blind to touch. However, many things that can not be seen through touch can be brought part of the way to the blind through the interpreting voice of seeing companions, or through museum docents; more will not usually be expected. And if reasonable arrangements are made to bring even a small number of objects within the reach of the seeing hand, this unusual privilege, plus the verbal or sometimes written interpretation accompanying them, will be an experience deeply appreciated and pleasantly remembered; and it will sometimes lead to the discovery and the fostering of life long interests.

For the members of museum staffs who instruct and guide the blind, there are compensations which only they can know. To be conscious of helping a person who is deprived of sight to fuller and finer living through the knowledge and love of the arts, is satisfaction of a high order. Although we know that, as Hector Chevigny, a writer who happens to be blind, has clearly said, "Sightlessness does not create a type of response new to psychology; that the problems of personality among those who can not see, do not differ in kind from those to be encountered in the generality of human experiences," yet because the opportunities to develop personality often differ so greatly between those who have and those who have not sight, to be able to help one of the latter toward understanding and appreciation multiplies the compensation.

Many museums will have in their own resources a great wealth of material to draw on. They can have exhibits based upon native materials which man has shaped into objects of use and beauty; collections of the tools he has used through the ages; exhibits based upon geographical areas; different art forms; objects of educational and aesthetic significance; and so on almost without limit.

There will be, in any well-worked-out museum plan, a study room for the blind members and there will be some special furniture devised for convenience, for saving time, for comfort, and especially for encouraging the member to come to the museum often and to get around by himself. However, until such details can be worked out, the usual museum furniture and facilities can be used. The main objective will be to encourage the blind visitor to come to the museum; then get the objects which interest him into his hands, with the desired interpretation, and the opportunity provided for leisurely exploration. There will also be services to blind individuals and groups outside the museum walls but, first, encouragement should be given to them to come and to know their museum, and as far as possible to let the museum know them.

Of course all persons who are blind, as those who see, are not interested in museums, but more are than we had thought. And it is not unlikely that in some cities the number of blind who will visit the museums, where they can touch some of the treasures and have them interpreted for them may, in proportion to their numbers, equal the visitors who can see, for the opportunities of the blind are so few compared to those available to seeing persons, that their eagerness alone will often carry them there. There is a natural and a growing hope on the part of the blind to share as fully as possible the privileges enjoyed by those who see, and in no country has this hope been realized as fully as in our own. To become a member of a museum and participate in its activities will be one of the most satisfying experiences which can come to some of our blind citizens.

As one thinks of our museums and their opportunities to extend their advantages to the blind, one fact is encouraging. There is not a museum in the land, however small and off the beaten path, but has some items, some material ready and waiting for the blind which can, with adequate interpretation, be used as soon as it is understood that the hand is often a wonderful substitute for the eye, and sometimes with even superior qualities of discernment.

Also, there has developed quite recently, especially in the United States, a great mine of tactually interesting and often beautiful objects in almost mass-production quantities such as has not heretofore been known, many of them replicas in both form and color of treasures in the art and in the natural history museums of the country, and in museums and private collections in other countries. These reproductions are so accurate that often, when they are of equal size with the original, the sighted can not distinguish the copy from the original. And there is reason to believe that we are just at the beginning of this rich flow of inexpensive replicas and reproductions perceivable and pleasure-giving to both eye and hand.

Some of these casts and reproductions of famous sculpture and other art forms have been put to a new and very unusual use in the Museum of Art for the Blind, dedicated in March, 1958, on the grounds of the Adult Training Center of the Florida Council for the Blind at Daytona Beach, Florida, sponsored by B'nai B'rith, the local chapter of the International Jewish Benevolent Organization.

The idea for this museum came from Henry Saltzman, a painter, sculptor, mosaicist, and art dealer of Daytona Beach. Mr. Saltzman had not been acquainted with blind persons, but one day several years ago, when out for a walk with his small daughter, he stopped to chat with a blind neighbor who, through lightly touching the head and face of the child, interpreted her features and her characteristics so sensitively that the father resolved to try to bring sculptural forms within the reach of blind persons.

He worked on the idea until he had assembled several suitable subjects, and when Louis Unitan, President of B'nai B'rith, was seeking a worthy project for the support of the Daytona Beach chapter, Mr. Saltzman was ready with a suggestion which they were glad to adopt.

The Adult Training Center of the Florida Council for the Blind, through the interest of its director, E. B. Hall, furnished a suitable building; Mr. Saltzman designed the interior, selected the replicas and reproductions, and installed them on uniform shelves with built-up pedestals to bring them into easy hand reach of adults and children. Then he had legends in print placed near one side of each subject, and legends in Braille on the other. The arrangement, running the full length of the gallery on both sides, is very attractive and there is maximum space for easy circulation.

Mr. Saltzman is the interpreter of the objects at the present time. He meets groups of teachers and blind individuals by appointment. Clients of the Adult Training Center for the Blind visit the museum, and blind children from the Center sometimes use the reproductions to guide them in their clay modeling. The museum is in its early stages of development but it has brought pleasure to many blind persons, and it is hoped to make the collection more easily available to both sighted and blind.

It should not be long until sustained services are established by American museums so that blind persons will feel as welcome as the sighted do, to take advantage of these great sources of knowledge and repositories of beauty. The blind should be quite as free as those who see, to join in the membership of the museums, and some of them, becoming qualified by both temperament and training, may join the working staffs of the museums. As they are doing in schools and other institutions, blind individuals will make their special contributions through museums to the knowledge and culture of the country. In fact, a note of prophecy is ventured here; that the blind will help raise the standard of museums' service to the whole community. We are just at the beginning of what we can learn from blind persons about the art and the technique of spoken communication. We who can both see and hear are not so sensitive as many blind persons are about the matchless qualities the human voice can attain, especially through the spoken word. In many museums the voice quality of lecturers and guides could be improved for everyone. If we who have both ears and eyes strain to hear the low, sometimes almost hushed voices, realized that the blind depend entirely on their hearing, and if we joined them in their desire for clearer voices and better articulation, it would be everybody's gain. To the blind, the gain would be immeasurable; to many of them the human voice is more wonderful than most of us can know.

CHAPTER 10

WRITING AND THINKING TOWARD BEAUTY
FOR THE BLIND

Hasty generalizations is one of the most com-
mon vices of the human mind.—PIERRE VILLEY

IN THE reading I have been able to do in the literature about
blindness and the blind, I could find but three authors who
have made a sustained study of the aesthetic life of the blind as
compared to that of sighted persons. One, the Frenchman, Pierre
Villey, whose book, *The World of the Blind,* contains a chapter
on The Arts, another the American, Thomas Cutsforth, whose
book, *The Blind in School and in Society,* has a chapter on The
Aesthetic Life of the Blind; and third, a translation from the
German of a work by the Hollander, G. Revesz, *Psychology and
Art of the Blind.* The first two authors have a special value in connection with our subject of Beauty for the Sighted and the Blind
because both are blind men. Dr. Revesz has written more fully
than anyone of whom I know on haptics and the aesthetic experience.

Neither Villey nor Cutsforth touch directly on the point of
beauty as stimulus to communication between sighted and blind
persons, or on the unlimited store of beautiful objects in both
nature and the arts which the blind might enjoy if they had access
to them. Both are much concerned with the measure of beauty
which the blind miss: Villey, with their lack of enjoyment in the
field of the fine arts, and Cutsforth with what he considers the
widespread error made by sighted persons who insist that the
blind like the same things, objects for instance, that the sighted
do. Because either or both authors might easily be interpreted as
disagreeing with the soundness of the main thesis of Beauty for

the Sighted and the Blind, which is that the mutual enjoyment of many (but by no means all) objects is possible, and that the main problem is to find the way and the opportunity for the experience, we shall consider their arguments briefly here.

I do not believe that the argument of either author is in conflict with what is claimed for our thesis, or that what they say in any way invalidates it. I would say, rather, that when carefully analyzed their arguments would seem to support it.

With Dr. Revesz it is different. Although at the end of his book he assures blind persons that they may practice sculpture (this being the only plastic art which he discusses), he is certain that "the blind artist will never be able to reach the same heights as the seeing one. He will never create new forms or open up new approaches or exert any marked influence on artistic trends. For that, seeing, artistic seeing, is indispensable; for only vision is capable of raising the sensory impressions into the sphere of aesthetic contemplation." This point of view is so opposite to that set forth in Beauty for the Sighted and the Blind that I feel it must be considered here.

In Pierre Villey's chapter on The Arts, he confines his discussion to the fine arts of painting, sculpture, and architecture and, limiting the discusion to the extent to which touch can replace sight, he points out the difficulties of the blind person with sculpture and architecture and, although allowing generously for the part the memory sometimes plays where blindness did not come too early in life, on the whole he does not believe that the blind can get much enjoyment out of sculpture and architecture through touch alone. He does say, however, that "no one can tell in what measure, aided by association of sentiments, he (the blind person) might thus enrich his sensuous enjoyments, and how near he might bring them to the aesthetic sentiments." And he later adds that the blind person may obtain from his sense of touch, experience in connection with sculpture and architecture which are "a commencement of aesthetic pleasure."

I believe that the main reason why Villey did not come closer to realizing the enjoyment of beauty for the blind, as we are declaring for it here, is that he limited himself in the beginning of his writing by bringing his observations into a chapter entitled The Arts, and he did what was common when he was writing in

the first quarter of this century, limited his discussion and observations to the fine arts of painting, sculpture, and architecture.

These fine arts, so often considered in what we might call their
classic forms, could not include that very extensive and often
fine source of creative expression, the handicrafts, which, if for no
other reason than their dimensions, that is, their handleable size,
bring many of them within the perception of touch. The handicrafts, open to all the blind who have the sense of touch,
constitute an inexhaustible world of objects enriched by the association sentiments to which both Villey and Cutsforth sympa-
thetically refer; but these authors do not seem to regard them as
important stimuli to the aesthetic experience, or as evoking the
awareness of beauty with which we are primarily concerned.
However, I believe that aesthetic growth seldom, if ever, begins
with an appreciation of classical architecture and sculpture; the
deep appreciation of these arts comes with maturity, and is usually a late development.

But Villey, after he concludes his observations on the fine arts,
comes close to the feeling with which Beauty for the Sighted and
the Blind is concerned when he says: "Marie Heurtin, the deaf-
blind girl of Larnay, in her days of untamedness, would delight in
touching certain objects for hours together. She, and several deaf
children, before their minds were trained, were subject to violent
jealousy if one of their companions had a more silky garment, or
some ornament which was more agreeable to the touch than they
had. One of these irresponsibles went so far as to pour milk over
her neighbor's collar. Does not this," Villey asks, "give evidence of
the germ of aesthetic pleasure which can be cultivated by the
mind and the heart?"

And again he comes very close when he says that the expressions used by the poets for interpreting "what is aesthetic in their
sentiments and even in their visual sensations, depend on the
impressions which come to them from all the senses, from the
least to the noblest. Warm, gentle, penetrating, sweet, fresh, are
words frequently used by them." He observes that Sully Prud-
homme made a list of qualifications which interpret both the perceptions of the senses and the various states of our sensibility, in
which the epithets of touch figure most frequently. "There are
about fifty of them and their power of expression is great." And

he adds, "What does this signify, if not that it is not only by the special relations of order and movement that it [touch] perceives, but also by specific notions such as polish, smoothness, silkiness, which touch alone can reveal to us, an aesthetic value which must not be despised." So Pierre Villey does not disagree with us; he only fails, or perhaps declines, to carry his observations and reasonings into the vast field of objects which we are here designating as handicrafts, countless numbers of which, because of their size and character, are available to exploration through touch, that surest notion-giving way for the blind.

A quick reading of Thomas Cutsforth's chapter might at first seem discouraging to the point of view held here because the author is so positive in his position that "touch and vision are two distinctly different forms of experience. Tactual perception, no matter how well trained, carries with it a meaning of literal realism which does not permit the grasp of ideal meanings." He cites what to him seems a thoroughly aesthetic response of a blind person to a stimulus which he believes the seeing person would not regard as an aesthetic stimulus at all. In this case the stimulus to the blind man was a well-preserved cavalry saber of the Civil War. I believe there is no reason to conclude that a sighted person could not share the aesthetic feelings for the cavalry saber which, with its many associations, it evoked in the mind of the author's blind friend.

What Dr. Cutsforth conveys in this and other parts of his chapter, "The Aesthetic Life of the Blind," one not only reads in his lines but between his lines. It is that sighted people are usually insistent that blind persons see or feel in an artistic or aesthetic stimulus what they, the sighted, see or feel. At several points the author condemns such a point of view in words better than I can conjure, but expressing not more than I feel, and I am obliged to him for what he has pointed out, which is the same thing that I am trying to say in connection with the mutual sharing of these objects by sighted and blind persons, that the aesthetic response is individual and its quality and worth are determined largely by the associations which the individual brings to it and with which he infuses it.

If ever there develops an uncomfortable feeling of tension between a blind and a sighted person on this point of aesthetic agree-

ment, I would, as one who sees, remind them that sighted arrogance, of which there are too many examples in the "art circles"
of the world, is just as unsparing in its operation among seeing
persons who differ in their tastes as between sighted and blind
persons; and no doubt Dr. Cutsforth can recall instances in which
some blind persons are equally intolerant of those who do not
agree with them or share their aesthetic reactions. The thought
at the heart of our experience, often expressed here, is that there
is no pressure upon anyone to enjoy what someone else feels is a
beautiful object; there is only the desire to give another the opportunity to enjoy it.

As to the nature of the aesthetic experience and its growth, no
better statement could be made than Dr. Cutsforth's which reads:
"Aesthetic growth does not take place so much through the senses
of perception as it does through the entire intellectual development. . . . Aesthetic appreciation is always relative to the wealth
of effective relationships it organizes about the stimulus pattern."

The third and most recent work bearing directly on the subject of aesthetic experiences of the blind, *Psychology and Art of
the Blind*, by G. Revesz of Holland, has been ably translated from
the German by Dr. H. A. Wolff.

Dr. Revesz holds that one who is blind can not, either as creator
or perceiver of a plastic object, enjoy the aesthetic experience
through touch; that this experience is only for those who have
eyesight. On page 325 of his book, as part of his summarizing
statement, he says, "The loss of vision does not render the practice
of plastic art impossible. But for finding aesthetic pleasure in
works of art, and for the creation of new forms, sight is essential."

In prefacing his reasoning, the author says that he is conscious
that his conclusions are new and revolutionary, for he is unable
to agree with the psychologists and workers with the blind who
assert that the blind possess the ability to enjoy plastic works
aesthetically and to judge their value, or with others who deny
any such ability to the blind. In his conclusion he hopes that he
has succeeded "in bridging the gap between the art of the blind
and the art of those who can see."

I can not agree with Dr. Revesz in his conclusion; nor do I think
that the evidence which he has gathered supports it. Moreover,
if his conclusion should find general acceptance it would set back

rather than advance the progress and welfare of many blind persons. But to deny is not to reason, and this very scholarly work deserves the most thoughtful consideration.

Although unable to agree with Dr. Revesz in his major conclusion, I admire him for the thoroughness of his research which contains much of great value to anyone interested in the psychology of blind persons or in the science of haptics, and I am distinctly indebted to him for bringing together, within the covers of one book, more information than has hitherto been assembled by anyone, as far as I know, on eminent blind sculptors of Europe and their work.

It is a happy fact for our discussion that Dr. Revesz states, about as clearly as one can in words, what he means by the aesthetic experience, a definition quite sufficient for our purpose here. He quotes from the German writer, M. Geiger, who in his work, *An Approach to Aesthetics,* traces artistic efforts back to two basic forms. One of these forms, or modes, he calls "effect of depth," the other "surface effect." The "surface effect" is related to the vital sphere, to the production of pleasurable sensory experience, while the aesthetic "depth effect" is related to the personality. "In the sphere of the deep Ego," as Geiger puts it, "and thereby passes from the stratum of pleasure into the stratum of happiness."

Dr. Revesz does not believe that blind persons can have this happiness, either in the creation or in the appreciation of plastic forms, because he insists that both are dependent on the sense of sight. I hold quite the opposite; I believe that blind persons in the things which they make and in the things which they touch can in many cases convey to others, and experience for themselves, that state of happiness which we call the aesthetic experience or beauty. They reach this, not through touch alone (nor could they through sight alone), but through the wealth of associations which is awakened when the message from the plastic object is conveyed to the brain through touch. This "wealth of associations" clearly brought out by the American psychologist Cutsforth, as determining the quality of the experience, seems to be overlooked by Revesz who gives the impression that the sense organ, the hand in this case, determines the experience. It is in any case the mind, and the stimulus to the experience can come by the hand through touch or by the eye through sight.

It was not my intention in this book to touch upon the creative work of blind artists or craftsmen, but to put the emphasis on appreciation and enjoyment, on the sharing of beautiful and significant objects between sighted and blind. But since Dr. Revesz relies so heavily upon the creative work of his sculptors to support his theory I will follow his examples as far as I can. I think he would have us understand that, while he confines his illustrations to sculpture only, he would have his conclusions apply to any forms of the plastic arts which the blind perceive through touch.

In this connection I would note that I think the aesthetic experiences of the great majority of us, in the field of plastic arts, come through other forms than sculpture, especially portrait sculpture, of which Dr. Revesz employs so many examples. Sculpture is not one of the popular arts, therefore most aesthetic experiences are with other plastic forms, such as clothing, articles of personal adornment, decorative articles of use and beauty, and objects closely associated with home and daily life. There can be no objection to Dr. Revesz choosing whatever form of plastic arts he feels suits his need best. We should, however, as we follow his reasoning through the many pages of evidence which he brings to the support of his conclusion, keep continuously in mind that this is a treatise on the art of sculpture and nothing more; for he does not, in any part of his book, bring in any material bearing on the many other forms of plastic arts with which sighted and blind are most concerned, the great division of man's arts which we call handicrafts.

It is fair to the subject, I think, to point out at the beginning that the title of Dr. Revesz' book, or that part of the title which reads, the "Art of the Blind," is in itself misleading, because there is no such thing. All of the arts thus far have been originated by those who see, and in the main advanced by those who see, with some very notable contributions by blind men and women, a subject we can not go into here, deserving as it is. We judge the arts, and that is especially true in the dissertation by Dr. Revesz, by standards of the seeing world. Every blind sculptor referred to by the author has striven to satisfy the eye of man, not necessarily to please him, but to be understood by him to a point of acceptance. The highly talented blind sculptor Masuelli said in substance that he was not trying to please anyone but was trying to be understood: art is, above all, communication. That we are on the way to forms of art that because of their qualities of haptic beauty, will be particularly acceptable to the blind, I have no doubt. But these forms designed for touch will depend for acceptance largely upon the cultivation of haptic aesthetics by those who see, as well as by those who do not, but who are conscious that there is such a thing as beauty through touch. A wider consciousness that there is such a thing as "tactile beauty" will develop as sighted and blind share experiences together.

In approaching his subject Dr. Revesz states that he will follow the reasoning of the supporters of "tactile aesthetics" who base their claims on three relevant arguments: One, the statements of blind persons when subjecting plastic works to touch; two, the modeling achievements of blind children; and three, the remarkable creations of blind sculptors. I think we can shorten and simplify our discussion by agreeing to omit the work of blind children because, important as the opportunity to model is for many of them, I do not think their products as a rule contribute much to the aesthetic aspects of our problem; therefore we will consider here only the two arguments which Dr. Revesz believes the proponents of tactile aesthetics most favor: the testimony of the blind, and the outstanding achievements of blind sculptors.

Dr. Revesz believes that we can not usually rely upon the testimony of blind persons concerning their aesthetic experiences because the experiences which they usually report are not their haptic perceptions but rather an "inevitable result of tuition received by the blind from the sighted"; and he gives two illustrations in support of his claim.

The first is the case of a blind man who asserted that he experienced aesthetic pleasure when the author showed him the bust of a beautiful youth, but which proved displeasing to him when taking it into his hands he found the material of the bust to be brittle and rough. This indicates, I think, that the blind man was prepared for the aesthetic appreciation by his seeing friend who introduced him to the bust, the examination of which would have confirmed and strengthened his appreciation of its beauty except

that it had some unpleasant textural qualities which the author
had not recognized, possibly because he did not examine it carefully through touch. Or, if he had, it is possible that his pleasure
in seeing it, the optical impression, was such that the texture of
the material seemed of no consequence to him; or he may have
been tactually quite insensitive.

Whatever the explanation, the fact remains that the blind man
was, through the interpretive explanation of his seeing friend, well
on his way to an aesthetic experience which would have been
completed had the material of the bust been haptically pleasing,
or as it might have been even exquisite if the materials had been
sensitively finished. The author's feelings about the beauty of the
bust, it would seem, were satisfied by the sight of it; but he should
not have been disappointed because someone else, whose tactile
standards were offended, could not agree with him that it was
beautiful.

Whatever conclusion is reached as to this experience the fact
remains, I believe, that the aesthetic experience is within the
reach of the blind person if to the aesthetic interpretation of his
sighted friend, is added the pleasure, or the happiness, of a beautiful texture for that most sensitive perceiver, the human hand.
Thus a blind person can have, when touching certain forms, an
aesthetic experience of high quality; this I have seen happen
many times. And who of us can not recall some object in finished
wood, polished stone, or bronze, beautiful to see, but when
touched ever so lightly by the hand, lifted to loveliness?

The second example which Dr. Revesz cites to prove the
futility of the sense of touch as a way to the aesthetic experience,
is the classic one, often quoted, of Helen Keller, and he gives
what to him are "fantastic statements" made by her "which seem
to have excited a considerable influence on the views of certain
psychologists of the blind."

"A medallion of Homer," Miss Keller says, "hangs on the wall
of my study, conveniently low, so that I can easily reach it and
touch the beautiful sad face with loving reverence. How well I
know each line in the majestic brow—tracks of life and bitter evidence of struggle and sorrow; those sightless eyes seeking even
in the cold plaster, for the light and the blue skies of his beloved
Hellas, but seeking in vain that beautiful mouth, firm and true

and tender. It is the face of a poet, and of a man acquainted with sorrow. And how well I understand his deprivation—the perpetual night in which he dwelt.

"I sometimes wonder," Miss Keller continues, "if the hand is not more sensitive to the beauties of sculpture than the eye."

Of this, and there is more in the quotation, Dr. Revesz says, "Nothing could be more evident than that this intelligent and gifted woman was perceiving the blind eyes of Homer not with her touching hand but with her 'seeing' mind." Yes, that is it, with her seeing mind, but made possible through her perceiving touch.

We can not follow in detail Dr. Revesz' speculations in this case of Miss Keller other than to agree with him that "it becomes clear how essential it is to find out by what means the blind reach their aesthetic judgments and by what factors they are guided." This statement itself would seem to be an admission by Dr. Revesz that the blind do have their aesthetic judgments, or that at least some do. And his statement that Helen Keller perceived "the blind eyes of Homer not with her touching hand but with her 'seeing' mind," is further testimony from the author that she, a blind person, did have this aesthetic experience. One recalls again the words of Santayana. "To feel beauty is a better thing than to understand how we come to feel it."

This leads again to the observation that the aesthetic experience is not the message which the hand or the eye carries from the plastic object perceived to the brain; it is the sum of the experiences of the mind which that message recalls, that determines its quality and its worth.

We now come to the most unusual, interesting, and what I think Dr. Revesz considers the strongest supporting evidence of his theory that blind persons can neither through their creation or their appreciation of plastic forms attain the aesthetic experience. For this evidence, which is largely on the artist's creative side, Dr. Revesz brings the reader the experiences of eight eminent blind sculptors of Europe; and while we can follow only a part of his experiences with two of them, we name them all for those who may wish to learn of these extraordinary blind persons in the field of sculpture.

The first four, the older ones, now dead, are Kleinhans, the

Tyrolean wood carver; Vidal, the sculptor of animals (a student of Bayre); Moudry, the modeler; and Gonnelli, known as "the blind man of Gambossi." The four living sculptors are the German, J. Schmidt; the Frenchman, G. Scapini, and the Italians, F. Bausola and E. Masuelli, all of whom lost their sight in the First World War.

From this list I have selected two, the oldest and the youngest, Kleinhans and Masuelli. The former, having died in 1853, required the most extensive research; the latter the author knew personally and worked with directly. The author knew well the sculpture attributed to each of these artists and admired some of it so much that I feel, as others have, that Dr. Revesz wavered a great deal between his admiration for their work, I think one might say his aesthetic enjoyment of it, and his desire and need to prove his thesis that blind persons could not have the aesthetic experience either in the creation or contemplation of plastic art through touch.

I have never had the privilege of seeing or touching a single one of their sculptures, but I am indebted to Dr. Revesz for making available to me through his book good photographs of the works of each, and I am thrilled by some of them "to the point of happiness," as I have been told others have been, and as I am convinced the author has been. So I submit the question: If we who have eyes to see are so stirred by the works of these blind sculptors, is it not likely that they, in creating them, had an aesthetic experience?

I am especially impressed by certain works of Masuelli for which Dr. Revesz, with characteristic honesty, expresses his admiration. But in his effort to support his conclusion, or to avoid weakening his conclusion, that a blind person can not create or enjoy the aesthetic experience, he attributes this phenomenon to the fact that the "artist is really living and working in a world of visual memory."

The author's analysis of the sculptor's work is admirable; it is sympathetic, intelligent, and quite thorough, and he admits, or rather affirms, that Masuelli in "the proportions and the correlation of parts, the attitude of the body, the expression of the face, suggests a sculptor who knows how to embrace the total impression in an artistic unity." And he adds, "These are definitely features hitherto found only in sculptural works of sighted artists."

This I believe to be an erroneous statement; it is, however, an admission that the author believes that at least one blind sculptor has had the aesthetic experience.

I quote too briefly some things which Dr. Revesz seems to believe support his thesis, but which seem to me to undermine it. He says, "Nobody is likely to deny the artistic value of these (Masuelli's) works, and hardly anybody would ascribe these figures, which conform so well to our aesthetic feelings, to a blind artist." A part of Dr. Revesz's explanation is "that all his psychological experience is intimately connected with his previous visual life. . . . It is to the vivid contact with the world of sight that he owes the ability to model."

To give only a few of the author's statements is hardly fair to his remarkable exposition of an artist he knew personally and some of whose work he watched in process. However, his final sentence is, "Masuelli's work is truly an aesthetic achievement." I think that this statement alone, although much more could be quoted, answers the main question, and confirms my own conviction that the author has proved that E. Masuelli had the aesthetic experience in his creative work, and that his sculpture often evokes a similar experience in the minds of those who behold it.

The Tyrolese wood carver, J. B. Kleinhans, whose sculpture has inspired large numbers of persons in Europe and elsewhere for over a hundred years, died in 1853 at the age of seventy-nine. The author had to rely upon the written record of his life and work, plus the evidence supplied by the works attributed to him. Some of his work, as most of that of Masuelli, made a strong appeal to Dr. Revesz, but there was one great difference between them. The Austrian carver was said to have lost his sight as a consequence of smallpox when he was four years old. Dr. Revesz could not reconcile this fact with the quality of his sculpture and spent much time in research on his life and work. All the other blind sculptors of high rank whom he knew had retained their vision until a comparatively late age, and some had practiced sculpture before they became blind. Dr. Revesz' study convinced him that all the work attributed to Kleinhans could not have been done by him; that much of it, if by him, could not have been done in the periods recorded; and the upshot of all the study was that much of the work attributed to the famous wood carver poses for the psychologist a problem which can probably never be solved.

We should keep in mind, as we consider the "Kleinhans problem" as Dr. Revesz has posed it, that he does not believe it is possible for one who has been born blind or who became blind at a very early age, to become a sculptor. Therefore Dr. Revesz can not accept the Kleinhans story as we get it from tradition, the steady growth of a blind boy from a simple wood carver at seven, carving a crude but surprising crucifix at twelve or thirteen, working at regular sculpture at twenty-two and from then on concentrating on the carving of religious subjects, especially crucifixes, at which he worked much of the time throughout his long life; the legend says that he produced over 300 of them. And so Dr. Revesz sees three possible avenues of approach to what he names the "Kleinhans problem."

First, that the sculptor was not blind practically all of his life as the records have it; second, that he became blind at a comparatively late age; and third, "that he retained traces of vision throughout his life." Dr. Revesz says, "It is difficult to decide which of these three hypotheses carries most probability. I personally am in favor of the last assumption." One must leave the author free to make his own choice of the answer to the problem which he himself has posed, but this uncertainty is one of the factors in the development of his very extensive thesis that makes his reasoning seem unconvincing to me, and why it would seem impossible for anyone to accept his major conclusion that a blind sculptor can not, as creator, have the aesthetic experience.

Dr. Revesz does not mean to be cruel in such a judgment of blind sculptors, he only means to be psychologically helpful. He does not say that blind persons can not learn and practice sculpture, indeed he assures them that they can, explaining that they can learn to measure, they can be trained, and he gives other advice; but one feels it is the advice of a sighted person to all blind persons, asking them to realize their limitations. Among his closing words are these: "The blind artist will never be able to reach the same heights as the seeing one; all his energy and talent will not help him to attain the highest spheres; they will remain closed to him. He will never create new forms or open up new approaches or exert any marked influence on artistic trends. For that, seeing, *artistic seeing*, is indispensable; for only vision is

40. THE HALL OF MAN: CHICAGO NATURAL HISTORY MUSEUM

"The Surf Rider" a Hawaiian Man, Sculpture by Malvina Hoffman, in the Hall of Man, was the first choice of a blind college student who was invited "to see," through touch, eight or ten subjects of his own choosing. See Story, page 175.

41. THE HALL OF MAN: CHICAGO NATURAL HISTORY MUSEUM

This "Bushman Woman and Baby" of Kalahari Desert, South Africa, a sculpture in bronze by Malvina Hoffman, was a subject of unusual interest to eight blind persons recently invited by the Museum "to see" several subjects of their choice in The Hall of Man. See Story, pages 172–177.

Chicago Natural History Museum

42. THE HALL OF MAN: CHICAGO NATURAL HISTORY MUSEUM

Of a small group of blind persons invited by the Chicago Natural History Museum to name eight or ten of the bronze scultpures by Malvina Hoffman which they would like "to see," by touching, all included in their choices the group of Malaysian Cock-Fighters, a man from Madura on the left and a man from Borneo on the right. The woman from Bali and the boy from Java in the background, were lookers-on like the blind guests, and did not get so much attention. See Story, pages 172–177.

43. THE HALL OF MAN: CHICAGO NATURAL HISTORY MUSEUM

This Solomon Island "Tree Climber" of Melanesia, one of the bronze sculptures by Malvina Hoffman in the Hall of Man or sometimes known as "The Races of Mankind," was a subject of both interest and amusement to a few blind persons who were invited "to see" him recently. The experience was very satisfactory for each guest was able to feel the climber and the tree from all sides and they sensed the seriousness and difficulty of the undertaking, as they discovered that he had no ropes, straps or other supports to help him ascend. A brief account of the visitors of the blind to this remarkable collection of bronze sculpture begins on pages 172–177.

capable of raising the sensory impression into the sphere of aesthetic contemplation."

There is no misunderstanding Dr. Revesz's conclusion, but it is, I submit, the conclusion of a man prejudiced not by ignorance, for his work is a model in research and in the arranging of facts, but prejudiced by the arrogance of eyesight, an arrogance which perhaps all of us who are not blind feel in some degree, and which we must strive to overcome because the conclusions it leads to are sometimes dangerous and damaging. The author reveals clearly in his book potentialities of blind persons which surprise and enlighten us and which he himself, a short time before, would not have believed; some things that as a psychologist he could only ascribe "to that impenetrable life of those who can not see." And yet he seems ready to close the gate to any further discovery, assuming that he has reached the end of understanding the blind through this study of them in relation to one of the great arts of man, sculpture.

It is perfectly clear that all his judgments in the world of the plastic arts are eye judgments, and we hear again the imploring voice of one who once had sight but is now blind, "I beg you to remember that the eye is not all of a man." Nor should all of man's creations be judged by or made to conform to the standards of those who see. There is not in this whole work by Dr. Revesz a single suggestion that some objects might well be made for the blind to feel; everything is for the sighted to see. I have already said that there is no such thing as an art for the blind only, nor will there ever be, but, in pointing out for us the extraordinary abilities and achievements of eight blind sculptors, Dr. Revesz has helped to lead us nearer to the time, which I think inevitable, when sculptors and other artists will create forms especially to be felt, gracious gifts to those who can not see, and welcome ones to those who can see but who have also reached a place in their culture where they know that there is such a thing as haptic beauty.

I can not conceal my feeling that the conclusion of Dr. Revesz' book, wherever accepted, will be very damaging in its influence on the blind and those who work with and for them, for the reason that it places such an arbitrary, and I think unsound limitation, on those members of society who can not see. In happy contrast I quote the distinguished American doctor Howard Rusk, a pioneer worker for the handicapped everywhere, who, speaking for his fellow physicians, says: "We never tell the patients that they can not do a thing until they have had a chance to try it."

To place such limitations on any human being is one of the greatest possible mistakes. I would bring to the support of my reasoning and my conviction the words of the American educator and psychologist, Victor Lowenfeld, from whose book, *Creative and Mental Growth*, I take these words. "It is one of my deepest innermost convictions that wherever there is a spark of human spirit—no matter how dim it may be—it is our sacred responsibility as humans, teachers and educators to fan it into whatever flame it conceivably may develop. . . . We as human beings have no right whatever to determine where to stop. . . . It is our basic philosophy to develop in every human being his uppermost potential creative ability regardless of the degree of his handicap. This excludes from the very beginning the question as to whether an individual is 'good enough' to do creative work."

"Touch and vision are two distinctly different forms of experience," but the notion of a thing gained by feel may be as satisfying as that gained by sight. But the fuller answer is that the aesthetic response is not from the perceptive sense alone, but from the "wealth of effective relationships which the mind organizes around the stimulus pattern."

No sighted person should be disturbed by finding a blind person enjoying a stimulus which is new or different to him, as for instance the blind young man who stated that perhaps the most enjoyable tactual experience he could have was the feel of several three-quarter-inch ball bearings forming different patterns in his hand; or perhaps the more familiar instance of the famous deaf-blind child, Laura Bridgman, enjoying more than any other plaything one of her father's old boots. Many of us who are sighted could, if we searched our memories or confessed our present secret enjoyments, find among our own treasures objects that could quite parallel in surprise the steel balls and the leather boot. Many a sensitive old Chinaman might be willing to exchange his favorite "feeling stone" for three or five ball bearings just for the tactile experience.

Here we are again near the crux of the aesthetic experience, and these varying stimuli to it illustrate the basic point always to keep clear, as between a blind and a sighted person, but quite as much between two sighted or even two blind persons. We are never insisting that any two persons feel the same way about the same object or stimulus, and never do we insist that someone else like what we like. But rather, we hope, we work, and we wish that another person may find something to see or feel which will bring him the kind of satisfaction which a certain favorite stimulus brings to us. And we now have conclusive proof that the world is full of objects which bring to those who see with their eyes and those who see with their hands, similar responses, thus yielding communication of high quality to both.

As for the mistaken fear that those who can not see can never enjoy the great aesthetic creations of man, one is reminded of a very sincere and studious man who had lost the sight of one eye, but was so grateful that the other remained intact, that he wrote a valuable book telling "the story of the wonderful power of vision," but it was rather sense-arrogant in pointing out some of the things which those who have no sight at all must miss. This quotation is from that book, *The Value and Importance of Sight*: "To the blind man, the inspiring and enduring paintings of a Michelangelo or a Raphael, the superb statues of a Phidias, of a Praxiteles, the chaste and elemental lines of the Gothic Cathedrals are non-existent. He is *restricted* to the brief and fleeting delights of music and song."

How much human energy is spent on telling others how much they miss. But, as in this case, it sometimes has its value. The lesson here is that most people with full vision have also missed all the great works mentioned above. No one person can have a full appreciation of many of the treasures of our boundless human heritage, but all who have a fragment of them are rich, and through sharing that fragment, enrich others. I know some persons who have never heard of Michelangelo, Phidias, or Praxiteles, or hearing, have forgotten, who have nevertheless walked with beauty all their lives. Some of these friends see, some do not —but deprived as they may seem, they have not missed everything. No one has spoken more thoughtfully about such matters than Will Rogers, who probably missed most of the splendors of our Greek and Roman heritage but who helped console us all in our mental limitations with his profound statement that "We are all ignorant; we are just ignorant about different things."

I am remembering two blind friends to whom some things declared by the author of *The Value and Importance of Sight* as "non-existent," are existent. One who has traveled over much of the world described to me his visit to the Parthenon, the inspiration it was to him to touch the marble with his hands, to feel the sunshine, as others felt it in this place ages ago, to recall some of the ancient happenings there—of which I had not known until he told me of them, thrillingly convincing me that the great temple of Athens was richly existent to him. The other, a boy who had never traveled far from his native North Carolina, recently went with a group of blind persons to California for a meeting of the American Association of Workers for the Blind, and stopped for a day at the Grand Canyon of the Colorado. His was as satisfying an account of the Grand Canyon as I can remember. He saw the superb natural wonder through the eyes of a guide and other friends and, telling me that it was one of his greatest experiences, he said, "Of course, never having seen anything in my life (he was born blind) I can't make a comparison, but I believe that I got as much pleasure from it—maybe more—than I could have if I had seen it only with my eyes."

The testimony of both these blind friends points up a factor of communication between sighted and blind so obvious that we have perhaps not stressed it enough: the sense of hearing. The great sense of hearing in the perception, education, and enjoyment of the blind can never be overestimated. Some blind persons get the highest pleasure from a painting, a landscape, the sea, or the heavens filled with stars through the word descriptions of a teacher or friend; which does not lessen the indispensability of touch as the most complete and satisfying means of comprehending and enjoying objects that can be brought within the reach of the hand. But this communication by hearing alone attests in a most convincing way, the truth which above all others this book would lift high, that blindness is not in itself either a mental or a spiritual barrier to a deep enjoyment of beauty.

And it would help our common cause immeasurably, that is the need of wider communication between sighted and blind persons, if everyone who has sight could realize the simple fact that through his sight and his personality, he has something unique and probably precious to share with a person who happens to be blind. Conversely, every person who is without sight, has, through that very fact, something unique and probably precious to share with those who happen to see. And through this communication which sighted persons should seek as eagerly as do the blind, each is almost certain to find growth, well-being and happiness.

CHAPTER 11

A GLANCE BACK AND A LOOK FORWARD

The Journey of a Hundred Miles Begins With a Single Step.
—OLD CHINESE PROVERB

ALTHOUGH it was at the Kansas Rehabilitation Center that we were able to give the objects in the Collection of Objects of Beauty for the Sighted and the Blind their fullest and best controlled use, there have been other opportunities to show a part or all of the collection to groups and to individuals. Many others, hearing of it, have expressed the wish to see it, but these showings have not yet been possible to arrange.

There were some who were doubtful at first of its "practical value," but seeing was believing, and I can not recall anyone who has seen it questioning the principle and worth of the project. The president of a large group of teachers of the blind who was persuaded to see a part of the collection with a few blind students, said afterwards, "I did not care to see the exhibition because I have felt that music was the only art that was accessible to the blind; but my mind has been changed as I have seen the pleasure they are getting through touch from what we usually think of as the visual arts. And I am for it." The executive secretary of a State Commission for the Blind wrote the Office of Vocational Rehabilitation in Washington after the collection had been shown to the clients in his State Rehabilitation Center, "I confess that I was a bit skeptical when the matter was first discussed last year. I am sure now that this skepticism was based on pure ignorance. We believe that this medium is extremely valuable," and he asked to have the collection again if possible.

It is, however, the opinion of the blind themselves with which we have been most concerned. They have given the strongest testimony of its worth. From some three hundred blind persons

170

who have seen a part or all of the collection, I think there has not been one negative response, and some of them have been heartening beyond expectation.

"Now I know what I did not believe yesterday," said a young blind teacher of the blind after she had seen the collection with friends and later had spent two hours with a few objects by herself. "I know now that the visual arts, as they are often called, are as much for us as for those who see. They belong to all, it is really as Miss Keller has said, a matter of our claiming them. There are some things which if one reads about them, or someone describes them, one can know quite well, even if never seen or touched; but those with sight will not be satisfied until they have seen them with their eyes, if it can be managed. And just so for those who can not see things with their eyes, they will not be satisfied without feeling them with their hands, if it can be managed. Now there is the promise that many beautiful things will be shared together. It is wonderful, the promise."

We talked on until very late; I wanted the thinking and feeling about the collection of one so thoughtful, one with such a passion for knowledge, and with such gratitude for every good thing that came her way. It was long after this visit that I learned, what I never had thought, that she had always been blind. "I have read," she said, "that seeing is believing, and I think this must be true, for I know, as someone has said of us, that 'tactuality is actuality,' or about as close to it as a single sense can be; but I don't believe we should limit our idea of anything to just one sense, if we can help it. To fully enjoy beauty we must bring everything we can to it."

A man of middle age who had lost his sight about two years earlier said in one of our visits at the rehabilitation center, "I am trying to learn to be a blind man, and it isn't too easy; but one thing that is helping is to discover here something I thought I had lost entirely when my sight went. I was sure that I could never enjoy beauty again—it was one of the things I had put on the shelf, something to be forgotten. But now I know better, I know that there need be no end to the pleasure from beautiful things I can touch. I am almost believing now that some of the things that I once took for granted, it was so easy to see them, may mean

even more to me through a more appreciative and leisurely cultivation."

Through a happy circumstance not anticipated when I began
this book, I have recently had an experience with blind persons
in their enjoyment of beauty that not only confirms much that has
been said here about the desire of the blind to share in creations
designed especially for the seeing world, but goes beyond any
claims heretofore made, by proving their ability to comprehend,
to enjoy, and sometimes to be stirred by life-size sculpture of
human forms.

It will be remembered that in the Collection of Objects on
which most of the experience recorded here rests, the objects
were of a size that could be taken into one or both hands, and
thoroughly explored. There was no claim made for objects beyond this size. However, there was one of the arts which I had
long wished to explore in which the objects would greatly exceed
in dimensions those we had brought together, and that was the art
of sculpture, especially sculpture of the human figure in life size.
It seemed reasonable to me that almost any blind person could,
through touch, perceive quite clearly representations of the human form in sculpture, and that some could probably make out
the stance or action and possibly the features of the human subject, because everyone would have a natural and immediate source
of reference or comparison in his own physical figure.

An opportunity to test this theory came through the invalu-
able co-operation of Dr. Clifford Gregg, Director of the Chicago
Natural History Museum, who granted me the privilege of taking
several blind friends to see, through touch, any of the sculpture
in the Museum's great Hall of Man, given over entirely to the
hundred creations in bronze by the distinguished American sculptor, Malvina Hoffman, a collection often referred to as "The Races
of Mankind."

Nowhere in the world could be found a collection of subjects
so suitable for this experience, and the privilege was deeply appreciated by the eight blind persons who were possibly the first
visitors, sighted or blind, to touch these bronze figures since their
installation in 1933. We chose carefully those who were to "see"
this famous sculpture, wishing to gain as clear an idea as possible
of the extent to which it might appeal to blind persons. There

A. Burton Carnes

44. NEEDLEWORK AND KNITTING BY A BLIND ARTIST

This doll's costume was designed and completely made by Miss Helen Siefert, born in Minatare, Nebraska, who became blind and deaf in her second year. The dress is of satin and the sweater was knit in yellow yarn. The stitches in the knitting are original, having been worked out by touch. The buttons on the sweater are ¼ of an inch wide. Miss Siefert, now at the New York Institute for the Education of the Blind, makes many of her own clothes and often mends the clothes of children. She can copy by feel almost any pattern in knitting or crocheting, and her work is as neat and accurate as any sighted person's could be. She sews also on a machine and uses carpenter tools; and takes great pleasure in creating new designs in her sewing and other needlework. She has a deep appreciation of the good craftsmanship of others and derives great pleasure from her own creations.

were two pupils in their teens, a boy and girl in the city high
school; a youth in college; two middle-aged men who were counselors to the blind; a husband and wife, of middle age, both blind,
quite widely traveled, who for years had been working with blind
people; and one man who remembered the dedication of the Hall
of Man when he had his sight, and recalled some of the figures,
but after he became blind had never expected to see any of them
again, for he knew they were not to be touched by visitors.

Each blind guest was accompanied to the museum by a sighted
person, and shown the sculptures individually, or sometimes two
together. There were no conflicts in schedules and there was time
enough, from one and a half to two and a half hours, to see from
seven to ten subjects of their choice and, if desired, to see certain ones twice, as some asked to do.

Before beginning the tour, a brief statement was made as to
where we were in the museum, and what we had come to see.
The Hall of Man, it was explained, is known throughout the world
as the finest and most complete presentation of the different types
of mankind to be seen anywhere.

All the guests were much impressed by the fact of the enduring
quality of bronze, and they were especially interested in a short
account of how the sculptor Malvina Hoffman had traveled around
the world to get these types, and pleased to hear that she had
written a book, *Heads and Tales,* a remarkable and very complete
story of the great adventure, and much more, and so important
that the Library of Congress had published it in Braille. (As I
write, one of our visitors is reading the Braille edition in four
large volumes.)

I gave a very brief description of the subjects I thought would
be of interest, giving each visitor some range of choice but almost
knowing in advance what proved to be true, that they would wish
to see all of them. I had selected several groups for their human
interest, educational content, and action; and a few single figures,
all of which could be examined from every side. Since all were
life-size figures and mounted on bases, the tops of a few were
higher than could be reached from the floor; but in these cases
the guards obligingly provided a small platform which enabled
those who desired to "touch everything."

These were fine days for us all. The procedure was similar to that for seeing smaller objects; one of us sighted persons would give a brief description and then the visitor would proceed to "see" by feeling it, as one might do if blindfolded, but with much more skill, often discovering details which had gone unnoticed by the interpreter. In the sculpture groups there was often considerable action, and this seemed to be detected almost as clearly through touch as through sight when, of course, the experience was preceded by the interpretation of the subject by the sighted companion which is always essential with any new object. Of the many sighted persons with whom I have in the past visited the Hall of Man, only a few, I believe, have carried away as definite, pleasant, and lasting impressions as some of these blind friends have done, although of course the blind visitors would "see" only a small fraction of the number of subjects viewed by the sighted in the same period of time.

All the guests wanted to know more about the artist, and how bronze sculpture is made, and each one told me that the feeling of bronze was most agreeable to the touch. Two at the museum asked if sculpture was ever done in other materials. As Miss Hoffman had included in addition to the hundred bronze subjects three heads in stone and one in marble, it was a great pleasure to give them an opportunity to feel the very beautiful portrait head of The Ethiopian Woman in black marble, which I know thousands of sighted visitors have longed to touch.

The teen-age boy and girl were much impressed by the small size of the Pygmies as compared to the rest of us, and had never dreamed that it would be possible for anyone in any medium to represent them almost as in the flesh, so faithful to their form and with such smooth and pleasant textures of the skin. There were three figures in the Wambuti Pygmy family in the Ituri Forest, Belgian Congo, the father playing a drum fastened to two saplings, the mother leaning against one of the trees holding her baby firmly, his legs astride her waist, half clinging with both hands and feet. One visitor was particularly intrigued by the sculptor's modeling of the baby's hands and feet and the natural spread of its toes. But it was another item in the composition that caused one of the counselors of the blind to ask to see the Pygmy family again. He must have spent ten minutes examining the musician's drum, explaining that before he became blind he played the drum and he wanted to see what this one was like. He had played several instruments and had his own band, and he laughed as he told us, "My trombone player was the laziest musician I ever saw," and he gave us, in strict confidence, the name of the lazy but otherwise very successful individual.

Another group which intrigued everyone was the South African Kalahari Bushman family; the father, a hunter with bow and arrow, the mother sitting near, her mind apparently on something else than her baby who was clamoring for her attention. She was perhaps waiting for her husband to bring down some game for supper, but the baby, swung in an improvised saddle of coarse cloth at her back, was not satisfied with his own situation and was squirming to improve it. The mother and baby got a lot of attention as their position was low and the guests could explore them in detail and on all sides. The baby was of primary interest but when they had finished with him and his small head of very kinky hair, they spent much time with the mother, her hair of larger kinks, her hand-woven headdress with small sea-shell decorations, her necklace of beads, and bracelets and anklets of metal. There is a good photograph of the Bushman mother and baby on another page. They are a part of the first group on the right as one enters the Hall of Man.

Included also is a photograph of what has long been one of my favorites in this superb collection of human sculptures, the Hawaiian Surf Rider. This subject means even more to me since the day I saw it with my blind young college friend who, after he had gone very carefully over the several subjects he had chosen to see, told me that this was his favorite of them all. And writing me two weeks later he said "The Surf Rider is still my first choice."

As we looked for quite a long time that day at the Hawaiian Surf Rider my friend pointed out the remarkable sense of balance in the figure, poised as though he might rise from the surfboard and fly away any instant. Then he showed me how swimming had developed this muscle and that in the legs and neck, lessons that he had learned from practice and which the sculptor had confirmed for anyone who could see or feel the beautiful bronze figure.

No one of our eight blind visitors seemed to get more out of their visit to the Hall of Man than the young college man whose greatest response was to this splendid athlete of the water. A good swimmer himself, and striving to be a better one, he gave me an interpretation of the figure which no one else had done and which I can never forget. I had met him when he graduated from high school, a boy who had lost both his sight and his hands in an accident three years before. But overcoming these almost overwhelming odds he had developed a sense of touch in his forearm which carried to his mind very much the same messages that the hand and fingers would. And besides, he had learned to read Braille with his lips. When the director of the museum gave me the chance to show some blind friends this collection, my thought immediately went to this young man, who had seen the smaller objects two years before, in the hope that these larger objects might mean even more to him. I was fortunate enough to find him home from college for a few days, and he and his mother immediately accepted the invitation to come to the museum. The result was another demonstration of the truth that no one can know the potentialities of another human being.

Two of our visitors, the blind husband and blind wife, distinguished workers with and for the blind, had never before had an opportunity to see an example of fine sculpture. They expressed the great personal pleasure which the experience had brought to them; but they were thinking even more of what it would mean to many blind persons they knew in our own and in other countries, if ways could be found by which the museums of the world could share a portion of their treasures with those who could know them mainly through touch. They saw the sculpture together, and one of their favorites, as it was with others, was the Malaysian Cock Fighters illustrated on another page.

Usually when I asked a visitor for the most effective sculpture he had seen, he would mention at least three, and some liked all they had seen. There was not one subject which was not favored by someone. And to the question, "Do you think that most any blind person would like this experience?" all answered in the affirmative.

This opinion was made clearer by one of them who said, "I think that there would be a greater proportion of blind persons who would enjoy sculpture, if they had a chance, than of sighted people, because there are so few opportunities for the blind to see what is around them. So what they do see, if it is explained to them, is usually more of a privilege. But beyond this is admiration for the skill, the ability to shape and the sense of form, and often the illusion of action which a sculptor can create; all this is wonderful for anyone who is blind to experience, as he can sometimes very fully by touch."

We have not had enough evidence to be sure of this comparison; but we have had enough to be sure that superior sculpture, intelligently interpreted, can be a fine experience for many blind persons.

The gains from the overall project of Beauty for the Sighted and the Blind have not all been for the blind but also, as we hoped, for the sighted persons who have been close to the work. One of those who had been charmed by several objects in the collection, and had followed some of the early experiences with the blind said, "Our blind friends have given me, if not a new sense of perception, surely an enhanced one, for every beautiful or interesting object I see now, I must take into my hands if possible, for 'feeling is believing' in a sense I never realized before. And now I am learning that to feel is often quite the best way of seeing many things. When a blind friend comes occasionally to my home, I try to have around some things that I have liked the feel of very much and that we may enjoy together." And she, a countrywoman, continued, "One of my blind friends, without knowing it, is also educating my sense of smell. The other day when she came, remembering her enthusiasm about fruit, I filled a bowl with apples and placed it on a table near her chair. As she sat down she exclaimed, 'Oh, apples for me, how I love them.' I had not mentioned them, though I had intended to, but she had discovered them. Taking in her hand one apple at a time, she smelled each one, saying, 'This is a McIntosh; this is a Stark's Delicious; this is a Winesap, probably from Virginia,' and she gave me, in about a minute, an enlightening dissertation on fall and winter varieties, convincing me that a good sense of smell was essential to the full enjoyment of apples.

" 'I can tell some varieties by their shapes,' she went on. 'Isn't an apple beautiful to feel? But that is too slow sometimes, so I get them the quick way, by smell.' And then we talked for a long time about fragrances, not only as ways of identification, but as pure aesthetic experience."

Most of us have given too little attention to this wonderful detector of delight, the sense of smell; many of us are negative to it, limiting our thinking, if we think at all, to the warning or protecting function of this discriminating sense. "I want to smell everything," a blind boy told me one time, "and I do when I am by myself. But my folks tell me it isn't good manners." We were alone together and he asked, "Could I smell that sandalwood fan again, that you showed us? I remember it almost better than anything."

Smell is undoubtedly the most reminiscent of our senses. Most of us will agree with the German philosopher Schopenhauer, who wrote: "We might call smell the sense of memory, in that it brings back to us more directly than any other sense, the specific impression of an event or scene from the distant past."

It is reminiscent, but the present effect also, however fleeting, is a high source of pleasure. Many thoughts about fragrances will come to each reader as he scans these lines. The thought I would leave is that the sense of smell, like the sense of touch, is one which the sighted and blind can share together, and we who see will probably learn from our blind friends more about these two senses, their practical and aesthetic values, than we could learn in any other way.

There is no experience which equals the sharing of blessings, but the greatest joy comes when they are balanced. There is between those who see and those who do not a kind of natural balance which is not usually thought of, but which the discerning will find. Those who lack sight will usually, because of its absence, develop more fully the remaining senses, especially those of hearing, touching, smelling; possibly of tasting, but of the first three, quite surely. And what they perceive is often of value to us who do not have to depend so much as the blind do on these senses, because sight serves us so well. We need to encourage our blind friends to share with us their aesthetic experiences through hearing, touching, and smelling. Just asking them will sometimes establish bonds of mutual pleasure. An instance came to me recently by way of a letter from a blind teacher of the blind in Maine, not directly to me, but through a mutual friend. The letter was a treat to all my family when I read it to them one evening; it seemed to us a fine bundle of compensations.

My new one-way friend, because while I have discovered her, she does not yet know of my interest in her collection of feels and smells, sent only a partial list of "Things I like to touch, and Good Smells"; seventy-one to touch and sixty-four to smell. Of these, she wrote, "Of course this is just a beginning, what I think of as I write."

Many of my favorites are in her list. I cull a dozen from it. They are: freshly baked bread, jelly being made, unless it boils over; carnations, lilacs, freshly cut hay, violets, rose geranium; linen closet full of clean linen, pine trees, sawdust, wood smoke, leaves burning in the fall, piles of apples in the orchard in the fall, and to make a baker's dozen from her list, little puppies, to which I will amend, little kittens.

Shall we not add to the past and present attributes of the sense of smell its lure to the future? Who will not think of a treasured odor he would like to smell again, or of fragrances which will come with his summer garden? How rewarding are the seasons in this Temperate Zone, to those who look forward to the smell of the wild grape blossoming in Kentucky, to wild crab-apple blossoms in West Virginia—or apple blossoms anywhere, to the native field roses of Oregon or, a personal preference, the fragrant blossoms of the linden tree. Every year in early summer, wherever I am, I try to get home in time for our annual visit to an old German farm in Connecticut, with its line of lindens in a long lane, all in bloom in late June or early July.

The new vistas which the Collection of Objects of Beauty for the Sighted and the Blind is helping to open on the aesthetic level, are bound in the evolution of progress to be followed by more vistas, to all forms of knowledge that can be perceived through touch and other senses related to it. This will continue, for the thoughtful members of society and our government will not halt until the opportunities for the blind are as nearly equal to those who have sight, as human intelligence and devotion can make them. We shall continue to hear the voices of the two young blind men, Hartman and Hall who, a hundred years ago, wrote the first book in America pleading for a better understanding of the blind, dedicating it to "The American Public Whose Philanthropic Heart Ever Moves at Humanity's Call."

Ways will be found, some not yet dreamed of, to help bring to those without sight, the things and the thoughts which mean most to those who have it. In this quest, it will be then, as now, that the human hand, with its touch of unlimited discernment and its power to shape and reshape man's environment, will continue to bring knowledge to the minds of the blind and beauty to their hearts.

IN ACKNOWLEDGMENT

In bringing this book to a close, I come to the most difficult part in the making of it, the endeavor to convey my appreciation to those who have contributed in many ways to an undertaking which they have made their own. My task is lessened some by the fine acknowledgments which Mary Switzer has made for both of us in her Preface; and I have been able in the Colophon to mention a few who have helped in the appearance, the form and the construction of the book.

Miss Switzer has named some of those to whom we are both deeply indebted. To these indispensable ones I must add the name of Mary Switzer herself, for she more than any other individual, except possibly Helen Keller, has understood best what beauty means when shared by the sighted and the blind together; and to the work which I have been able to help get done and partly recorded in these pages, her's will always remain the greatest single contribution. I must also include here my debt to her associates on the Staff of the Office of Vocational Rehabilitation of the Department of Health, Education and Welfare for their encouragement and their help since the beginning of the project with them.

Only a blanket acknowledgment can be made here to some who have supported the idea and purpose of the book and who, through their confidence and cooperation have given it strength and growth. Among these are officers and members of the following organizations: the Russell Sage Foundation; the American Foundation for the Blind; the American Association of Workers for the Blind; the

National Federation of the Blind; the National Rehabilitation Association; the New York Institute for the Education of the Blind; Perkins Institution for the Blind; the New York Association for the Blind; the Chicago Natural History Museum; the Smithsonian Institution; the American Association of Museums; the Cleveland Society for the Blind; the Cleveland Museum of Art; the New York Society for Ethical Culture; the Pennsylvania Working Home for the Blind; the Industrial Home for the Blind, Brooklyn; the Illinois Industrial Home for the Blind; the Hadley School for the Blind; the Kansas Rehabilitation Center for the Blind, Topeka, Kansas; the Catholic Center for the Blind, Boston Massachusetts; the North Carolina Commission for the Blind, Raleigh, North Carolina; the Columbia Lighthouse for the Blind, Inc., Washington, D.C.; the Southern Highland Handicraft Guild; N. W. Ayer and Son and the American Bible Society.

I am especially grateful to those individuals and organizations whose loans and gifts have helped so much in building up the Collection of Objects of Beauty for the Sighted and the Blind. Among these are: the American Museum of Natural History; the Metropolitan Museum of Art; the Brooklyn Art Museum; the Art Institute of Chicago; the Museum of the American Indian, Heye Foundation; the University Museum of the University of Pennsylvania; the Indian Arts and Crafts Board; Georg Jensen; the Alva Studios and many individuals.

And last but far from least, is my gratitude to those friends, both sighted and blind, too many to be listed here, who have helped in their personal ways to bring about what this book records—and much more. He who scans these pages will not see many of their names; but they, I hope, will read between the lines, as I have often done while writing them, and feel my gratitude for their friendship and their help over these good years through which we have known each other, and, looking toward the future, have worked together.

INDEX

THIS BOOK

BEING ABOUT BEAUTY, IT SEEMED FITTING TO USE IN ITS MAKING, TYPE FACES, SKILLS AND MATERIALS which combined would commend it to those who are sensitive to the graphic arts, and who know that finished books do not just happen. The selection of the six type faces for this book has given me special pleasure on two counts. First, for the opportunity to use beautiful type faces by American alphabet designers of distinction; and second, for the privilege of bringing under the covers of one book the typographical creations of six friends over the years, thus recalling associations with them in the American Institute of Graphic Arts, The Stowaways, The Typophiles or in some other relationship in the making and enjoyment of good books.

These artists (for type designing is one of the most useful and beautiful of the arts) are Will Dwiggins, in whose Caledonia the text is set; Rudolph Ruzicka, whose Fairfield is used in the chapter headings and quotations; the title page is set in Centaur designed by Bruce Rogers; the dedication page in Laurentian designed by William Dana Orcutt; the page of quotations in the front of the book in Fred Goudy's Deepdene; and this Colophon in Cornell type designed by George Trenholm.

The illustrations are credited to the several photographers, most of whom contributed them; but my greatest debt is to Bert Carnes who photographed all the objects of Beauty from the Collection which appear in the book and gave them to our mutual cause.

The designs for the jacket, the book covers, frontispiece and the end papers were done by Martha Eaton.

Credit is due the following companies: H. Wolff Book Manufacturing Company, Inc., for composition, presswork and binding; Colorplate Engraving Company for the color frontispiece; Latham Process Corporation for engraving and printing the illustrations by offset; Henry Lindenmeyr & Sons for S. D. Warren's Olde Style paper; the Holliston Mills for the Novelex binding cloth; the Algen Press for printing the jacket, frontispiece and end papers; Becker Brothers Engraving Company for the binding dies.

All these and other details were brought into organization and harmony by Fred J. Royar of St Martin's Press.   A. H. E.

Wilmington Public Library
Wilmington, N. C.

RULES

1. Books marked 7 days may be kept one week. Books marked 14 days, two weeks. The latter may be renewed, if more than 6 months old.

2. A fine of two cents a day will be charged on each book which is not returned according to the above rule. No book will be issued to any person having a fine of 25 cents or over.

3. A charge of ten cents will be made for mutilated plastic jackets. All injuries to books beyond reasonable wear and all losses shall be made good to the satisfaction of the Librarian.

4. Each borrower is held responsible for all books drawn on his card and for all fines accruing on the same.

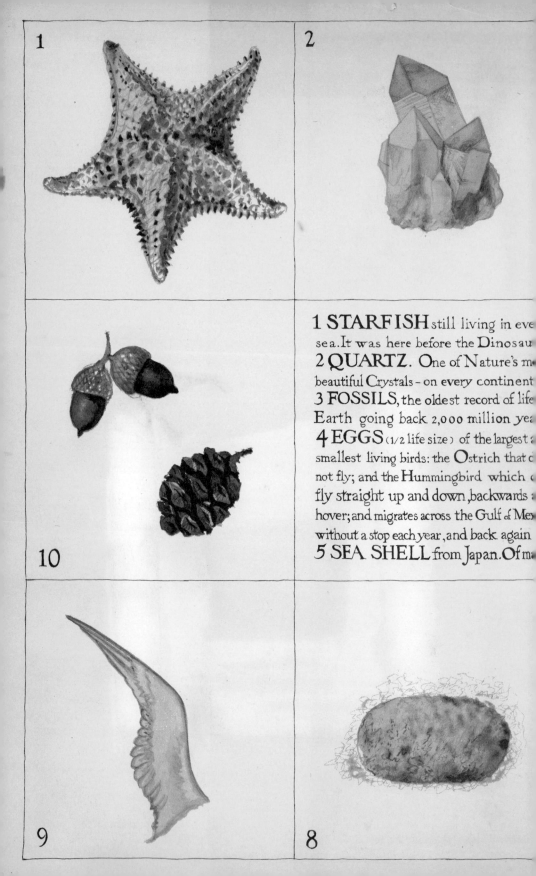

1
2

1 **STARFISH** still living in eve
sea. It was here before the Dinosau
2 **QUARTZ**. One of Nature's m
beautiful Crystals – on every continent
3 **FOSSILS**, the oldest record of life
Earth going back 2,000 million yea
4 **EGGS** (1/2 life size) of the largest a
smallest living birds: the Ostrich that c
not fly; and the Hummingbird which c
fly straight up and down, backwards a
hover; and migrates across the Gulf of Mex
without a stop each year, and back again
5 **SEA SHELL** from Japan. Of m

10

9
8